THE FORTUNE IN YOUR FUTURE

THE FORTUNE IN YOUR FUTURE

DAVID C. VEENEMAN

McGraw-Hill

New York • San Francisco • Washington, D.C.
Auckland • Bogotá • Caracas • Lisbon • London
Madrid • Mexico City • Milan • Montreal • New Delhi
San Juan • Singapore • Sydney • Tokyo • Toronto

McGraw-Hill

A Division of The McGraw·Hill Companies

Copyright © 1998 by The McGraw-Hill Companies, Inc. All rights reserved. Printed
in the United States of America. Except as permitted under the United States
Copyright Act of 1976, no part of this publication may be reproduced or distributed
in any form or by any means, or stored in a data base or retrieval system, without the
prior written permission of the publisher.

1 2 3 4 5 6 7 8 9 0   DOC/DOC   9 0 3 2 1 0 9 8

ISBN 0-07-067353-5

The sponsoring editor for this book was Andrew Seagren, the editing supervisor was
Donna Namorato, and the production supervisor was Suzanne W. B. Rapcavage. It
was set in Palatino by Carol Barnstable of Carol Graphics.

Printed and bound by R. R. Donnelley & Sons Company.

The Star System of Investing, The Star Workshop, and *Star portfolios* are trademarks and
service marks of Veeneman Associates and may not be used without permission.

Ibbotson Associates data used with permission. ©1998 Ibbotson Associates, Inc. All
rights reserved. (Certain portions of this work were derived from copyrighted works
of Roger G. Ibbotson and Rex Sinquefield.)

This publication is designed to provide accurate and authoritative information in
regard to the subject matter covered. It is sold with the understanding that neither
the author nor the publisher is engaged in rendering legal, accounting, or other
professional service. If legal advice or other expert assistance is required, the services
of a competent professional person should be sought.

> —*From a Declaration of Principles jointly adopted by a Committee of the
> American Bar Association and a Committee of Publishers.*

McGraw-Hill books are available at special quantity discounts to use as premiums
and sales promotions, or for use in corporate training programs. For more
information, please write to the Director of Special Sales, McGraw-Hill, 11 West 19th
Street, New York, NY 10011. Or contact your local bookstore.

 This book is printed on recycled, acid-free paper containing a minimum of
50% recycled de-inked fiber.

To Liza Veeneman, who spent many
evenings reading through investment theory
and bad jokes. She said in two sentences
what it took me two hundred pages to say:
"Sure, I'd like to earn 50 percent on my
money—Who wouldn't? But you don't
get something for nothing;
pigs get slaughtered in the end."

CONTENTS

PART ONE

ANYONE CAN DO IT

Chapter 1

The Fortune in Your Future 3

Save regularly, invest wisely, and you can retire with $1 million.

Chapter 2

The Law of Large Numbers 15

Investing is about risk and reward. Get the right balance, and you'll be on your way to becoming a successful investor.

Chapter 3

Keep It Simple 37

Growth versus value and other investing debates aren't important for most investors.

Chapter 4

Investment Building Blocks 51

The pros and cons of savings accounts, CDs, money market funds, guaranteed investment contracts, bonds, and stocks.

Chapter 5

The *Star* System 73

Spread your savings, use time to protect yourself, understand your attitude, and regulate your investments.

Chapter 6

Using the *Star* Portfolios 89

Pick the *Star* portfolio that's right for you.

PART TWO

PORTFOLIOS FOR EVERY INVESTOR

Chapter 7

The Mattress 101

What's the safest place to stash your money? In a mattress. A very conservative portfolio for investors who want to avoid risk.

Chapter 8

Belt and Suspenders 109

Figuratively speaking, a portfolio for investors who wear a belt and suspenders to bed so their pajamas won't fall down. For those who don't like surprises.

Chapter 9

The Shallow End 117

Enough water to swim, but not enough to drown. A safe portfolio that provides a modest and consistent return.

Chapter 10

The Jogger 125

A slow and steady portfolio that earns a decent return, although there may be a bump or two along the way.

Chapter 11

The Center Line 133

The perfect portfolio for the middle-of-the-road investor. But remember, traffic can hit you from both sides.

Chapter 12

Partly Cloudy 141

The sun may be out in the morning, but it may storm in the afternoon. A portfolio for investors who want a good return and can tolerate occasional setbacks.

Chapter 13

Over the Hump 149

We're taking on more risk now, but the returns are better too.

Chapter 14

The Sports Car 157

You can hit top speeds, but watch out for road conditions. For long-term investors who don't mind a few down years.

Chapter 15

The Deep End 165

For investors who thrive on risk and are looking for big returns.

Chapter 16

The Black Diamond 175

For experts only. Heavy exposure to international stocks means constant volatility, but the returns can be huge.

Chapter 17

The Sky Dive 185

For thrill-seekers. Requires unshakable faith, endurance, and a touch of wild abandon.

PART THREE

THE CARE AND FEEDING OF YOUR PORTFOLIO

Chapter 18

Animal Crackers 195

Shopping for mutual funds is like shopping for animal crackers: the contents are mostly the same—the differences are in flavor, price, and packaging.

Chapter 19

We'll have Funds, Funds, Funds Till Daddy Takes the T-Bird Away 213

Choosing the right mutual funds for your portfolio.

Chapter 20

Changing the Oil 235

Evaluating the performance of your funds and deciding if changes are needed.

Chapter 21

Midcourse Corrections   253

Rebalancing your portfolio as your investments grow and your goals change.

Chapter 22

Reaching for a Star   265

Review of key concepts. Now it's up to you.

Appendix A

How the *Star* Portfolios Were Created   269

Appendix B

What a Return Will Earn   275

Appendix C

Step Transfer Worksheet   281

GLOSSARY   285
INDEX   299

THE FORTUNE
IN YOUR FUTURE

PART ONE

ANYONE CAN DO IT

1

CHAPTER

The Fortune in Your Future

Save regularly, invest wisely, and you can retire with $1 million.

There's a fortune in your future, a millionaire in your mirror. It's not pie in the sky, and it will take time, desire, and commitment. But if you want to, there is no reason that you should not retire with at least a million dollars. You will probably retire with more. Much more.

The headlines we read every day seem to say just the opposite. The safety net is gone, they say. Guaranteed company pensions are a thing of the past. Social Security may not be around when we need it. "Americans will live their golden years in poverty!" they scream. Well, don't believe it. Americans will live their golden years in Miami.

More American workers are retiring with more money today than at any time in our nation's history. They are doing it without the guarantees and benefits of our parents' generation. They are doing it on the strength of their own savings.

There is no reason that you should not retire with at least a million dollars. If you are 30 years old and you plan to retire at age 65, then all you have to do is save about $3,500 a year between now and the time you retire and earn an average of 10 percent a year on those savings. It's that simple.

"Simple?" you say. "What's so simple about coming up with $3,500 a year? I'm having a tough time just making ends meet!"

Coming up with the $3,500 is probably the hardest part. But come up with it. Beg, borrow, or steal it if you have to, but do it. The rewards are unbelievable.

COMING UP WITH YOUR MILLION

There are all kinds of ways to come up with the money you need, even if you don't earn a lot. A few years ago, I presented an investment seminar, *Common-Sense Investing for Common-Sense People*, at a factory in Pennsylvania. A company had asked me to come in and deliver the seminar for their employees. The company had just added some new investment options to its 401k plan, and employees needed help.

After one of the sessions, a young woman came up to me and asked for some help. She introduced herself as Karen and said she worked part time. Karen and her husband had two kids, she said, and they were doing all right. Karen's husband was a trucker. According to her, "The money's pretty good, and the work is real steady."

Karen and her husband were doing well enough, in fact, that she had thought about quitting when she had her second child the year before. But she didn't like the thought of not working. "You never know when things might turn down," she said. So Karen decided to keep working part-time.

At first, she had just planned to do it for a while, long enough to build up a nest egg to tide them through tough times. But she found she really enjoyed working. She liked the job, and most of her friends were at the plant. Karen worked half-days in the accounting office, and by the time day care was taken out of her take-home pay, she figured they were clearing about $11,000 a year from her earnings.

"I'm 27 right now," Karen continued, "and I'm thinking that I'll keep working until I'm 35 or so. What I'm trying to figure out is, if we do this, and if we want to retire at age 55, would we have enough to do it?"

I was hooked. I had never heard of anyone doing what Karen was doing. She seemed surprised. "It just seems like common sense," she said. I asked Karen how she planned to invest her savings. She had enjoyed the seminar, she said, and she wanted to go with a middle-of-the-road mix of stocks and bonds.

I'm a sucker for a compliment. I told Karen I would work up some quick numbers and meet with her later in the day.

Later that afternoon, when Karen came by the office I was using at the plant, I had her sit down. "You may find this pretty hard to believe," I began. "I had to double-check the numbers myself, just to be sure I hadn't made a mistake.

"If you save about $11,000 a year from last year until you're 35, and if you earn an average of 10 percent a year on your savings, then by the time you turn 55, you are going to have somewhere around $1 million."

Karen sat in silence. After a moment, she said "You're kidding me."

"No," I said, "I'm not kidding. I knew it would be a lot, but I didn't know it would be that much."

Karen put her hand to her mouth and stared out the window for a moment. "I can't believe it," she said. "A million dollars, and from a part-time job!"

Karen is not the only person who has found her million. The wife of a friend of mine teaches aerobics. As a part-time job, it's more of a hobby than a real moneymaker—she clears only about $5,000 a year. But they bank every penny of it. By the time they retire, they expect those savings to have grown to over $500,000. And that's in addition to his pension and 401k savings.

WHAT'S WRONG WITH INVESTING

"All right," you say, "Karen came up with the money on the front end. But how is she going to invest it? She doesn't have the background to invest that kind of money."

True enough. Karen had her high school degree, and her husband had his GED, but neither of them had any college education. And that made them pretty typical of the thousands of people who attended one of our *Common-Sense* seminars.

We once did a series of seminars at a manufacturing company in Tennessee. Like many companies, this one had added investment options to its 401k plan. Employees were confused about the new investments, and the company wanted someone to explain investing in plain English.

At one particular session, we began by asking participants what they saw as being wrong with investing. What was it that kept them from feeling comfortable? There was an uncomfortable silence while participants waited to see who would speak first. Finally, a middle-aged man in the back of the room spoke up.

"Investing is too complicated!" he said. I asked him to tell us more. "It just seems to take too much time," he added.

I asked how many people in the room felt that investing was too complicated. About three-quarters of the hands went up. I asked for some more thoughts on how investing was complicated.

"I don't know anything about stocks and bonds," a younger woman on the left chimed in. "Everything I hear sounds like gobble-dygook, and half of what I hear seems to contradict the other half."

"Fair enough," I answered. "Let's talk for a minute about what it takes to be a successful investor. Maybe that has something to do with what makes it seem so complicated. Somebody tell me what you have to be able to do to invest successfully."

A man on the right raised his hand. "You have to know which funds to be in at the right time," he said.

"Does everyone agree with that?" I asked. A lot of heads nodded. I wrote on the flip chart "KNOW RIGHT FUNDS" and "KNOW RIGHT TIME." "Okay," I continued, "what do you have to be able to do to know which fund to be in and when to change?"

A younger man in the middle spoke up. "You have to be able to figure out what's going to happen next. You know—figure out when the market is going to go down so you can get out of it."

Another man in front added his opinion. "That's what I don't like about stocks and bonds," he said. "It feels like gambling."

"GAMBLING" went up on the flip chart, and I asked him to tell us more. "Well, I don't know what's going to happen next," he said. "But the people who run funds are supposed to know, aren't they? But it seems like the funds are always down, like the people running them don't know what they're doing." I wrote "PREDICT THE FUTURE" on the flip chart, to scattered laughs.

I asked if anyone else felt like investing was a gamble. There was some nervous laughter, and someone from the back called out, "Are you kidding?" Over the laughter, I could tell we had hit a nerve. But there was still something we hadn't gotten out yet. I asked for someone to tell us more about how investing is a bet.

A man in a short-sleeve shirt and a tie stood up in back. Everyone turned around to watch him—he seemed to have a lot of influence with this crowd. I found out later he was in the plant accounting office. "The way I see it," he began, "the stock market is a lot like a football pool. I make my picks on Wednesday, and I throw in my 5 bucks. Then I go home on the weekend and watch the games. If I made good picks, I pick up some money on Monday morning."

"When was the last time you won the pool, George?" someone called out from the side of the room. The audience broke up in laughter.

"Well, that's my point!" George continued. " I'm not sure I can pick investments any better that I can pick football teams. Playing a football pool is one thing, but I sure don't want to gamble with my retirement savings."

Bingo! That's what I had been looking for. After thanking George for sharing his views with us, I described a common nightmare scenario. "You wake up one morning, and you find out the market crashed. Then you learn you have lost your savings—they're gone."

"Isn't that what happened in the Great Depression?" a woman asked from the middle of the room. Lots of heads began nodding.

"My grandfather lost everything he had," someone else added. More head nodding. "LOSE EVERYTHING" went up on the flip chart.

"Okay, that's quite a list." I said, intending to move on. But a hand went up on the right side of the room.

A tiny woman stood up. "There's something else," she said. "I keep my money in a bank because I feel like I know what's going on. With the stock market, you don't have any control. You could have a million dollars one day, and nothing the next. I just can't live with that kind of uncertainty."

I had to pause for a moment—I hadn't thought about that. "CONTROL" and "UNCERTAINTY" went on the flip chart. "Anything else?" I asked, wondering exactly when I had lost control of this audience.

Fortunately, the participants cut me a break. No more hands went up. "Okay," I said, reading off the flip chart. "The main problems with investing seem to be that it's complicated, it takes too much time, and it feels like gambling. You don't feel like you have any control, and you're concerned that something will happen and you will lose all your savings. Is that a fair statement?"

Lots of head-nodding. "Suppose I could show you a way to invest that got around these problems?" I began. "Suppose I could teach you a simple way to invest that didn't feel like gambling and where you didn't have to worry about losing your savings. What would you say?"

"How about fresher breath and whiter teeth, while you're at it!" someone called out from back. The room broke up again.

Desperate times call for desperate measures, and I kept a $100 bill in my wallet for just such an occasion. I pulled it out. "I'll tell you what," I said. "I have in my hand a fairly tattered $100 bill. In the next couple of hours, I think I can teach you that system. We'll take a vote at the end. If you don't agree at least two-to-one that I have succeeded, I'll raffle off the $100 bill to someone in this room. Fair deal?"

The audience agreed, and we jumped into the seminar. Now, the reason the hundred-dollar bill was a bit worn was because I had used it a lot. In fact, I had been carrying it around for a couple of years. I had never had to raffle it off at the end of the seminar, and I didn't that day in Tennessee, either. At the conclusion of the session, the participant evaluations agreed four to one that we had kept our promise.

WHAT THIS BOOK WILL DO FOR YOU

I make the same promise to you that I made to the seminar participants in Tennessee that day. If you will spend a couple of evenings with this book, I will teach you a simple system for managing investments. You don't need an MBA to use it, and it doesn't require much time. It does take the gambling out of investing, and it will leave you in complete control of your savings. You will have every confidence that you will never wake up to find your savings have disappeared. That's a promise.

The name of the system is the *Star system. Star* is an acronym. You will see in this book that it stands for a number of things. For right now, let's just say it stands for "Saving to avoid risk" because that's what a lot of people really want to do.

There's an old story that is credited to Will Rogers, the Roaring Twenties entertainer. Someone asked him at the height of the great bull market what he thought of returns in the stock market. "To tell you the truth," he said, "I'm more concerned about the return *of* my money than the return *on* my money!" That's saving to avoid risk.

Does that mean we're promising high returns without any risk whatsoever? Not at all. As you will see, there are many kinds of risk. But the risk that many people want to avoid is what we will call *gambling risk*, the out-of-control risk that makes people worry about losing their money. The *Star system* makes that kind of risk go away, and it enables you to control the other types of risk involved in investing.

Most investing books are about return. Not this one; it's about risk. The point of this book is, "Control risk, and return will follow." We're going to show you how to control risk and how to estimate the *return*, or investment earnings, you can expect from your investments.

There is a little-known fact about investing: It is about 90 percent common sense. The *Star system* reduces investing to its common-sense principles and lays them out for you in an easily understood way.

We aren't talking about dummied-down investing. The system we will teach you is used by most of the country's major pension plans to run their multi-billion-dollar funds. I can't claim to have invented it. In fact, no single person invented the system. It was developed over a period of years by a number of people. Two of these developers, William F. Sharpe and Harry Markowitz, received the 1991 Nobel Prize in economics for their contributions to the system.

HOW THIS BOOK WILL DO IT

The *Star system* is based on one very simple premise: *Over 90 percent of your risk and return comes from asset allocation.*

Huh? What the heck is *that* supposed to mean? Well, it's probably the best-kept secret in all of investing. Half the reason is that it sounds like gibberish. Well, more than half. More than one investment type has gone stark raving bonkers trying to explain the idea to regular people—those without graduate degrees in finance. Yet the basic idea is ludicrously simple.

Let's have a race. We're going to race 20 miles down a wide, straight road with no traffic. Our first entry will be a brand new bicycle—a ten-speed-racing model, top of the line. Jan Ullrich, the winner of the 1997 Tour De France (the Super Bowl of bicycle races) will ride the bicycle. In case there is any question, Ullrich can beat virtually any other bicycle racer on the planet.

Our second contestant is an automobile. We'll make it a 4-year-old Volvo wagon. It has a couple of rust spots on the right rear quarter panel. A soccer-mom with two kids is driving the car. We have told her we'll pay her kids' college expenses if she wins the race, so she *wants* to win.

Who would you put your money on? No matter how good our bicycle racer may be, there is no way he is going to beat a car. He may get off to a faster start, and he might even manage to lead the car for a short distance. But pretty soon, the car is going to overtake him and leave him in its dust. In the end, it's not really a fair competition. Ullrich might win at a half-mile, but not at 20.

That's what *asset allocation* is all about. Over the long haul, stocks have historically earned more than bonds, and both have earned more than bank accounts. And there is every prospect for that to continue into the indefinite future.

Is it guaranteed? No. Is it highly probable? Most experts think so.

Let's go back to the seminar in Tennessee. When I asked the audience what someone has to do to be a successful investor, they seized on two things:

- You have to be able to pick the right funds.
- You have to know the right time to switch between funds.

That's certainly one way of investing. And it is one that probably works pretty well for some investors. Let's call them *traders* because they look to make money through frequent trading of their investments. Most people would agree you need to be very knowledgeable to win at that game, and you need to spend a lot of time managing your investments. A little luck doesn't hurt, either.

But is that the only way to invest? Absolutely not. Most of the people in the Tennessee seminar were *savers,* a different kind of investor. They like a feeling of security, of being in control. They are more concerned about the return *of* their money.

The *Star system* is a saver's approach to investing. The *Star investor* relies on the mix of stocks, bonds, and other investments to control risk. The mix also determines how much return to expect over the long haul.

Did you notice we didn't say anything about switching around between funds or trying to guess where the market is going next? That's because the *Star* investor doesn't do that, for two reasons:

- Nobody, not even the pros, really knows where the market is going next. It's called the *Breakfast Barometer*, and we'll talk more about it later.
- Over time, different funds of the same type start to look alike. Whether we're talking about a Volvo or a Ferrari, the car will always beat the bicycle. That's called *reversion to the mean*, and we'll talk about that too.

So, look what we have done so far. If asset allocation holds true, then pick-and-switch investing is a sucker's game. That's what savers have been saying all along. What the savers missed was the fact that there is a whole other way to invest, one that doesn't involve pick-and-switch. That's what the *Star system* is all about.

"Not so fast," you say. "Are you telling me that an intelligent manager can't outperform the market?"

I won't tell you they *can't*, but over the past 10 years or so, most haven't. A series of landmark studies concluded that picking and switching, even by pros, makes relatively little money. More on that later, too.

"I'm not sure I'm buying this," you say. Good; you're skeptical. A healthy dose of skepticism is probably your best friend in the investment world. You continue, "It sounds like you're saying I should blithely hang onto my funds, even while the market is crashing down around me. That sounds nuts!"

Investing is common sense, but it's not necessarily intuitive. Neither was driving when you first got behind the wheel. We're going to spend a fair amount of time on this later. For right now, let's just say that every study that has ever been done has concluded that most investors are better off sitting tight when the market blows up.

This picture of investing is probably very different from any you may have heard before.

- For most people, picking and switching is a waste of time. And sometimes it can cost them real money.
- Don't spend a lot of time poring over your investments—it will only make you crazy. Set a long-term target, and stick with it.

That's what we're going to teach you to do in this book. We said before that *Star* stands for a lot of things. One of the things it stands for is "Strategic targeting and regulating." This book will teach you how to set a long-term investment mix that is suited to your personal goals—that's the "strategic target." Then we will teach you how to keep your investments on target as time goes by and market conditions change—we call that "regulating" your investments, much as a faucet regulates the flow of water. If you put your learning into practice, you will gain control over investment risk, and you will probably end up earning more on your savings than you are earning now.

WHAT'S IN THIS BOOK

The first part of this book, "Anyone Can Do It," explains the *Star* approach. We will start out with a look at what makes the *Star system* work. Researchers have argued for years that investments are no more predictable in the short run than the next toss of a coin. But over the long haul, their performance is as predictable as the number of tosses that will come up heads. That's the key to taking the gambling out of investing.

We will then look at the overriding philosophy behind *Star:* Keep things as simple as possible. Many of the high-sounding debates in which investors get involved have far less impact on investment performance than staying focused on three basic principles, which we call the *three laws of investing.*

Next, we will cover the fundamental building blocks from which all investments are built. There are five to choose from. Once you understand them, the maze of funds we face becomes amazingly simple. Finally, we will walk through the four investment strategies at the heart of the *Star system.* Armed with this knowledge, you will be ready to roll up your sleeves and go to work.

The second part of this book, "Portfolios for Every Investor," presents 11 model portfolios to help you set your all-important investment mix. We will show what's in each portfolio, and we will show how the portfolio has performed decade by decade over the past 70 years. For example, if you want to see how a particular portfolio performed during the Great Depression of the 1930s, it's in there. If you want to see how another performed during the "Crash Nobody Heard" in the 1970s, that's in there, too. This section of the book amounts to a reference tool you can use to find a mix that best suits you, your goals, and your "ouch factor."

Your investment mix may determine 90 percent of risk and return, but the devil is certainly in the other 10 percent. If you swim 90 percent of the way across the English Channel and then drown, you're still dead! And that's where Part 3, "The Care and Feeding of Your Portfolio," comes in.

Part 3 is your portfolio cookbook. We will cover the types of funds available and the pros and cons of each. We will show you how to find the right funds to fill the "slots" in your portfolio and how to decide whether those funds are performing as you had expected. Then we will show you how to keep your investments on track—how to "regulate" your portfolio. *Regulating* a portfolio means making the midcourse corrections needed to keep your investments in line with your goals and keeping risk at a comfortable level. The two key strategies we will cover in this section are *rebalancing* and *step transfers*. These strategies will ensure that you are the master of your investment destiny.

HOW TO USE THIS BOOK

You don't have to read this whole book to benefit from it. In fact, I would encourage you to browse through it, skip around, and hit only the parts that you find valuable. For example, the next two chapters are intended for readers who want to know *why* investments aren't predictable in the short term and *why* simplicity is the key to successful investing. These chapters will benefit those who find these notions somewhat odd. If you view them as common sense, you could easily skim the chapters or skip them altogether.

Don't skip Chapters 4 through 6. Chapter 4, "Portfolio Building Blocks," covers *asset classes*, the understanding of which is absolutely essential to understanding strategic investing. Chapters 5 and 6 explain the *Star strategies* and how to build a *Star* portfolio.

Part 2, "Portfolios for Every Investor," is intended to be an investor's reference. You don't need to read each chapter. Look at each portfolio just enough to get a flavor for its mix, its risk, and its return. There is a chart at the beginning of each chapter to help you do that. Then go on to the next portfolio.

Part 3, "The Care and Feeding of Your Portfolio," will take you through a step-by-step process for building and maintaining your portfolio. It's a must. Some of the information in this section will be a little challenging. We didn't pull any punches, and we didn't dummy it down. But we did make it straightforward and practical. Work through the examples, and use the step-by-step guides to set up your own portfolio. You will find that you have gained the knowledge and confidence to invest like a pro.

2

CHAPTER

The Law of Large Numbers

Investing is about risk and reward. Get the right balance, and you'll be on your way to becoming a successful investor.

Walking through an airport last week, I ran across a financial magazine with a screaming headline. "**SELL STOCKS NOW**," it read. Could be pretty good advice. The stock market was at a record high, and a lot of experts were predicting some kind of correction in the near future.

Or it could be pretty bad advice. The stock market had rolled on to record highs for years by this time. When the Dow hit 4,000, the same magazine had the same headline. Some months later, after a brief hiccup, the Dow shot to 5,000. I saw the same headline around the time the Dow broke through 6,000. And merrily it marched along, all the way to 8,000.

Will the market keep going up forever? Of course not. Oops, change that—of course it will! Actually, both are correct. Over the past 200 years, common stocks have grown with the world economy. They just haven't grown in an unbroken string.

It's important to understand a big distinction—between what happens 5 weeks from now and what happens 5 years from now. Five weeks from now, who knows where the market will be?

It turns out that statisticians, who reputedly can put almost anyone to sleep, probably come as close as anyone. Now, *statisticians* sounds rather technical and just a bit intimidating. But as bright as these folks are, what they do isn't all that complicated. (It's *how* they do it that boggles the mind.) So let's skip all the formulas and as much of the jargon as we can. In fact, since these people eat numbers for breakfast, let's call them *number crunchers* and leave it at that.

THE BREAKFAST BAROMETER

Anyway, number crunchers use a yardstick called *serial correlation*. It measures how well you can predict what will happen tomorrow on the basis of what happened today. A serial correlation of 1.0 means you can use what happened today to predict tomorrow with dead certainty. A serial correlation of –1.0 means the same thing—it just says that what happens tomorrow will be the opposite of what happens today.

A serial correlation of 0 means there is no real connection between today and tomorrow—they are *independent events,* like two tosses of a coin. In other words, what happened today isn't useful in predicting what will happen tomorrow. You might predict it, but if you do, it's luck, not skill. No matter how skillful one is, nobody can consistently predict the next toss of a coin.

So, what are we getting at? It probably comes as no surprise that number crunchers figured out the serial correlation of the stock market. First, they went back to 1926, to make sure the Great Depression was included, and they calculated the serial correlation of the Standard & Poor's 500 Index from month to month. It came out close to zero—.09, to be more precise. (Number crunchers love precision, even though they measure things that aren't precise, only probable. In this case, we're referring to the serial correlation of monthly S&P 500 returns between January 1926 and June 1997.) In other words, a reasonable person would have no more that 9 percent confidence in anyone's prediction of what will happen next month based on what happened this month. Put another way, there is only a 1-in-11 chance they will be right.

Of course, a lot has happened in the past 70 years. The economy has changed, and so has the stock market. When we throw in all those old months, we could be comparing apples to oranges. So let's look back again, but this time we will only go back 30 years. What do we see? The serial correlation actually *drops* to .01. The longer data are actually 9 times more reliable than the recent data, although that's like saying you are 9 times as likely to be struck by lightning as hit by a meteor. Neither is very likely.

What if we compared year to year, instead of month to month? Does the future become any more predictable? Not really. Whether we go back 30 years or all the way back to 1926, we get the same result—a serial correlation of –.01. In other words, if the market goes up, there is a chance it will go down next. But not at all a strong chance. [We could use longer periods, such as 5 years. But there are so few of these (only 14 between 1926 and 1996) that we lose the benefit of large numbers.]

PREDICTING THE FUTURE

Does that mean you can *never* predict what's going to happen tomorrow? Of course not. If there is a massive earthquake in California, it's a pretty safe bet the stock market will have a pretty rocky day. What number crunchers tell us is that nobody can predict the future *consistently*. In other words, nobody can predict *when* that earthquake will occur. (Earthquake examples may seem a bit extreme, but that's exactly what happened in Kobe, Japan, in the heart of Japan's industrial district.)

And that means the disclaimer you read on every piece of investment sales literature, that past performance is no indicator of future earnings, is quite literally true. They aren't just "weasel words" written by a lawyer in the home office. There are a thousand systems for predicting the stock market, from hemline indicators to the Elliott Wave Theory. (The Elliott Wave Theory is a technical system for predicting stock market performance. It claims that the stock market moves in a series of waves.) If the breakfast barometer holds true, then their value is questionable at best.

HEADS OR TAILS?

Okay, what do we make of all that? Let's go back to the coin toss. It's a stronger comparison than you might think. Professor Burton Malkiel, in his book *A Random Walk Down Wall Street*, makes the point forcefully in a story about an experiment he had his students conduct.[1] He had them toss a coin a number of times and plot the results on graph paper. If the coin landed heads, they plotted an *uptick*, an increase in price of one-half point. If the coin landed tails, they plotted a *downtick*, a decrease of one-half point. He suggested to his readers that they run the same experiment.

It is an illuminating exercise. Professor Malkiel claims there's a pretty good chance your chart will show many of the "trading patterns" that technical analysts are so fond of. I have repeated the experiment a number of times and find Professor Malkiel's claims eerily on point. An example of such a chart is shown in Figure 2–1.

Friends in the business have pointed out double bottoms, double tops, resistance points, breakouts, and head-and-shoulders patterns. So the next time someone touts a system for predicting the

FIGURE 2–1

Coin Toss Results

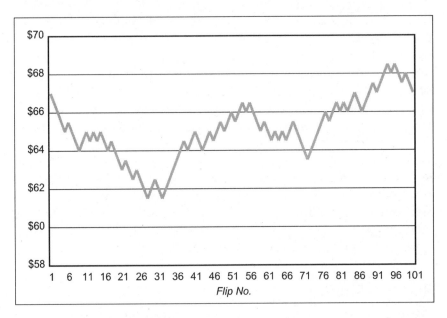

---

1   Burton Malkiel, *A Random Walk Down Wall Street*, 6th ed., W. W. Norton, New York, 1996.

market, you might ask him or her how good it is at predicting coin tosses.

There's a calculator on the www.veeneman.com Web site, *Random Plot.xls*, which will toss the coin a hundred times and plot the results on screen for you. If you have any friends who are serious chart-watchers, show them results from the program and tell them it shows recent price movements in some stock or another. Then ask them to interpret the results for you. It's a fair bet they really will find technical indicators, like head-and-shoulders patterns and resistance-point breakthroughs, in the chart.

Now, that doesn't mean there isn't anything an intelligent investor can do. Let's go back to the coin toss. Even though we can't predict the next toss of the coin, how about the next 100 tosses? What percentage will come up heads? If you have ever had the pleasure of a number cruncher's company for more than 5 minutes, you probably know the answer is "about 50 percent." That's called *playing the probabilities.*

PLAYING THE PROBABILITIES

Playing the probabilities is what statisticians do. The more you toss the coin, the more certain it is that 50 percent of the tosses will come up heads. At 100 tosses, the percentage can run anywhere from 46 to 54 percent, or "about 50 percent." At 1,000 tosses, it really starts zeroing in on 50 percent—the range runs from 49 to 51 percent. And at 10,000 tosses, you'll hit 50 percent on the nose just about every time![2]

It's called the *law of large numbers,* and it's the basis of much of what number crunchers do. Actuaries, whom you might think of as statistical undertakers, use it to predict the number of people who will die this year. Given a large enough group, they're amazingly accurate. In fact, there is an old gag on the subject:

> **Q:** What's the difference between a regular actuary and a Mafia actuary?

---

2   Most people have better things to do than sit around tossing coins all day, so there is a program on the www.veeneman.com Web site called *Coin Toss.exe.* This simple little program lets you tell it how many times to toss the coin. It will tell you the number and percentage of heads and tails that result. As you increase the number of tosses, you can watch the *law of large numbers* (discussed later in this chapter) start to kick in. It's a very worthwhile exercise, particularly if you are really bored.

A: A regular actuary can tell you how many people in a
crowded football stadium will die during the coming
year. The Mafia actuary can tell you who they are.

Remember the cliché about life insurance? "I'm betting that I'm
going to die, and the insurance company is betting I'm not." Well, if
you think about it, the insurance company isn't betting at all. As long
as they have about 10,000 customers or so, they know almost exactly
how many death claims will come in over the next year. They just
don't know if you will be in that group.

That's nice, but what does it have to do with investing? Just
about everything, as it turns out. Think of every day in the stock
market as a single coin toss. We know from the number crunchers
that we can't consistently predict the next day. But string a bunch of
those days together, and we can start predicting results the way
actuaries predict heart attacks. We can't predict what will happen
tomorrow or the next day, but we can begin to make fairly accurate
estimates of what will happen over the long haul.

HOW LARGE IS LARGE?

How many days does it take to start making accurate predictions?
You could have a million trading days, and you still wouldn't be able
to *predict* tomorrow or the day after accurately because of what we
said earlier about serial correlations. But here is what you can do.

We can get the number crunchers to do a particular calculation
called an *expected return*. If we ask them what stocks of large U.S.
companies are expected to earn per year, they will tell us it would
probably be somewhere around 13 percent per year. That's not
necessarily next year—it's *any* year. We'll get to what that means
shortly.

But before we do, let's stop for a moment. Aren't we contradicting ourselves? We have just finished saying that the past can't be
used to predict the future. Isn't that just what we are doing? Well, if
we stop at the expected return, that is *exactly* what we are doing. And
we know that doesn't work. In fact, the number cruncher would
probably point that out to us, only it would sound like a foreign
language.

Let's take another look at the expected return. We said that
stocks will *probably* earn *somewhere* around 13 percent per year.

That's because the 13 percent is nothing more than an average of the investment's historical returns. (Believe it or not, there are two different types of averages that number crunchers use. They use a simple average, the one you and I learned in school, to estimate likely future returns. But they call it an *arithmetic mean*. Which just goes to prove that you can make *anything* complicated.) Number crunchers tell us the average of an investment's past returns is the most *likely* estimate of future returns. But it doesn't mean you will ever earn exactly that amount in any one year. It's just an estimate we can use to compare different investments.

And it's not guaranteed. I may expect to play golf this weekend, but if it rains, I won't be on the golf course. (On the other hand, my friend Doug will be there anyway.) And as we know, it rains all the time in the stock market. Like the coin toss, there is a 50-50 chance we'll actually earn the expected return. But there is an equal chance we will earn something more or something less than that.

So, by itself, an expected return is not very useful. What we need is some way to measure the chances that things might not turn out as we expect. There are a number of esoteric measures, none of which is very intuitive. For example, when was the last time you ran into a standard deviation? But these measures *can* be used to come up with a yardstick that is more realistic. One very good yardstick is the degree to which the return might be higher or lower than what we expect.

THE RANGE OF AN INVESTMENT

Let's look at another example. Instead of stocks, let's say we put our money in the bank. Most of us are familiar with 90-day certificates of deposit. They are federally insured, and they are considered to be among the safest and most conservative investments in the known universe. These investments have an expected return of 4.9 percent. What many savers find attractive about CDs is that they probably won't vary much from that return. 95 percent of the time, the return shouldn't be lower than 3.3 percent or greater than 6.5 percent.[3] That's a pretty narrow range. Even if we don't see the expected return, the return we do see won't be very different. In other words,

---

3 Ranges are calculated using *confidence levels*, which are explained in the *glossary*.

TABLE 2-1

Returns and Ranges for Two Different Investments

Investment	Expected Return, %	Range, %
90-day CDs	4.9	3.3–6.5
Large U.S. stocks	13.0	−19.4–52.6

if we get a surprise, it will be a small one. Our CD investment is very predictable. Most people interpret that as low risk.

Now let's go back to our stock example. We said large U.S. stocks have an expected return of 13 percent per year. Although that's the "most likely" return, we probably won't hit it on the bull's-eye. The best we can say is that our actual return should be somewhere around there.

It probably comes as no surprise that stocks have a much broader range than CDs. 95 percent of the time, the actual return on large U.S. stocks could run as high as 52.6 percent, or as low as −19.4 percent (yes, that's a *loss* of almost 20 percent). In other words, the range is all over the board, and we can't be at all sure what to expect!

With both the *expected return* and the *range* of an investment, we can begin to compare different investments on an apples-to-apples basis. An example of such a comparison is shown in Table 2–1. We can use these two pieces of information to sort out those investments that we can expect to pay the highest long-term return for the amount of risk involved. More on that later.

IS GOOD NEWS RISKY?

Some people have a tough time equating risk with unpredictability. After all, there is a roughly even chance our actual return could be *higher* than what we expect. That's a surprise, but it's the kind we would all like to get! Hardly what most of us think of as risk. We worry about losing money, not making it.

But think about it for a second. I can put my money in CDs, where I can be pretty sure that, over the long haul, I will make somewhere between 3 and 6 percent. On top of that, the U.S.

government guarantees my account. You can't get much more predictable than that.

On the other hand, I can put my money in lottery tickets. If I do, my return can range anywhere from losing my money to winning millions. That's about as uncertain a proposition as you will find. If you didn't have at least *some* chance of hitting the jackpot, you would never buy the ticket. And if winning was anything but uncertain, the lottery would be out of business the day it opened its doors. Gain and loss are two sides of the same coin—both add up to risk.

THE FIX IS IN THE MIX

So far, we have assumed we would invest all of our money in either stocks or certificates of deposit. The range on CDs is comfortably narrow, but the expected return is awfully low. It barely keeps pace with inflation. On the other hand, the expected return for stocks is attractive, but the range is awfully wide.

President Harry Truman was faced with a similar dilemma in 1948, while listening to government economists present their economic forecasts. [Economists and statisticians have a lot in common. Some (mainly economists) claim statisticians are economists with personality deficits.] One after another, they presented reasons that the economy would flourish in the coming year. And one by one, they paused and intoned, "On the other hand ..." and then proceeded to give equally compelling reasons that the economy was about to go into the doldrums.

After a couple of hours of this, President Truman finally snapped. "What I really need," he barked, "is a one-handed economist!"

The answer, obviously, would be to split your investment between CDs and stocks. That's why investment types constantly harp on us to diversify our investments.

But how do we figure out which funds to use and how much to put in each fund? That's what the *Star portfolios* later in this book will answer.

For now, let's just say that we can control both the expected return and the range by adjusting the mix. For example, if we split our investment between CDs and stocks 50-50, the 1-year range would be –8.3 to 28.1 percent. Although that's still a pretty broad range, it's much narrower than the range for stocks alone (–19.4 to 52.6 percent).

The expected return for the mix would be 9.0 percent. That's not as high as the expected return for stocks alone, but it's nearly double the expected return for CDs alone. (And now you know why investment types have been harping on you to diversify for all these years.)

We'll see later that adjusting the mix is one of the most powerful means at our disposal for controlling risk. As we noted at the end of the first chapter, the investment mix determines over 90 percent of risk and return. When we get to the *Star portfolios,* we will have five different *asset classes,* or types of investments, to work with, rather than the two we used in this example. That will give us a lot more flexibility in matching risk and return to individual needs. But you will see that the process of choosing a portfolio is no more complicated than the example we looked at above.

WALL STREET IS A ZOO

We started out this chapter with the law of large numbers. We saw that we can't predict what is going to happen next, but we can start making *probabilistic forecasts* once we have a lot of information about a particular type of investment. The law of large numbers affects investing in another very important way, as well. The number crunchers tell us that over time, all investments *revert to the mean.* That means that sooner or later, the law of averages catches up with everyone, even geniuses.

We'd all like to think that a smart investment manager in going to do better than a dumb one. And by and large, that's true. Every time I go up against the pros, I get my clock cleaned. But every time the pros go up against a chimpanzee, they get *their* clocks cleaned. Don't ask me how I would do against the chimp.

So, what's going on here? Do monkeys really beat Wall Street professionals, or is this just another one of those urban myths, like alligators in the sewer system? Well, this one's true. My cousin knew a guy in Toledo who had a friend who saw it happen. I'm just kidding about that, but it really is true. NBC ran the experiment on its *Dateline* series a couple of years ago. But it wasn't really fair; the deck was stacked in the monkey's favor. More on that later.

THE MONEY PIT

Let's get back to reversion to the mean. That says the law of averages catches up with everyone sooner or later. But won't the smartest investment managers always beat everyone else? Here is a story that may shed some light on the subject.

One of the firms I worked with was a Wall Street investment management firm. Our meetings were generally held at their main office in the World Financial Center near Wall Street. To get to the conference room where we held our meetings, we walked down a second-floor corridor with a picture window that overlooked "The Pit." That's where the portfolio managers spent their days.

The Pit was about the size of a basketball court, with two banks of computer consoles that ran its length. Enormous video monitors and display screens were mounted on the walls. And yes, it did look like the NORAD command center. There were about 200 traders and managers working The Pit at any time. Every one of them, I was told, had at least an MBA from an Ivy League business school. The best and the brightest, yet they seemed to spend most of their time milling around. But when news broke, they earned their keep.

I enjoyed stopping at the picture window on the way to the conference room. You could always tell when news was about to break because the traders would drift back to their consoles. I think they had a sixth sense. The buzzing in The Pit would die down, and for a few moments it would become almost quiet. Then, as the news broke, there was a loud clicking as the traders hit the keys on their consoles to trade on the news.

Now, this little scene is repeated hourly all over New York, every day. And it's repeated in London, Tokyo, and all around the world. Thousands of experienced traders, all trading on the same information, at the same time. They don't all trade the same way. Some buy and some sell. But every one of those trades amounts to a financial vote on what the news means. The votes affect the price of a stock or bond. And everyone in the game worldwide knows what price everyone else is trading at. When news breaks, within seconds the market adjusts the price of the stock or bond to reflect the news. Any one of those traders can be wrong, but all of them? It's unlikely.

DO NOT PASS GO

For the system to work as it's supposed to, all those MBAs have to get the news at the same time. So what about those who are crafty enough to trade ahead of the news? Don't they do better than everyone else? Isn't that what the smart money does?

Yes, there are those who trade on "inside information." And when they get caught, they go directly to jail. They do not pass Go, they do not collect $200. Investment trading is one of the most heavily regulated industries on Earth. For example, I once wondered why brokers don't have e-mail. I was told it's because e-mail is considered written communication, and every written communication from a broker has to be reviewed by a manager.

So, if money managers, by and large, trade on the same information, how does one stock fund do better than another? It all comes down to style and risk, and sooner or later, the law of averages catches up with all of them. And that brings us back to the chimpanzee.

THE J. FRED MUGGS FUND

Years ago, long before *Dateline* ran its experiment with the monkey, a chimp starred on the *Today* show. It's true; in the early days of the show, it was hosted by Dave Garroway (a respected journalist) and a chimpanzee named J. Fred Muggs. This was about the same time Milton Berle regularly hosted the most popular weekly series on television wearing a dress.

Anyway, NBC has long had a thing for chimpanzees, so in 1993 they ran an experiment. They asked primary school students to pick a portfolio of stocks. They had a chimp pick a portfolio by pointing at the stock page of *The Wall Street Journal*. And somewhere, they found a Wall Street money manager who was a good enough sport to join the contest. The manager they recruited was no dummy. He was, and still is, a bright, capable money manager.

After several months, the results were tallied, and the three contestants finished in the following order:

- The schoolchildren
- The chimp
- The Wall Street professional

Or, in other words; the champ, the chimp, and the chump.

The Wall Street pro was a *really* good sport because he allowed himself to be interviewed on the program. He was asked such insightful questions as, "So, how does it feel to be beaten at your job by a monkey?" He laughed and said things just went that way sometimes.

But it wasn't really a fair contest. The chimp, and the schoolchildren for that matter, had a definite advantage. We can safely assume that at least the chimp didn't know what it was doing when it picked its stocks. So it stands to reason the chimp picked stocks at random.

If you pick Fortune 500 stocks truly at random, a little bit of magic begins to occur. The number of stocks you pick drives the magic. Somewhere around 20 well-diversified stocks, you begin to duplicate the performance of the market. And that's the way the *Dateline* game was run. The Wall Street professional wasn't really being pitted against a chimp. He was being pitted against the *market*.

The same experiment has been run any number of times by different academics. They typically choose their stocks by throwing darts at the financial pages. These "dartboard portfolios" have beaten the investment managers in most of these studies.

There is no real surprise in all of that. Over the past 20 years, the stock market has beaten over two-thirds of stock mutual funds. In recent years, the stock market[4] has regularly beaten as many as 85 percent of all stock fund managers.

It's no scandal, really, if you accept the premise that over 90 percent of your return comes from the asset class, and not the manager. There simply isn't much room for an investment manager to add value. A manager's contribution is often so relatively minor that the fees they charge can easily eat it up.

SMOKE, MIRRORS, AND INDEXES

If investing comes down to coin tosses and probabilities, then it raises some disturbing questions:

- Are investment managers worthless, or worse? Is Wall Street a huge shell game?

---

4   In this case we're talking about the market for large U.S. company stocks, as represented by the Standard & Poor's 500 Index.

- Some managers consistently beat other managers, and they consistently beat the indexes. How can that be, if investing comes down to tossing coins?

One of the hot debates over the past few years has occurred over *index funds*. These funds differ from other types of funds in that they don't try to beat the market. They try to *duplicate* it. For example, the manager of an S&P 500 Index Fund doesn't try to pick stocks that will outperform the average company. Indexers are very skeptical about anyone's ability to do that, for all the reasons we have already discussed.

Instead, the index fund buys all the stocks in the index. (Actually, most index funds use a variety of options and futures contracts to achieve the same result. It lowers their costs and actually increases the efficiency with which they track the index.) The fund will mirror the performance of the index and, consequently, the market. You will never beat the market investing in an index fund, but the market will never beat you either.

There is a wide variety of index funds. Many are based on the Standard & Poor's 500 Index, which measures the market performance of 500 of the largest publicly traded companies in the United States. There are also index funds that track bond indexes, smaller-company stock indexes, and so on.

Index funds offer two potential benefits to investors:

- An index fund comes as close as one can to a guarantee of market performance. There is no chance that a manager's misstep will cost the investor money. (A classic misstep by an active manager occurred in February 1996. Jeffery Vinik, then the lead portfolio manager for Fidelity's flagship Magellan Fund, became convinced the stock market was about to slide. He moved 20 percent of the $56 billion fund's investments from stocks to bonds. The stock market ignored him and continued to plow ahead, and as a result, Magellan trailed the market for months.)
- Index funds appeal to the skinflint in all of us. The fees are often one-sixth of those charged by comparable funds that are "actively managed."

Index funds are based on a simple proposition: If managers can't, as a rule, beat the market, then why pay their high fees?

Index funds languished for years. "The only guarantee is guaranteed mediocrity," according to the active management community. My friend Carl put the challenge another way at lunch a few months ago. "Do you mean to tell me," he asked, "that an intelligent and experienced market professional can't beat the averages? That's absurd!"

I will be the first person to admit that it does sound awfully strange. Doesn't it stand to reason that someone doing research would do better than someone who doesn't?

But we are forgetting something. Suppose *everyone* does research? Suppose the market is crowded with MBAs huddled over computer networks, hitting their keys within seconds after news breaks. In effect, they *are* the market. In trying to beat the system, they are only trying to beat themselves. If most of them were stupid and only a few were bright, there might be some chance for a clever manager to exploit some inefficiency. But no one has ever claimed these folks are stupid. Their collective drive and intelligence is what makes it all but impossible for any of them to be king of the hill for more than 15 minutes.

And that leaves us with the indexers. They simply buy the market and hold it. They reap much of the benefit of the work that goes on in trading pits all over the world. And that drives some active managers crazy. "They're freeloaders!" is a common cry. "If the market weren't as efficient as it is, there is no way they could approach the performance of active management, much less surpass it."

That may be true. But it brings home our basic point. At times, the market may not be terribly efficient. The crash of 1987 shows how frantic and irrational the markets can be, and much of the time they appear to be driven solely by fear and greed. By and large, however, those thousands of traders, brokers, and portfolio managers operate as a pretty efficient system. As Professor Malkiel observes:

> No scientific evidence has yet been assembled to indicate that the investment performance of professionally managed portfolios as a group has been any better than that of randomly selected portfolios.[5]

It may very well be that there simply isn't very much room, not more than a percentage point or so, for active managers to add value.

---

5 Burton Malkiel, *A Random Walk Down Wall Street*, 6th ed., W. W. Norton, New York, 1996, p. 184.

Don't get too carried away with the idea of riding the coattails of the market. There are a *lot* of markets, and they aren't all as efficient as the market for large U.S. stocks seems to be. Index funds don't work as well in these less efficient markets. For example, they don't have nearly as strong a track record in the market for smaller U.S. stocks. These smaller companies aren't followed as intensely as their larger counterparts, and they aren't traded as frequently as the largest companies. While thousands of pin-striped MBAs spend their days researching the biggest and the best, there do seem to be opportunities for hard work to pay off with smaller stocks.

In other words, index funds aren't a panacea. They seem to work very well in some markets but not as well in others. And that brings us to our second question: If at least some markets are efficient enough to limit an investment manager's opportunity to add value, then how come some funds still beat others?

RISK IS A FOUR-LETTER WORD

We see it all the time. "The Izzobaf Large Cap Equity Fund outperformed 98 percent of its peers over the past 3 years." How can that be if investing boils down to playing probabilities?

To answer that question, we need to turn to Professor William Sharpe, one of the unsung heroes of the Investing Revolution. (Well, not quite unsung. He won the 1991 Nobel Prize in Economics for his work in developing the Capital Asset Pricing Model, which is where we are headed next. He is also one of the best-known academics in investing and finance.) Professor Sharpe was the prime developer of what is known as the *Capital Asset Pricing Model,* or CAPM. Entire books have been written about CAPM, so anything we say about it here will invariably oversimplify things. But the gist of CAPM is as follows:

There are two kinds of investment risk: *company risk* and *market risk.* (CAPM theory calls these risks *unsystematic risk* and *systematic risk,* respectively. Market pros use the term *market risk* to refer to another kind of risk. To keep things simple, we are going to drop the jargon in favor of the more easily understood terms.) Both types refer to mishaps that can cause the value of an investment to fall.

Company risk is the risk that the stock price of a company I invest in will fall because of something that happens to the company. Izzobaf Industries' microwave ovens suddenly begin exploding; it's a safe bet that their stock will take a serious hit. But the stock of other microwave oven manufacturers may actually go up. *Market risk* is the risk that the stock price will fall because of an event that occurs outside the company's control. The United States slides into a prolonged recession; the entire stock market will probably sink like a stone.

I can get rid of company risk by diversifying, spreading my investments among a number of different stocks in a number of different industries. If I own one company's stock and that company goes bankrupt, I lose all my investment. If I own two stocks and one company goes broke, I lose only half my investment. If I spread the money among 20 stocks, only 5 percent of my investment is exposed to any single company. At around 20 well-selected stocks, company risk literally begins to disappear.

I can never get rid of market risk. It's always there, and it's the price I pay for the return I receive on my investment. The rising tide lifts all boats, and when the tide goes out, all boats fall. It's that simple.

Let's say investors can choose between two investments, both of which have the same return. The only difference between the investments is that one is riskier than the other. Which one will they choose? The less risky investment, of course. All those MBAs huddled over their consoles are chasing the highest return at the lowest risk. The result is that for every level of return, there is a corresponding amount of risk an intelligent investor will be willing to take on.

If you accept all that, then one conclusion is inescapable: *To get a higher return, you will have to take on more risk!* This proposition is at the heart of CAPM, and of modern investing in general. Boil down all the models and all the equations, and it comes down to this: There is no free lunch.

ALPHABET SOUP

If that's the case, then there are few ways a manager can beat the market: The most obvious is to add more risk to your portfolio. It stands to reason that, if risk goes up with return, then the reverse is also true. Add more risk, and return will follow, at least over the long haul. It's like a machine—dial in more risk on the console, and the machine cranks out more return. This risk can be measured and compared to the risk of a market index, like the Standard & Poor's 500. The ratio of the two is called *beta*.

The market, by definition, has a beta of 1.0. An investment that is riskier than the market will have a higher beta. For example, an investment with a beta of 1.2 is 1.2 times, or 20 percent, riskier than the market. Now comes the key question: *So what?*

We said risk goes up with return and that every level of risk has its corresponding level of return. That means if we know the risk, we can predict what the return *should* be. For simplicity's sake, let's assume risk and return follow each other on a 1-for-1 basis. In other words, an investment with a beta of 1.2 should earn 20 percent more than the market.

What if that's not the case? What if the investment earned 22 percent more than the market? The difference between the actual return and the return predicted by the fund's beta is called an *alpha*. (In classic CAPM theory, an alpha is the amount of company risk in a return. Diversification virtually eliminates company risk. Consequently, alphas should not exist in a well-diversified portfolio.) Investors view alphas two ways:

- The 22 percent return is higher than was predicted by the beta. The 2 percent alpha is an *excess return* that didn't come from risk. In other words, the manager really did add value to the return.
- Betas are calculated over a period, such as 3 years. The alpha suggests the fund was more aggressive during the most recent period than it was over the period used to calculate the beta.

According to the first view, there may not be a free lunch, but there are peanuts at the bar, and the manager did a pretty good job of scooping them up. A manager that generates a positive alpha has earned its keep over an index fund.

Proponents of the second view argue that the alpha represents added risk, not added value. By this view, the alpha represents an inconsistency in the fund's management style. (In the heyday of CAPM, an army of investment consultants made the rounds of pension funds measuring the betas and alphas of their investment managers. In recent years, CAPM has started to show its age. Academics have found holes in the theory, and the general consensus these days seems to be that CAPM doesn't do as complete a job as originally thought of explaining how investment markets work. But it is still accepted as a sound working model of risk and return.)

THE EFFICIENCY ASSUMPTION

The second view assumes that *all* return comes from risk. For that to be the case, investment markets would have to be 100 percent "efficient." The *efficient market hypothesis* (It's a hypothesis because there remains room to argue both sides. No one has come up with conclusive evidence that would close the book one way or the other.) has been the subject of great debate for over a generation:

- The extreme (or "strong") view of market efficiency says that there is nothing the portfolio managers in The Pit could do to add value to their portfolios. Even inside information wouldn't help them because it is already factored into the price of the investment.
- A less extreme (or "semistrong") view says that the portfolio managers in The Pit are so good at what they do that all *public information* is factored into the prices of stocks and bonds within seconds after being released. Consequently, there are no undervalued stocks (or bonds). Every stock's price fully and fairly reflects everything that is known about its issuer.
- The least extreme (or "weak") view says that the portfolio managers in The Pit are good, but they aren't perfect. They do make their share of bad calls, and that leaves *some* room for an astute analyst to find undervalued stocks. It just doesn't leave much room to do so.
- The *Star system* adopts the semistrong view of market efficiency, even though there is ample evidence to support the weak view. The reason is that the opportunities to add value are limited, and they are overwhelmed by other factors.

THE FIRST LAW OF INVESTING

Woody Allen once said that "80 percent of success is just showing up." In investing, it may be closer to 92 percent. A series of academic studies has looked at how much investment managers really contribute to investment returns through investment picking and market timing. The leading study was performed in 1987 and updated in 1991.[6] It concluded the following:

- Market forces determine about 92 percent of an investment's performance.
- Activities by managers, such as investment selection and market timing, determine only the remaining 8 percent of performance.

In other words, if my actively managed stock fund earned 10 percent last year, 9.2 percent of those earnings was driven by market forces beyond the fund manager's control. I earned that return *just by being in stocks*, just for showing up. The manager determined only the remaining 0.8 percent.

That means that *asset allocation,*—how I divide my investments among basic categories such as stocks and bonds—is by far and away the most important factor in determining both risk and return. It also leads to the *Star system's* first law of investing:

Law 1: There is no free lunch—a higher return means greater risk.

Given everything we have seen in this chapter, that's really just common sense. Money doesn't appear out of nowhere, and the stock market is efficient enough that undervalued stock opportunities are few and far between, at least where large stocks are concerned.

SMOKE, MIRRORS, AND RISK

Let's go back to our original question: If asset allocation accounts for 92 percent of risk and return and if there is not much room for managers to beat the market, then how do they do it? The answer should be pretty obvious by now. In many cases they do it by taking on more risk than the market.

That means we need to modify our original statement. There is not much room for managers to beat the market *at the market level of risk*. Beating the market is actually pretty easy, at least over the long haul. Simply take on more risk. What's tough is beating the market without taking on more than the market level of risk.

---

6   Gary P. Brinson, L. Randolph Hood, and Gilbert L. Breebower, "Determinants of Portfolio Performance," *Financial Analysts Journal,* July–August 1986, p. 39, and Gary P. Brinson, Brian D. Singer, and Gilbert L. Breebower, "Determinants of Portfolio Performance II: An Update," *Financial Analysts Journal,* May–June 1991, p. 40.

Here is another way of looking at it. Remember the Volvo and the soccer-mom from the first chapter? The bicycle may not be able to beat the Volvo, but a Lamborghini driven by Danny Sullivan, winner of the 1985 Indianapolis 500, would leave it in the dust. But a Lamborghini costs one heckuva lot more than a Volvo, and Danny's services don't come cheap. If you want to go faster, it's going to cost you more. But the most important thing to remember is this: Both cars will leave the bicycle in the distance. There is a lot less difference between the two cars than there is between the cars and the bike.

GETTING A HANDLE ON RISK

So what does all that mean for the investor? It's not enough to look at a manager's return, although that's all you ever see in their marketing materials. Return doesn't really mean anything unless you also know the risk that goes along with it. The *Star* system uses two measures of risk:

- It uses the *range* of an investment's return as one measure of risk. An investment with a range of –4 to 12 percent is riskier than one with a range of 1 to 7 percent. This yardstick is used to compare the risk of different mixes, or asset allocations.

- It uses beta to set return targets for the funds in a portfolio. Funds that perform differently than their betas predict may be more or less risky than the investor had anticipated.

Both measures can be used to set strategic targets for a portfolio and regulate its performance. That's one of the *Star* acronyms—"Strategic targeting and regulating." As we move through the book, you will learn how to set investment targets for your portfolio and how to regulate the portfolio, to keep it on a steady course toward those targets.

3
CHAPTER

Keep It Simple

Growth versus value and other investing debates aren't important for most investors.

We spent a lot of time in the last chapter debunking what might be called "the myth of performance." Mutual fund companies and other investment managers go to great lengths to distinguish themselves from one another and to sell their market-beating performance. But we saw that many academics are skeptical about investment mangers' ability to add more than modest value to your investments. If asset allocation really does account for 92 percent of performance, then there simply may not be room for managers to add more than modest value.

We also saw that it really hasn't been hard to beat the market in the last few years. Simply add risk and stir. By widening the range we are willing to live with, we can increase the expected return. As long as the market continues to boom, we will come out on the top end of the range. But the number crunchers tell us that, sooner or later, things will probably even out.

In this chapter, we will look at a couple of other debates that seem to occupy investment people inordinately. These debates sound awfully important, but in the end they may amount to much sound and fury, signifying nothing.

HOW MANY ANGELS CAN DANCE ON THE HEAD OF A PIN?

In some respects, these debates amount to an argument about how many angels can dance on the head of a pin. When I was a kid, Father McGee used to come into our religion class once a week. He told us a story once, about how theologians used to argue how many angels could fit on the head of a pin. And then he asked us if it really mattered. "The most important things," he said, "are really pretty simple. Don't get caught up in ivory-tower debates of dubious consequence."

He taught us something else, too. We should watch out, he said, for people who tried to sway us with these debates. He was fond of the Shakespeare quote, "The devil can quote scripture for his purpose."[1] A healthy dose of skepticism, he said, would take us a long way.

And so it is with investing. A good snake-oil salesperson (and that includes authors of investment books) can cite statistics to support just about anything, as we will see in both of the Great Debates we discuss in this chapter. The first debate is over whether risk goes down over time. If it doesn't, then virtually everything you know about investing is wrong. The second debate is preceded only by religion or politics in the number of heated discussions it has generated. That's the argument over whether growth investing or value investing performs better over the long haul.

What we will see is that both of these debates don't amount to very much in the end. They sound important, but they are greatly overshadowed by three simple, common-sense investment principles, which we call the *three laws of investing.* You saw the first one in the last chapter. We will introduce the second and third here.

TIME HEALS ALL WOUNDS

It has long been conventional wisdom that risk goes down over time. It's in virtually every primer on investing ever written. The longer you have until you need your savings, the less you can be hurt by short-term swings in stocks and bonds.

By and large, that's just common sense. For example, let's say I invest $1,000 in large U.S. stocks. We saw the likely results in the last chapter. Over a 1-year period, my most likely return is 13.0 percent, but I could earn anything from a high of 52.6 percent to a low of –19.4 percent.

---

1   William Shakespeare, *The Merchant of Venice,* act 1, sc. 3.

But what does that mean? Let's say the worst happens, and 1 year after making my investment, I find that I have lost 19.4 percent. That means I have only $806 left of the original $1,000 I invested. Ouch!

At this point I have two choices: I can cash out the investment, take my losses, and go home, or I can stick with the investment. If I stick with the investment for another 4 years, or a total of 5, here is what happens:

- First, the return range narrows. The high for a 5-year period would be 25.8 percent, and the low would be –5.9 percent. The high isn't as high as the 1-year high, and the low isn't as low as the 1-year low.
- Second, my worst-case loss diminishes. If the worst happens and I end up losing an average of 5.9 percent, I will have $823 at the end of the 5 years. Even in the worst case, I am better off than I was at 1 year. Maybe not much better off, but better off nonetheless.

If I hang onto my stock investment for 10 or 20 years, the situation continues to improve, as Table 3–1 shows. If I hang in there for 10 years, then even in the worst case I should end up with about what I started with. I may not have made money, but at least I didn't lose any of my investment. And if I stick it out for 20 years, then even in the worst case I can expect to just about double my money.

Of course, what we have been talking about are worst cases. If stocks earn their expected return, then I should have $1,845 after 5 years, $3,404 after 10 years, and a whopping $11,589 after 20 years. And that's why investment types say that the longer you have until you need your money, the less you can be hurt by risk. For just about

TABLE 3–1

How Longer Time Frames Affect Potential Losses

Time Frame, Years	Range, %	Worst Case— What's Left, Dollars
1	−19.4–52.6	806
5	−3.8–27.9	823
10	0.3–22.7	1028
20	3.3–19.1	1909

any period of time of 10 years or longer, there is very little chance of losing your initial investment, and there is at least an even change of tripling your money or better.

RISK GOES DOWN OVER TIME, OR DOESN'T IT?

But every once in a while, you hear a number cruncher challenge the conventional wisdom. Usually, it's in an article with a title like "The Fallacy of Time Diversification."[2]

These articles make the point that while the range of your *rate of return* does narrow over time, it doesn't matter. They point out that the *dollar range* actually gets wider over time.

Let's go back to our example using large U.S. stocks:

Let's say you put $1,000 in large U.S. stocks. As we have seen, over a 1-year period, you can expect a return of between –19.4 and 52.6 percent. In dollar terms, your $1,000 investment could shrink to $806 by the end of the year, or it could grow to as much as $1,526. That's a spread of $720 between the high and the low.

Over 5 years, the range is from –3.8 to 27.9 percent. The return range has narrowed, so risk has gone down, right?

Not according to the naysayers. With that 5-year range, your $1,000 could shrink to $823 or grow to as much as $3,428.[3] That's a *dollar range* of $2,605, which is over 3½ times as large as the dollar range over 1 year. The dollar range is *increasing* with time, which means risk is going up!

If we calculate the dollar range for 10 and 20 years, we will see the dollar range continue to widen. Table 3–2 shows the results. So which is right? Both and neither. Like so many other things in life, it all depends on how you look at it. And the whole argument may amount to debating how many angels can fit on the head of a pin. The return ranges we have been looking at show, get ready for this, the *average annualized compound rate of return*. Still awake? It means

---

2 I'm not inventing this title. It is the title of an actual article from the June 1997 issue of *The Journal of Financial Planning*.

3 There is a calculator on the www.veeneman.com Web site that you can use to figure out dollar ranges. It's called *Dollar Ranges.xls*. Enter a time frame and a return range, and the calculator will show the dollar range at the end of the time frame. There is also a demo on the Web site called *Tulips and Trumpets.xls*. This demo shows, year by year, how a return range can become narrower while its corresponding dollar range becomes broader.

TABLE 3–2

Dollar Ranges and Spreads for Large U.S. Stocks over Different Time Frames

Time Frame, Years	Dollar Range	Spread, Dollars
1	806 – 1,526	720
5	823 – 3,428	2,605
10	1,028 – 7,736	6,708
20	1,909 – 33,141	31,232

we're looking at an average return *per year*. That allows us to make apples-to-apples comparisons over different periods. And by that measure, risk does go down over time.

Even so, the *dollar range* will still go up over time. *Compounding*, the process by which money grows, is a lot like rolling a snowball downhill. The longer you roll the snowball, the bigger it gets. So by that measure, a longer hill means a bigger snowball.

THE ONE-HANDED ECONOMIST

Feeling confused? You're not alone. Does risk go down over time? We're back to Harry Truman and the pressing need for a one-handed economist. Well, here's a one-handed answer to the question. It is illustrated by the graphs that appear in the figures that follow.

As Figure 3–1 shows, the stock market has lost money in 20 out of the past 71 years. Put in $1,000 today, and you have a better than 1-in-4 chance of ending up with less than that 1 year from today. But what happens if you hold on to your stock for a total of 5 years? Let's go back over those same 71 years and see how many times you would have lost money. We'll start a new 5-year period each year, so our periods will overlap, and we will end up with 65 of them. Figure 3–2 shows the results. It turns out that over 70 years, there were only seven times when you would have lost money. In other words, in 13 of those 20 years when the market lost money, it had regained its losses in an additional 4 years. And in nearly every one of those cases, it not only regained its losses but also went on to make money for the 5-year period.

F I G U R E 3–1

Large U.S. Stock Gains and Losses, 1-Year Periods, 1926–1996

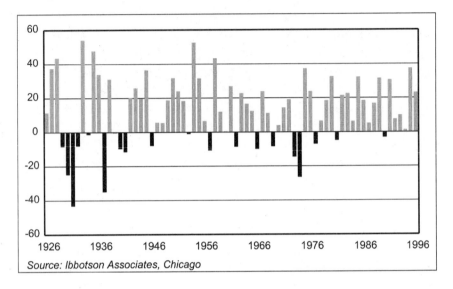

Source: Ibbotson Associates, Chicago

F I G U R E 3–2

Large U.S. Stock Gains and Losses, 5-Year Periods, 1926–1996

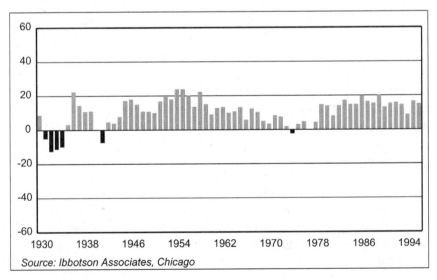

Source: Ibbotson Associates, Chicago

The same holds true for longer periods. Suppose you held onto your money for 10 years. Figure 3–3 shows those results. There are only two periods (both beginning during the Great Depression) where you would have ended up with less than you started with. In other words, in five of the seven periods when the stock market didn't make up its losses after 5 years, it made them up in 10.

Finally, there has never been a 20-year period when the stock market has ended up lower than it started. That doesn't mean it's guaranteed not to happen, but it's very unlikely. Figure 3–4 shows the record. So, if you put your money in the stock market, there is a 1-in-4 chance you could have less than you started with at this time next year. If you ride out the storm and don't jump ship, there is only about a 1-in-10 chance you won't be ahead in 5 years. If you have 10 years, the risk of loss goes down to about 1 in 33, and if you have 20 years, you come as close to a guarantee as you're ever going to get.

RIDING OUT THE STORM

Are we cheating here? We just finished saying that risk has two tails—the upside and the downside. But that takes us right back to

FIGURE 3–3

Large U.S. Stock Gains and Losses, 10-Year Periods, 1926–1996

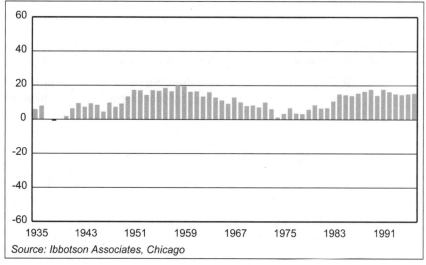

Source: Ibbotson Associates, Chicago

FIGURE 3-4

Large U.S. Stock Gains and Losses, 20-year Periods, 1926–1996

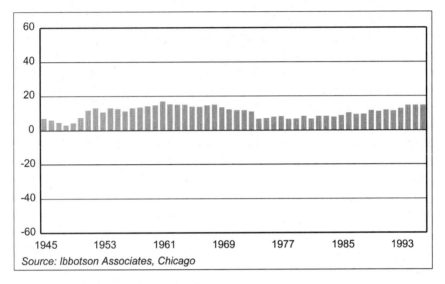

Source: Ibbotson Associates, Chicago

the "Do we use the average return or the ending value?" debate. As we were saying, angels dancing on the head of a pin. What we can say is this:

- Your risk of ending up with less than you started with does go down the longer you hold on to an investment.
- The return range narrows over time.

In most people's book, that qualifies as risk going down over time. And that brings us to the *Star* system's second law of investing:

> **Law 2**: Risk goes down over time—the longer you have until you need your money, the less you can be hurt by short-term swings in the stock and bond markets.

HEMLINES AND THE STREET

We have been discussing one of the great teapot tempests of the past few years, whether risk goes down over time. As we saw, the answer turns out to be largely common sense. From a technical standpoint, risk may not to go down over time. However, common sense tells us that we can't be hurt by near-term swings in the stock market if we don't need our savings for another 20 years, and the numbers bear that out. So, the whole debate boils down to an argument over how many angels can dance on the head of a pin. It becomes a distraction, and it diverts our attention from asset allocation, which determines better than 90 percent of our performance.

A number of investment debates revolve around different "styles" of investing. Wall Street and the fashion industry have gone hand in hand for generations. There used to be a popular stock market barometer called *the hemline indicator*. When hemlines on women's dresses got shorter, the story went, the stock market boomed. When hemlines got longer, it tanked.

The hemline indicator actually worked for quite a while after World War II. But it fell apart when hemlines ceased to be a one-size-fits-all fashion statement. As silly as it was, the hemline indicator was probably no sillier than the Super Bowl indicator, or any of the other indicators that have been popular in the past 50 years.

THE GREAT GROWTH VERSUS VALUE DEBATE

When we talk about style, we aren't talking about hemlines or colors, though. We're talking about different approaches to the same sorts of investments. Take one of the great debates among common-stock investors: Which is better, *growth investing* or *value investing?* For years, investors have argued the merits of one over the other. And, in fact, you can make strong cases for either one.[4]

GROWTH VERSUS WHAT?

Growth versus value may be a burning issue in investment circles, but it isn't something that most of us are likely to bump into in our everyday lives. Most of us have never even heard of growth investing or value investing. So first, some definitions may be in order.

Growth companies are the ones investors expect to grow faster than the average company in the stock market. Microsoft is a good example of a growth company. These companies tend to be the darlings of Wall Street, and investors eagerly bid up their prices. *Value companies*, on the other hand, are the ugly ducklings of the

---

4   If you want to see the numbers on the growth versus value debate, you can download the worksheet *Growth vs. Value* from the veeneman.com Web site.

market. Investors expect them to grow more slowly than the average company. These stocks are less in demand, and consequently they generally trade at a lower price.

Companies can, and often do, move back and forth between the growth and value groups. It all depends on what investors are willing to pay for their stock. A good example is IBM. It was one of the hottest growth stocks of the 1960s and 1970s, but it fell out of favor in the late 1980s when it was overtaken by the personal computer revolution. Its stock price fell to less than half its former level, and IBM was widely thought to be a "fallen angel."

To value investors, it was a potential diamond in the rough. They began buying its shares and profited handsomely when a new IBM management team engineered a turnaround in the early 1990s. Subsequently, its stock price rose as more investors renewed their optimism for the company, and it moved back into the growth camp.

IN THIS CORNER . . .

The Great Growth versus Value Debate revolves around the following: Will you as an investor come out ahead buying growth stocks, even though they are more expensive than average? Or is the better strategy to look for fallen angels in the market, overlooked bargains in the form of companies poised for a turnaround? There are no records of duels having been fought over this dispute, but the debate has been fierce, nonetheless.

THE CASE FOR GROWTH FUNDS

Growth investors are convinced of the superiority of their approach. In 7 of the past 10 years, they will tell you, growth stocks have outperformed value stocks. In fact, if you had put money into stocks any time between the beginning of 1987 and the end of 1990, you would have been better off putting your money in growth stocks. If you had put $1,000 in growth stocks on January 1, 1987, you would have had $4,254 by the end of 1996. Put the same $1,000 in value stocks, and you would have had only $3,954 at the end of 1996.

THE CASE FOR VALUE FUNDS

"Foul ball!" cry the advocates of value investing. "If you had put that same $1,000 into stocks in nearly any of the 12 years before 1987, you would have been better off in value stocks." And, in fact, that's true. You would also have been better off in value stocks if you had put your $1,000 in value stocks between 1991 and 1993.

And if we look at the longer term, the case for value stocks becomes even more compelling. Let's say you had invested your $1,000 on January 1, 1977. Put those dollars in value stocks, and you would have $16,660 by the end of 1996. Put them in growth stocks, and you would have only $12,909. And that's including the past 10 years, when growth stocks have modestly outperformed value stocks. In other words, the superior performance of value stocks between 1976 and 1986 far outweighs the growth stock performance since then.

AS THE DUST SETTLES

This is generally the point at which the two camps start screaming about manipulated numbers and begin throwing things at each other. So, which of them is right? We can debate the subject endlessly, and it is questionable whether we will ever come to any conclusion two investors would agree upon. Both sides can cite convincing statistics for their case. And, as Mark Twain pointed out, there are three kinds of liars: "liars, damn liars, and statistics."

In the end, it all becomes a game. We can make the result come out any way we want, by carefully choosing our starting and ending dates. If we invest on this date, growth wins. If we invest on that date, value wins. (For example, I can make the case in favor of value stocks seem very convincing by moving the starting date back 2 years, to January 1, 1975. A $1,000 investment in value stocks on that date would be worth $32,231 at the end of 1996, while the same investment in growth stocks would be worth only $19,357.) And sometimes, we can make the numbers come out one way by assuming we put in $1,000 in a lump sum and another way by assuming we put in $1,000 per year. After a while, it all starts to sound like angels dancing on the head of a pin. (Of course, to a value investor, it comes down to *fallen* angels dancing on the head of a pin.)

So who wins the debate, growth investors or value investors? As my 16-year-old daughter likes to say, "Don't sweat it. It really doesn't matter that much!"

Now, at this point you really should be shaking your head. "How can you say 'don't sweat it' when there are literally thousands of dollars riding on this decision?"

TABLE 3-3

Value of a $1,000 Investment at the End of 1996

Investment	Invested 1/1/87, Dollars	Invested 1/1/77, Dollars
Value stocks	3,954	16,660
Growth stocks	4,253	12,909
Bonds	2,479	6,675

Look at Table 3–3; it compares bonds to both growth and value stocks. No matter whether we choose 10 years or 20 years, both growth and value stocks beat bonds by a wide margin. Which is better, growth or value? We don't really know. But we do know that *both* beat bonds consistently.

THE MORAL OF THE STORY

And that's precisely the point. Investors sometimes get awfully hung up in very complicated debates over what may end up being relatively small points.

Arguing growth versus value is like arguing over which brand of gasoline is better for the Volvo in the last chapter. Personally, I don't care as long as the gas is any good at all. I just want to make sure I'm in the Volvo, and not sitting on a bicycle arguing fine points.

Many of the arguments over different styles of investing amount to relatively little in the larger scheme of things. Most of us will come out much further ahead in the long run if we simply forget about growth versus value or technical arguments about whether risk really goes down over time. As we saw in Chapter 2, *asset allocation,* or how we spread our investments among some very fundamental types of investments, determines over 90 percent of our investment performance. That's the *Star* system's third law of investing:

> **Law 3**: The "fix is in the mix"—asset allocation determines over 90 percent of the performance of your investments.

THE HOBGOBLIN OF HOBGOBLINS

Although the Great Style Debate may be vastly overblown, style is very important in one respect. An investment manager should be able to articulate an investment style and stick to it through thick and thin. Otherwise, the manager is simply trying to outguess the market. And as we saw in the last chapter, that's like trying to outguess a series of coin flips.

A manager with a consistent style works within the law of large numbers. Let's go back to the coin toss. If I try to call the next toss of the coin, I'm either going to be right or wrong; close doesn't count in this game. A manager with a consistent style won't try to guess the next toss of the coin. Instead, he or she will pursue essentially the same strategy whether the market is up or down.

Pursuing this sort of long-term strategy is more like flipping the coin a couple of thousand times. As the number of tosses grows, I can make more accurate estimates of the total number of heads or tails simply by playing the probabilities. Close not only begins to count; it becomes very important! You don't have to hit the bull's-eye to do quite well.

A classic example is Peter Lynch, who achieved fame and considerable fortune running Fidelity's flagship Magellan Fund in the 1970s and 1980s. He was an object of fascination to the financial press, which portrayed him as the shrewdest trader in the history of American finance. One might imagine Lynch wading into the trading pits with six-guns blazing, buying and selling whole companies in a frenzy of brilliant wheeling and dealing. Then, in 1992, William Sharpe, who achieved fame in academic circles,[5] ran a study of Magellan during Lynch's tenure.[6] He compared it to a supposedly stodgy, steady-as-they-go fund. What he found was amazing. Lynch was not a gunslinger; quite the opposite—he doggedly pursued an unwavering strategy. Sharpe concluded that Lynch was so consistent in his approach to the market that over 97 percent of Magellan's performance could be attributed to the *type* of stocks he bought, to his *style*.

---

5   Not to mention the 1991 Nobel Prize in Economics for his contributions to the development of the Capital Asset Pricing Model (see Chapter 2).

6   William F. Sharpe, "Asset Allocation: Management Style and Performance Measurement," *The Journal of Portfolio Management*, Winter 1992, p. 7.

We have been saying that over 92 percent of risk and return are attributable to asset allocation. In fact, Lynch's record shows that the percentages can run even higher. It also shows that very successful money managers need not be cowboys or gunslingers.

KEEPING IT SIMPLE

In short, one of the most successful money managers of the 1980s was also one of the most consistent. We will revisit this subject later in the book, when we talk about how to select an investment fund or manager. We'll show you how to judge for yourself whether a manager follows a consistent strategy or is blown around by the winds of the marketplace.

But for now, just remember two things:

- Keep things simple.
- Keep them consistent.

Sometimes it's very hard to avoid getting caught up in debates that sound very important. As a kid, I really *wanted* to know how many angels could dance on the head of a pin. So I asked Father McGee. He looked thoughtful for a moment, then said, "Three hundred and forty two." I was feeling quite impressed with this answer when he shrugged his shoulders and said, "That's probably as good an answer as any other." Then he chuckled and headed down the hall.

Simplicity and consistency are the keys to a successful, goal-oriented investment strategy. In the next chapter, we will begin introducing the *Star* system, which you can use to simplify your investing and navigate a steady course through the storms that rock investment markets.

4

CHAPTER

Investment Building Blocks

The pros and cons of savings accounts, CDs, money market funds, guaranteed investment contracts, bonds, and stocks.

We have covered a lot of ground. We saw in Chapter 2 that investing can largely be boiled down to probabilities. We can make probabilities work in our favor, and we can use them to control risk. We saw that risk and return are two sides of the same coin; to earn a higher return, we have to live with more market risk. There is no free lunch.

In Chapter 3 we saw the virtue of simplicity. Market risk can be reduced to the second law of investing: It goes down over time. Investing doesn't have to be complicated, and many of the hot disputes in the investment world may amount to little more than arguing about how many angels can dance on the head of a pin. The reason, we said, was the third law of investing: The fix is in the mix. Or, in academic terms, asset allocation accounts for over 90 percent of investment performance.

But we have yet to talk about a couple of questions that are pretty important to the investment approach we are explaining:

- What the heck is an asset class, anyway?
- Which ones am I likely to run across, and how will I know one when I trip over them?

That's where we're going in this chapter.

WHAT'S AN ASSET CLASS?

At the beginning of each seminar, I try to get a feel for how much the audience already knows. One of the questions I ask is whether anyone knows what an asset class is. At one corporate seminar, a man in the middle of the room raised his hand and said, "That's what this is, isn't it? My manager said I should come to the asset class so I could make more money on my 401k."

That's one kind of asset class, but there is another kind that's a lot more important. To investment types, an *asset class* is a very basic investment category. Here are the major asset classes most investment professionals agree upon:

- Stable values
- Bonds
- Stocks
- Real estate
- Precious metals
- Commodities

As an individual investor, you are most likely to encounter the first three: stable values, bonds, and stocks. They include the vast majority of mutual funds and other investment vehicles available. In this chapter, we are going to talk about those three asset classes and the various investments in each. The last three are more exotic, and you are not likely to run across them.

The advantage of approaching investing from the standpoint of asset classes is that it allows us to simplify investing dramatically. Instead of having to talk about 57 different varieties of stock funds, we can simply talk about stocks. As we have said repeatedly, the percentage of savings you allocate to stocks is far more important than which of the 57 varieties you choose.

OWNERS AND LOANERS

As we look at asset classes, you'll find you can invest in one of two ways:

- You can lend your money out and earn interest (become a *loaner*).
- You can buy something that you expect to increase in value (become an *owner*).

We're going to look at a lot of different investments, but they're going to boil down to those that make you a loaner and those that make you an owner. As you look at each asset class, ask yourself: Does it make you a loaner or an owner, and how does that affect the risk involved? We'll come back to owners and loaners later.

STABLE VALUES HAVE NOTHING TO DO WITH HORSES

Let's start with *stable values.* A stable value is any investment that looks, acts, smells, and tastes like a savings account. A classic example of a stable value is . . . a savings account.

A stable value makes you a loaner. When you deposit money in a savings account, you aren't turning it over to the bank for safekeeping. If that were the case, the bank would charge you for their services instead of paying you interest. Your deposit amounts to a loan from you to the bank. When you withdraw money from your account, the withdrawal amounts to a repayment of the loan by the bank. Stable values got their name because (and this should come as no surprise) their *values* remain *stable* even as market conditions change. Here's what that means.

If I put a dollar into stocks or bonds, the value of my investment will rise or fall with the market. If the market goes up, my $1.00 investment could grow to $1.10 overnight. And that's on top of any dividends or interest I might receive. Of course, the opposite could occur, as well. If the market falls, the price of my investment could drop to $0.90 or less. That's the market risk we talked about in Chapter 2.

Stable values aren't subject to market risk. Markets may boom or crash, and the dollar you put in stable values will always be worth a dollar. In investment parlance, a stable value doesn't "break the buck." To many people, that implies safety and security. That brings us back to the first law of investing: Risk goes up with return. Low risk means low return, and stable values pay the lowest return of the three major asset classes.

Since stable values look so much like a savings account, and since they aren't subject to market risk, most people assume they are protected from loss. Well, that's not quite the case. The Federal Deposit Insurance Corporation (FDIC), an arm of the federal government, insures most bank accounts, but other types of stable values are not guaranteed. It's unusual for a stable value investment to lose money, but it can and does happen.

STABLE VALUE INVESTMENTS

There are several different types of stable value investments. Here are the ones you are most likely to run into.

SAVINGS ACCOUNTS

Let's start with the easiest stable value to recognize. We all know what savings accounts look like. You go down to the bank, you give them your money, and they pay you interest. That's about as easy as it gets. A savings account is a loan from you to the bank that must be repaid on demand; that is, whenever you show up at the bank to withdraw your money.

Savings accounts are thought to be just about the safest kind of investment there is because the government guarantees them. There's a maximum of $100,000 to the guarantee, which applies to all accounts in a person's name at any single bank. If you plan to keep more than $100,000 in a savings account, you should first ask yourself "Why am I doing this?" As we'll see later, keeping that kind of cash in a bank account can cost you a lot of earnings.

But let's suppose you need a couple of hundred grand in a bank account. You have a couple of choices. You can split the money between two different banks, so that each account is under $100,000. That isn't a bad idea, even without figuring in deposit insurance. We'll see later that diversification is the best way to reduce risk, and besides, you may get an extra toaster out of the deal.

The second way to increase your deposit insurance coverage is to split the money between two accounts, one in your name and one jointly between you and your spouse. That's not a bad idea, either. We'll see later that a joint account makes a lot of sense. But it's still a good idea to keep the accounts at separate banks, just in case.

CERTIFICATES OF DEPOSIT

Commonly called CDs, these investments are almost identical to savings accounts. You give the bank your money, and they pay you interest. The U.S. government guarantees your savings, the same as a savings account. The only difference with a CD is that you agree to lend your money to the bank for a certain period of time. How long? It can be anywhere from 3 months to 5 years or more.

Why should you agree to let the bank keep your money for a longer time? Because they'll pay you to do it. Take the rate on a savings account. Generally, it runs about 3 percent. That's how much the bank has to pay people just to get their money in the first place.

Now, as we all know, interest rates go up and down with the economy. When the economy goes up, interest rates usually go up, too. When they go up too high, the economy slows down, and eventually that brings down interest rates.

The nice thing about a savings account is that you'll start getting a higher rate tomorrow if interest rates go up. You aren't "locking up" your interest rate. Of course, it works both ways. If interest rates drop, your rate goes down, too.

With a CD, you lock in an interest rate for the "term" of the CD. For example, let's say you buy a 1-year CD today that pays 5 percent. If interest rates go up to 6 percent tomorrow, you're out of luck. You are stuck with your 5 percent interest for a year, until your CD matures. Of course, if interest rates go down to 4 percent tomorrow, you have lucked out because you get to keep your 5 percent rate until the CD matures.

So, when you lock up a rate, you are making what amounts to a small bet that interest rates *won't* go up before the CD matures. To get you to make that bet, the bank has to offer you more money—a higher rate. They have to pay you to take a risk, in this case the risk that interest rates will go up and you'll be stuck with a lower rate. The longer the CD, the longer the lockup, and the more the bank has to pay you to do it. It's another example of risk and return going hand in hand. We will see the same phenomenon later when we look at bonds.

What happens if you cash in a CD before its maturity date? You incur (ominous sounding music should rise from the background at this point) *a substantial penalty for early withdrawal.* I always thought that meant a toe, or a finger, until I once had to cash in a CD early. I forfeited all the interest on the CD, and I only got back $98 of the $100 I had invested in the CD. We'll see why that is when we look at bonds later.

One more thing to keep in mind about CDs—not all of them are guaranteed by the U.S. government. If you invest in CDs and you count on the government guarantee, check carefully to make sure the CD you buy is insured by the FDIC.

MONEY MARKET FUNDS

As an individual, you are likely to go to the bank or a finance company if you need a short-term loan. But what if you are the U.S. government or a major corporation? You may need to borrow millions, or even billions of dollars. There aren't many banks that could handle loans of that size.

That's why the *money market* exists. The U.S. government can meet its short-term needs by selling *treasury bills* (or T-bills), and major corporations can meet their needs by selling *commercial paper*. Both types of "paper" mature in less than a year, generally in around 90 days or so.

Money market funds invest in T-bills and commercial paper. They generally pay rates that are a little better than savings accounts, and they don't involve a rate lockup. In other words, they look a heck of a lot like savings accounts. However, there is one major difference. Money market funds aren't guaranteed by the government as savings accounts are. And that's true even though many of these funds invest in T-bills issued by the government. That's one of the reasons money market funds pay a little more than savings accounts. They are a little bit riskier.

GIC

GIC stands for *guaranteed investment contract*, which is a misnomer if ever there were one. The word *guaranteed* gives us all a warm, secure feeling, which is one reason these investments have been so popular with 401k and other company savings plans over the past 15 years.

Insurance companies issue GICs. They use them to borrow money from the public. Since the contracts are called *guaranteed* investment contracts, they must be guaranteed by someone, right? And so they are. The insurance company that issues it guarantees a GIC. That's like my cousin Eddie guaranteeing that he will pay me back the $100 he wants to borrow from me. I don't want Eddie's guarantee—I want someone else's! So, despite their name, GICs aren't guaranteed. Not by the government, and not by the employers that offer them in their company savings plans.

Nonetheless, GICs remain very popular investments in these savings plans. (For tax reasons, GICs can't be offered outside company savings plan.) One of the big reasons for that is that GIC funds look like savings accounts or money market funds, but they generally pay as much as 2 percent more. That seems to violate the first law of investing, that risk goes up with return. GICs don't *appear* to have any more risk than savings accounts, yet they pay a higher rate of interest. What gives?

GICs have a gimmick that lets them pay the higher rate. Most GICs provide that employees can withdraw their money or move it to other investments at any time, *as long as they don't all try to do it at once!* In other words, there are limits to the amount that can be transferred from a GIC fund or withdrawn from it.

In most cases, these limits aren't an issue. People who put their savings into GICs tend to "set and forget." They hardly ever move their money. So the insurance company knows it will keep most of the money in a GIC for 3 to 5 years. In short, GICs are more like CDs than savings accounts.

So, what does all that mean to you? In most cases, GIC withdrawal restrictions will never affect you. However, if you are ever laid off from your job as part of a large layoff, the insurance company could invoke the restrictions. If you were counting on savings in a GIC fund to tide you over while you find a new job, you could have trouble getting to those savings immediately.

BONDS HAVE NOTHING TO DO WITH SPY MOVIES

So far, we have seen that stable values make you a loaner, rather than an owner. The loan is generally for a very short term. In most cases, you can get your money back whenever you want it.

Bonds are another kind of loan. These loans last anywhere from 1 to 30 years or more. You can invest in individual bonds, which are purchased through investment brokers, or you can invest in *bond funds*, which are offered by mutual fund companies, insurance companies, and banks.

Remember how we said that the government and major corporations use T-bills and commercial paper to borrow for short-term needs? A *bond* is a loan for longer-term needs. The next time your brother-in-law hits you up for 20 bucks, make him issue you a bond. Better yet, make it a convertible subordinated debenture. It's guaranteed you'll never hear from him again.

Companies and the government use bonds to finance big projects, like power plants. In the 1980s, companies used so-called junk bonds to buy other companies. These bonds were much riskier than more traditional bonds, and they paid higher rates of interest.

Junk bonds were the rage for a few years, until the market collapsed and the people behind the bonds went directly to jail without collecting their $200. Junk bonds are still around, but they're not as popular as they once were. And they're definitely not for the faint of heart.

So, a company or the government comes to you and me with its hand out, like a brother-in-law. Unlike the brother-in-law, this borrower agrees to do two things. First, they agree to repay the loan on a specific date in the future. Second, they agree to pay interest on the loan until they pay it back. The interest rate is fixed at the outset, like a CD, and it remains fixed for the life of the bond. Like a CD, a bond has an interest rate lockup. The difference is that most bonds have a much longer term than CDs.

THE GOING RATE

So how does the interest rate get set? Is there a government agency that sets the rate that bonds can pay? Nope. The interest rate is whatever the market will bear. It's called the *going rate of interest.*

The reason it's called the "going rate" is that it's always going somewhere—either up or down. When the economy is booming, every business in the world wants to borrow money to expand its business and cash in. There are often more borrowers than there are people willing to lend money. After all, in boom times, you and I are busy spending our money instead of investing it in bonds.

If there are more borrowers than lenders, the lenders are going to charge more for their money. That's why, when the economy heats up, interest rates heat up, too. The going rate goes up. Now, at some point, interest rates will climb so high that businesses can no longer afford to borrow like crazy to make more stuff, and you and I can no longer afford to borrow like crazy to buy it. The economic boom generally doesn't grind to a screeching halt. More often, it just runs out of gas.

That causes two things to happen. First, businesses get more cautious. They cut back on their borrowing. So there's less borrowing going on. Second, consumers become more cautious; they spend less and save more. That means there is more money to lend, at just the time when people are less interested in borrowing it. And that drives interest rates down.

It's called the *business cycle,* and it drives both the stock and bond markets. We will see in the rest of this chapter that, as interest rates rise and fall, so do the values of different types of investments.

PAIN AND GAIN

So, when is the best time to invest in bonds: when interest rates are going up or when they are going down? A 1996 Gallup survey[1] asked that question of 800 401k plan participants. Only 25 percent of the survey participants knew that the best time to buy bonds is when interest rates are going down.

What? Wouldn't the best time to buy into a bond fund be when interest rates are going *up,* to get the benefit of the higher interest rates? Nope. In fact, that's about the worst time to buy bonds. Here's why.

Remember the interest rate lockup we talked about in connection with CDs? Well, bonds have the same interest rate lockup. Let's say I buy a 30-year, $1,000 U.S. government bond today. Let's also say the going rate on these bonds is 7 percent. The instant I buy that bond, I lock in that 7 percent rate *for the next 30 years.*

Suppose the going rate goes up—say, to 8 percent. I'm stuck with a 7 percent bond, while another investor could go out and buy a new bond with just about the same term that pays 8 percent. If I hang on to the bond for 30 years, I will come out okay. I can turn in my bond to the government at that time and get my $1,000 back. And I will get 7 percent interest on the bond every year until then.

But suppose I need to sell the bond before then? For example, I might need to pay college expenses for my kids, or I may just decide the bond was a bad investment. Would I be able to sell it for the $1,000 I paid for it? Probably not. My bond pays only 7 percent, instead of the 8 percent going rate a buyer could get on a new bond. That means a reasonably intelligent buyer will give me less than $1,000 for my bond.

---

1   December 1996 survey by the Gallup Organization, sponsored by the John Hancock Life
    Insurance Company.

In fact, I'll probably get only about $890 for my bond.[2] When interest rates went up, the value of my bond went down since I had locked in a lower interest rate. But suppose the going rate had gone down to 6 percent instead? In that case, I would have locked in an interest rate *above the market.* I would have no trouble at all selling my bond for $1,000, should I be foolish enough to choose to do so. On the open market I could probably get about $1,140 for my bond. When interest rates went down, the value of my bond went up since I had locked in an interest rate above the going rate.

Changes in interest rates don't just affect some bonds; they affect all of them, even government bonds. If interest rates go up, the value of my government bond will fall, just like any other bond. That's the essence of market risk. Even though the government can't go broke, I can still lose money.

TO MARKET, TO MARKET . . .

The fact that bond values rise and fall as interest rates change is what makes them different from stable values. Remember how we said that stable values never break the buck? In investment parlance, that means they are carried at *book value,* the amounts that you originally invested.

Bonds, on the other hand, are carried at *market value.* That means your investment account statement will show the value of your bonds (or your bond fund) as the price you *would have* gotten if you had sold them on the date of the statement. That's the market value of your bonds, and that's the value your account statement will show, whether you actually sold your bonds or not.

LOCKING IN A LOSS

Simply because my account statement shows a drop in the value of my investments, it doesn't mean I have actually lost any money. We said earlier that I could hang on to my bond for the full 30 years and get my $1,000 back when it matures. Or I could wait for interest rates to fall to 7 percent or less and sell the bond. I lose money only if I sell

---

2   Assuming it still has about 30 years to maturity. There is a calculator, *Bond Value Estimator.xls,* on the veeneman.com Web site that will calculate the *present value* of a bond.

my bond to someone else while the going rate is higher than the rate on my bond. That's called *locking in a loss.*

When you invest in bonds (or stocks, for that matter), you have to be willing to live with market risk. There is no getting around it; it's the reason bonds and stocks pay a higher return than stable values. Once again, it's the first law of investing: If you want more return, you have to live with more market risk.

So how do you control this risk? As we said early on, pay close attention to your time frame. If you are saving for a child's college education in 10 years, a 30-year bond may not be a good idea. If you are a bond investor, a 10-year bond may be a better fit.

TYPES OF BOND FUNDS

Bond funds come in all shapes and sizes. The different types of bond funds you are likely to encounter are summarized in Table 4–1. We said that governments and large corporations use bonds to borrow money from the investing public. You will see that major distinction between different funds. Some funds invest exclusively in *government bonds,* and others invest solely in *corporate bonds.* Still other bond funds, called *mixed funds,* invest in both government and corporate bonds.

T A B L E 4–1

Commonly Encountered Bond Funds

Bond Length, Years	Government Bonds	Corporate Bonds	Mixed
1–5	Short-term government bond fund	N/A	N/A
5–10	Intermediate-term government bond fund	N/A	Intermediate-term government and corporate bond fund
10+	Long-term government bond fund	Long-term corporate bond fund	Long-term government and corporate bond fund

Bond funds are also grouped according to their length. Some funds invest in *short-term bonds*, those that mature in 5 years or less. Others invest in *intermediate-term bonds*, those that mature in 5 to 10 years. And still others invest in *long-term government bonds*, those with maturities longer than 10 years.

Why is that important? The longer the bond, the longer the interest rate lockup. For example, let's say I buy a $1,000 5-year bond that pays 7 percent interest. If interest rates go up to 8 percent, the value of my bond will fall to about $965. That's a much smaller drop than we saw with the 30-year bond because the interest rate lockup is for a much shorter period. So, as you might imagine, "long" bonds pay higher interest rates than "short ones."

THE BIGGEST LEMONADE STAND IN THE WORLD

If a bond makes you a loaner, a *share* of *common stock* makes you an owner. When you buy stock in a company, you are literally buying a piece of the company. It's a lot like the lemonade stands you had as a kid with your two best friends. One kid brought the lemonade, the second one brought the card table, and you swiped some paper cups from your mother's pantry. At the end of the day, you divvied up the money you made three ways.

General Motors isn't that different from your lemonade stand. But, instead of three owners, they have thousands, scattered all over the globe. Each owner of a corporation has a certain number of shares of the company's stock. For example, let's say a corporation has 1,000 shares of stock outstanding. If you own 100 shares, you own 10 percent of the company's stock.

As an owner, you are entitled to your share of the company's profits at the end of the year, just as with the lemonade stand. Your share of the profits is your *dividend* on your stock.

Stocks differ from bonds in three very important respects:

- Stocks don't have a face amount.
- They don't have a maturity date.
- They don't pay a fixed rate of interest.

Remember, we said that stock makes you an owner, not a loaner. You are entitled to your share of the company's profits. And if the company is ever liquidated, you are entitled to your share of the company's assets.

Running a company with thousands of owners could be an incredible nightmare. Most small businesses have a tough time getting by with just two or three owners. So a *board of directors* runs a corporation. It is the board's job to represent the interests of the owners of a company, its shareholders. The board is elected by the shareholders, and it, in turn, hires and fires the senior management of the company.

THE TINKERBELL FACTOR

If stock doesn't have a face value, a maturity date, or an interest rate, how does one tell what it's worth? A stock is worth only what people think it is worth. Remember the play *Peter Pan?* About halfway through the second act, the pixie, Tinkerbell, is poisoned by Captain Hook. Peter Pan turns to the audience and asks if they believe in fairies. "If you believe," he says, "then Tinkerbell will live!" Of course, we all believe, we clap like crazy, and Tinkerbell lives.

That's not too different from the stock market. It is driven by what investors expect companies to earn in the next several years. If investors feel optimistic about the economy, then they buy stocks. After all, a strong economy means higher earnings, which means larger dividends. Consequently, investors bid up the prices of stocks, which causes the entire market to rise. And if investors are especially optimistic about a particular company, they bid up the price of that company's stock. We saw how that happens with growth stocks in the last chapter.

On the other hand, pessimism drives down stock prices. If investors believe the economy is headed for recession, they generally sell stocks and buy bonds. A weaker economy means lower earnings, which makes stocks less attractive. But it may also mean falling interest rates, which would be good news for bond investors. The exodus of investors drives down stock prices.

ROLL TIDE, ROLL

That's the reason stock and bond markets rise and fall with surprising regularity. Some pundits have referred to the "tidal forces in the investment markets," and it's not a bad metaphor. Investment people are fond of an old cliché, "A rising tide lifts all boats." When the stock market is on the rise, it tends to take all stocks with it, and when it falls, it likewise drags all stocks down. That's one of the reasons asset allocation is so important. It doesn't so much matter *which* stock you are invested in as long as you are invested in stocks. The same holds true for bonds. And that's the key to the *Star* system.

TYPES OF STOCK FUNDS

Just as there are different types of bond funds, so there are different types of stock funds. The major types you are likely to run into are summarized in Table 4–2. Stock funds are generally grouped by the size company in which they invest and their fundamental investment style. (For years, the mutual fund industry grouped its funds by "investment objective," such as "preservation of capital" or "growth and income." Although these classifications still appear in marketing materials, there is a trend toward "size and style" classification among financial planners and other investment advisors. Institutional investors, such as pension plans and endowment funds, have long used the size and style approach.)

It may seem somewhat odd to use growth and value styles as a basis for grouping funds when we argued in the last chapter that the debate between the two camps of stock investors amounts to little more than a tempest in a teapot. Be that as it may, many of the fund evaluation services (such as *Morningstar Reports*) use this factor to classify funds.

In addition, the growth versus value distinction can be useful in deciding whether a manager has pursued a consistent style. A manager with a 5- or 10-year track record of investing in one type of

T A B L E   4–2

Commonly Encountered Stock Funds

Company Type	Growth Stocks	Value Stocks	Mixed
Large U.S. companies	Large U.S. growth funds	Large U.S. value funds	Large U.S. stock funds
Smaller U.S. companies	Smaller U.S. growth funds	Smaller U.S. value funds	Smaller U.S. stock funds
Large foreign companies	N/A	N/A	International stock funds

stock or another is more consistent than one who flip-flops between the two, depending on which way the winds happen to be blowing in the market.

The second major factor used to group stock funds is the type of companies in which they invest. The differences between these various types of companies are significant enough that most investment professionals divide stocks into three "subclasses": *large U.S. stocks*, *smaller U.S. stocks*, and *international stocks*.

LARGE U.S. STOCKS

These are the stocks we discussed in the last chapter. *Large U.S. stocks* are, not surprisingly, the common stocks of large companies headquartered in the United States and traded on major U.S. stock exchanges such as the New York Stock Exchange. There is no magic formula that determines how large a company has to be to belong to this club. By convention, most investment professionals use the 500 largest, publicly traded U.S. companies. One reason for choosing the top 500 is that it corresponds to a widely used market index called the *Standard & Poor's 500*, or simply, the *S&P 500*. This index has been widely used to measure the performance of large U.S. companies for over 40 years. The track record extends back to 1927 if one includes a smaller predecessor index.

LARGE INTERNATIONAL STOCKS

The second major stock category is *large international stocks*. These are the stocks of large companies headquartered outside the United States, whose shares are traded on foreign stock exchanges. International stocks don't generally follow the large-stock–smaller-stock distinction we see in the United States—most international stocks fall into the large-stock category. Nor do we see the growth versus value distinction that is made with U.S. stocks. For the present, stocks are stocks, at least in the international realm. (There is another subclass, *emerging-market stocks*, that is made up of companies in countries just now joining the international economic community. Emerging-market funds have not yet come into wide use, and there isn't a generally accepted market index for tracking them, so we haven't included them in the *Star* portfolios.) No doubt that situation will change in the future.

The *MSCI EAFE* is the most widely used index for tracking the performance of international stocks. EAFE stands for "Europe, Australia, Far East," which is where the most actively traded foreign companies are located.

One problem with international stocks is that they haven't been around very long. While stock markets have existed in Europe for as long as they have in the United States, the EAFE index wasn't created until 1970, and there wasn't a great deal of study given to international investing before that time. In fact, it is only with the rise of Japan as a global economic power that much thought has been given to the subject at all.

Consequently, it is hard to draw firm conclusions about international stocks based on the available data. The conventional wisdom says that large Japanese and European companies are not fundamentally different from large American companies. Stocks are stocks.

But there is a significant difference in their economic environment—European and Japanese companies are less vulnerable to shifts in the U.S. government's economic and monetary policy. For this reason and others, international stocks tend to rise when U.S. stocks are in decline, and vice versa. For example, in 1997, the U.S. stock market galloped to new highs. The stampede in Asian markets was for the doors, as the economies of Japan and Korea hit the skids. In other words, international stocks are a great way to diversify an investment portfolio. Instead of investing all of a stock allocation in U.S. stocks, spread some of the allocation among international stocks.

Is the conventional wisdom borne out by the data? Figure 4–1 compares U.S. and international stocks. Over the 26-year period, U.S. stocks earned an average return of 12.28 percent per year, while international stocks earned an average of 12.89 percent per year. That's not much of a difference, and it tends to support the contention that, from a return viewpoint, international stocks are similar to U.S. stocks. The two different types of stock appear similar from the standpoint of risk, as well. Table 4–3 compares the return ranges for the two types of investments. The ranges for international stock are no wider than those for U.S. stock. In fact, they are just a bit narrower, despite the higher return for international stocks.

In Chapter 2, we looked at serial correlations to see if what happened today can be used to predict what will happen tomorrow.

FIGURE 4-1

Large U.S. Stock and Large International Stock Returns, 1970–1996

Source: Ibbotson Associates, Chicago

TABLE 4-3

Return Ranges of Large U.S. and International Stocks

Time Frame, Years	U.S., %	International, %
1	−19.4–52.6	−14.0–48.8
5	−3.8–27.9	0.0–27.8
10	0.3–22.7	3.7–23.3
20	3.3–19.1	6.4–20.2

We can also use correlations to measure how much diversification will improve by adding another investment. The correlation between U.S. stocks and international stocks is only .47. That means the two types of investment move up and down together only 47 percent of the time. A little over half the time, large U.S. stocks and international stocks move at different rates or in different directions. That suggests that international stocks really are a pretty good diversifier.

So, what we have seen is that the greatest benefit of acquiring international stocks is that they can add diversification to a portfolio. They provide a way to reduce overall market risk without giving up a lot of return. But remember, we have only 26 years' data on which to base these conclusions. The situation could very well change over the next decade.

SMALLER U.S. STOCKS

When we talk about smaller U.S. companies, we aren't talking about garage startups like Hewlett Packard or Wal-Mart in their earliest days. Instead, we are talking about companies a bit further along in their life cycle. Both Hewlett Packard and Microsoft lived among the ranks of smaller U.S. companies during their corporate adolescence, after they had established themselves but before they had broken into the ranks of the largest American businesses. Smaller U.S. companies are the tier below the S&P 500.

There are about 2,000 companies in this group. The index most often used to measure their performance is the *Russell 2000*. Frank Russell Co., which maintains the index, follows the 3,000 largest companies in the country. The S&P 500 companies are at the top of the list, followed by 500 other companies. That takes us to the 1,000th company, which is where the Russell 2,000 begins. It includes the 2,000 companies from number 1,001 to 3,000.

Why track smaller companies separately from larger companies? For years, most investors assumed that smaller U.S. companies were simply smaller versions of large companies. Stocks are stocks, the reasoning went, and small companies probably grow at about the same rate as larger companies.

Then academics began to take note of what came to be called the *small-stock effect*. Small stocks, it was believed, didn't grow at the same rate as large stocks. Over the long haul, *they grew faster*. And since risk and return go hand-in-hand, it stood to reason they would be more volatile in the short run.

That made sense from a theoretical standpoint. Investing in smaller-company stocks certainly *seemed* riskier than investing in the largest companies in the country. So it stands to reason that small stocks would return more than large stocks over the long haul.

The theory was borne out by the data. If we look back to 1927, the difference is astounding. (The Russell 2000 Index dates back only

FIGURE 4-2

Large and Small U.S. Stock Returns, 1970–1996

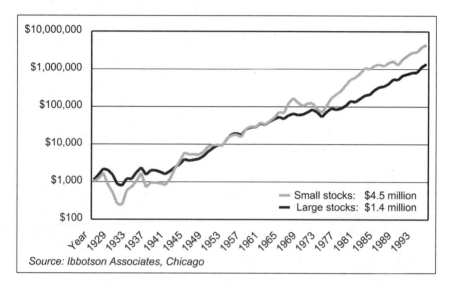

Source: Ibbotson Associates, Chicago

to 1978. For the longer view, we will use a small-company index maintained by Ibbotson Associates, Chicago.) Figure 4–2 shows the results. If we had invested $1,000 in both large and small stocks at the beginning of 1926, our large-stock investment would have grown to $1.4 million by the end of 1996. But our small-stock investment would have grown to over three times as much, or $4.5 million, by the end of 1996.

And so the following became conventional wisdom: Small stocks are riskier than large stocks in the short run, but they earn a higher return over the long haul. But look at the chart more closely. Small stocks haven't always outpaced large stocks. In fact, smaller companies actually lagged behind larger companies during the Great Depression, and they broke even with large stocks only through the mid-1960s. While they moved ahead in the late 1960s and early 1970s, they lost most of their gains between 1973 and 1975. By the mid-1970s, small companies had earned only a modest return over large companies. At that point, the small-stock effect looks more like the Great Growth versus Value Debate—a teapot tempest of little real consequence.

FIGURE 4–3

Large and Small U.S. Stock Returns, 1975–1983

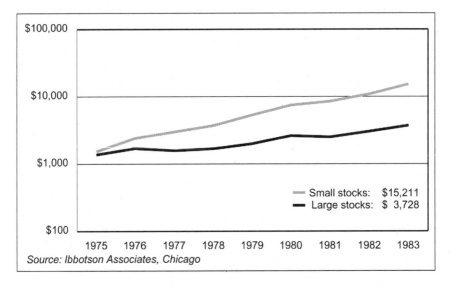

And then something extraordinary happened. Small stocks took off, and they took off like a rocket! From 1975 to 1983, small stocks outperformed large stocks by a wide margin. If you had invested your $1,000 at the beginning of 1975 instead of 1926, by the end of 1983 you would have had the amounts shown in Figure 4–3. A large-stock investment would have more than tripled your money, but a small-stock investment would have grown it 15 times over!

Now the difference between $3,700 and $15,200 may not seem very important in the larger scheme of things. But if you began the year with about $60,000 (which is roughly what the $1,000 invested in either investment in 1926 had grown to), then the next 9 years' performance makes a huge difference. It accounts for most of the spread we saw in Figure 4–2.

Professor Jeremy Siegel, in his book *Stocks for the Long Run*,[3] argues that if these 9 years are excluded, then the small-stock effect doesn't exist. Small stocks don't outperform large ones. Professor Siegel concludes that the Great Small-Stock versus Large-Stock De-

---

3   Jeremy J. Siegel, *Stocks for the Long Run,* Richard D. Irwin, Homewood, Ill., 1994, pp. 79–86.

bate is much the same sort of teapot tempest we saw in the Great Growth versus Value Debate.

It's hard to dispute his conclusions. Up to the end of 1974, there is no convincing evidence that small stocks outperform large ones. Was the extraordinary decade that followed a one-time fluke? Or was it the product of a very long term cycle of technological change that began in the 1950s and only bore fruit between the mid-1970s and the mid-1980s? And can that cycle repeat itself? If so, small stocks may very well outperform large ones on a consistent basis. It may simply take an extraordinarily long time for them to do so.

5
CHAPTER

The *Star* System

Spread your savings, use time to protect yourself, understand your attitude, and regulate your investments.

Now that we have the building blocks, let's look at how to use them to build an investment portfolio. A portfolio is nothing more than a mix of investments—there is really nothing complicated about it. There are two steps to creating a portfolio:

- Decide on a mix, using the *Star* strategies. In Part 2, we will provide a series of model portfolios that you can use to set your mix. You can use one of these portfolios as is, or you can use one as a starting point for setting your own mix.
- Fill the mix with investment funds that match the asset classes in your mix. Once you have set your mix, this step becomes a pretty straightforward and simple process. We will cover the process in Part 3.

A portfolio is like a car. Once you build it, you have to maintain it. If you don't, it will break down sooner or later. But you don't have to take your car in for service every day, or even every month. And you don't have to maintain your portfolio any more frequently. For most people, brief maintenance once every 3 months or so does nicely.

Maintenance doesn't have to be complicated either. You wouldn't overhaul the engine of your car every 3 months. An oil change would be more like it. It works the same way when you maintain a portfolio. As we said in Chapter 3, keep it simple.

FIXING THE MIX

We have said several times that the most important step in building a portfolio is fixing the mix—that is, coming up with the portion of your assets you will allocate to different asset classes. Investment professionals call this step *asset allocation*. And, as we have also said, this step determines 90 percent of the long-term performance of your portfolio.

The *Star* system uses four investment strategies (S-T-A-R) to help you fix your mix:

- **Spread** your savings among different types of investments.
- Use **time** to protect yourself against risk.
- Understand your **attitude** toward risk.
- **Regulate** your investments.

Let's look at each strategy.

SPREAD YOUR SAVINGS

Who was the greatest investment advisor in history? It isn't Warren Buffett, and it wasn't Bernard Baruch, the Wizard of Wall Street. It was your grandmother. She probably gave you the Best Piece of Investment Advice Ever Given: Don't put all your eggs in one basket.

It's that simple. Put all your money in one stock, even the company stock in your savings plan, and you are taking one heckuva risk. Put it in a stock *fund*, and you're taking less risk because you have spread your savings among a number of different stocks. But you still have all your savings in a single asset class, *stocks*. As we saw in Chapter 3, that means your investment earnings over a single year can run anywhere from –19.4 to 52.6 percent.

By spreading your savings among several asset classes, you can control risk—you can make the range wider or narrower. Consider a simple example. Table 5–1 shows the 1-year earnings ranges for different mixes of two different asset classes: stocks and stable

TABLE 5-1

Return Ranges for Different Mixes of Stable Values and Stocks

Stable Values, %	Stocks, %	Earnings Range (1 year), %	Expected Return, (1 year), %
100	0	6.2–9.3	7.7
80	20	1.6–16.3	8.8
60	40	–4.1–25.0	9.8
40	60	–9.5–34.0	10.9
20	80	–14.6–43.2	12.0
0	100	–19.4–52.6	13.0

values.[1] The first row of the table shows a 100 percent stable value mix; the rows in between shift progressively from stable values to stocks. The last row shows a 100 percent stock mix.

As you can see, the ranges grow wider as the stock component of the mix grows larger. That means market risk increases as we increase the stock percentage. At the same time, the expected return increases as well. But the most important thing to see is how you can gain control over risk by selecting the mix that matches the amount of market risk you feel you can live with. Once you have decided on your risk tolerance, the expected return follows naturally. That's the essence of the *Star* process, and it's the reason *diversification* is the first and most important *Star* strategy.

USE TIME TO PROTECT YOURSELF

The second *Star* strategy is this: Use time to protect yourself against risk. We talked a lot about this strategy in Chapter 3. We can debate the question of whether risk really goes down over time, but no one would disagree that the longer you have until you need your savings, the less you can be hurt by the short-term swings of stocks and bonds.

---

1 For stable values, we use the Ibbotson Associates U.S. 90-day T-bill index, and for stocks we use the Standard & Poor's 500 Index.

TABLE 5-2

10-Year Stock Market Performance at the End of 1997

Time Frame, Years	Return, %
1	23.1
3	19.7
5	15.2
10	15.3

Sometimes it seems as if time doesn't really matter. Table 5–2 shows the 10-year performance history of the stock market.[2] Why be concerned with your time frame in the face of a track record like this? Why, you could put your Christmas club money in stocks and make out like a bandit!

That's the reason we don't use the historical returns that are almost universal in the mutual fund industry. They can be very misleading. We have been fortunate enough to live through one of the greatest bull markets in history. It has continued in an almost unbroken string since 1982. Any historical figures will reflect performance only during that bull market, even figures that go back 15 years.

"But wait a minute," you might say. "There was a major stock market crash in 1987. Surely that event would show up in the historical figures, wouldn't it?" As it turns out, it doesn't. The 1987 crash was preceded by such a strong surge in the stock market that stocks earned just over 5 percent for the year, despite the crash.

The point is, watch out for historical numbers. If the period they cover doesn't include at least one prolonged market downturn, the figures don't give a complete picture of what you might expect.

So, are we back in the game of picking our time periods carefully to manipulate the results? If we rely only on the short-term history, we are. Suppose we had looked at the same figures at the end of 1981? Table 5–3 shows what they would have looked like. It's

---

2   We are using the Standard & Poor's 500 Index to represent the stock market, so what we are really talking about is large U.S. stocks.

TABLE 5-3

10-Year Stock Market Performance at the End of 1981

Time Frame, Years	Return, %
1	−4.9
3	14.3
5	8.1
10	6.5

a very different picture, and not nearly as attractive as the first. In fact, it was so dismal that at the end of the 1970s, *Business Week* magazine proclaimed "The Death of Equities" on its cover.

That's the reason most academics use stock and bond returns that go all the way back to 1926. Those returns include both the Great Depression of the 1930s and the miserable performance of the 1970s. These returns can be used to calculate the return range estimates we have used up to this point.

HOW TO USE YOUR TIME FRAME TO SELECT A MIX

Here is how to use your time frame and the return range estimates to set your investment mix. Remember the stable value stock mixes we looked at earlier in the chapter? Let's take another look at them. This time, we will add the return ranges for 5, 10, and 20 years. The results are shown in Figure 5–1. Let's say you are saving for college education expenses for a child now in the eighth grade. Your child will start college in 5 years, so you set that as your time frame. You would like to earn around 12 percent on your money, but other than that, you don't have any preconceptions about how you want to invest.

Now look at the mixes in Figure 5–1. Mix E has an expected return of 12.0 percent, so it meets your target return. But if you look down the column, you can see that over a 5-year time frame, mix E could lose: −1.5 percent. The odds of that happening are pretty slim—only 5 percent, but it's a possibility nonetheless. So the question becomes, is that an acceptable risk for you? If it is, then mix E meets your time frame requirements.

FIGURE 5-1

Stable Value and Stock Mixes

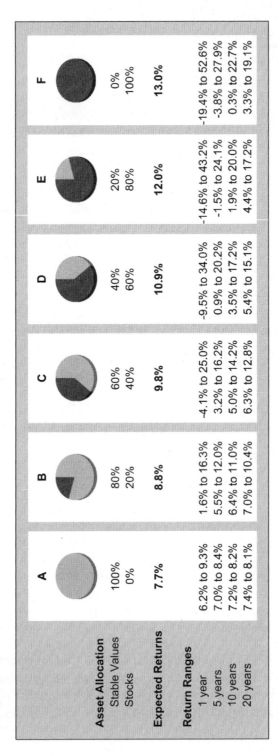

	A	B	C	D	E	F
Asset Allocation						
Stable Values	100%	80%	60%	40%	20%	0%
Stocks	0%	20%	40%	60%	80%	100%
Expected Returns	**7.7%**	**8.8%**	**9.8%**	**10.9%**	**12.0%**	**13.0%**
Return Ranges						
1 year	6.2% to 9.3%	1.6% to 16.3%	-4.1% to 25.0%	-9.5% to 34.0%	-14.6% to 43.2%	-19.4% to 52.6%
5 years	7.0% to 8.4%	5.5% to 12.0%	3.2% to 16.2%	0.9% to 20.2%	-1.5% to 24.1%	-3.8% to 27.9%
10 years	7.2% to 8.2%	6.4% to 11.0%	5.0% to 14.2%	3.5% to 17.2%	1.9% to 20.0%	0.3% to 22.7%
20 years	7.4% to 8.1%	7.0% to 10.4%	6.3% to 12.8%	5.4% to 15.1%	4.4% to 17.2%	3.3% to 19.1%

UNDERSTAND YOUR ATTITUDE

If a mix meets your time frame requirements, then it has passed the first hurdle to being an acceptable portfolio for you. But there is another hurdle yet to jump—your *Ouch Factor*.

The Ouch Factor measures your sensitivity to fear. Fear and greed are what get most investors into trouble. Vernon Hodge, one of the most successful stable value managers in the business, tells a story about a speech he gave at a conference in the early 1980s. Vernon, who is a bit of a number cruncher, had just finished a presentation on "mean-variance optimization" and how it could be used to construct "efficiently diversified" portfolios.

At the end of the presentation, a crusty senior investment manager raised his hand, and was recognized. "I don't know much mathematics beyond what I learned in high school," he said. "But I have been in the investment business for 25 years, and I think I know what moves the investments markets."

FIRG AND GIRF

Every head in the room turned to see what the investment manager would say next. "It's FIRG and GIRF!" he drawled. The audience wore a puzzled look as Vernon asked the manager to explain FIRG and GIRF. "FIRG," he said, "stands for 'fear inevitably replaces greed.' GIRF stands for 'greed inevitably replaces fear.' Fear and greed go 'round and 'round, and that's what makes the markets go up and down."

Vernon said the manager got a huge laugh with that little story. I heard it about 15 years ago, and it has stuck with me ever since, along with an old Wall Street cliché: "Bulls get rich and bears get rich, but pigs and chickens get slaughtered."

I think there is more fundamental wisdom in FIRG and GIRF than in any model ever created by number crunchers. If you take nothing else away from reading this book, take away FIRG and GIRF. They will keep you out of more trouble than you will ever know.

THE LESSONS OF THE MARKET

The stock market crash of 1987 shows plainly how investors can get whipsawed by fear and greed. Figure 5–2 shows the tumultuous stock market of 1987. The market had one of its best months in history

FIGURE 5–2

The 1987 Stock Market Crash

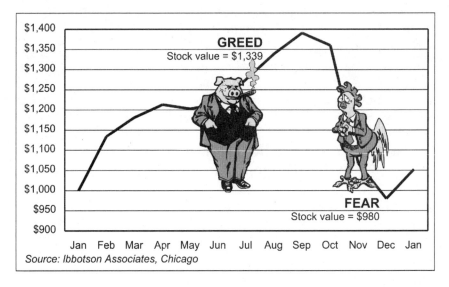

Source: *Ibbotson Associates, Chicago*

in January, returning 13.4 percent for the month. That's more than it earns in the average *year*. February and March were solid winners, with above-average returns. The market paused for a breather in April, and lost a little ground. May was a so-so month, and then the market took off again.

By the time June rolled around, market pundits were nearly unanimous in their pronouncements that the market was headed for new record highs. And that attracted a lot of money into the market. Much of it came from individuals investing through 401k and other employee savings plans. They didn't know it, but they were jumping in at the very top of the market.

ODD LOTS AND FREE RIDES

There is a widely followed market indicator called the *odd-lot indicator*. This indicator assumes the small investor, who buys in odd lots, buys into the market at or near the top and sells at the bottom. That certainly seemed to happen in 1987.

Certain investors look for a free ride in the market. They don't want to invest in stocks because of the market risk involved. But in their view, there are certain times when the stock market isn't risky at all. And one of those times is when "everyone says the market is going up."

After all, doesn't it stand to reason that if the public expects the market to rise, people will bid up prices, causing it to rise? A market mania is a self-fulfilling prophecy. All the shrewd investor has to do is jump in, ride the market on the way up, and jump out before the bubble bursts. What could be simpler? There is nothing simpler than getting GIRFed.

A lot of these free riders didn't jump in until June, and from then to the end of the year, the news got worse and worse. July was a good month, and August turned out pretty well, although there were a few rough days. The market lost about 2 percent in September, and then it fell apart in October. In that month alone, the stock market lost almost one-fourth of its value. In November, it lost nearly another 10 percent. The shrewd investor who had jumped into the market with $1,000 at the end of June was left with only $768 by the end of November. And by the end of November, many of them had had enough. They pulled what was left out of the stock market, licked their wounds, and went home. In short, they got FIRGed.

SINGLES AND DOUBLES

That's not to say everyone lost money in the 1987 crash. A lot of people made money. Some savvy professionals made killings. And there were a lot of individual investors who rode it out with no problem and actually made a little that year.

Babe Ruth was one of the greatest baseball players of all time. In 2 incredible years, 1927 and 1928, he hit 114 home runs, world records in their time. What a lot of people don't realize is that Ruth also set another league record in each of those years—the record for the number of strikeouts. That's right—the home-run king was also the strikeout king.

Even so, Ruth still managed a batting average of .354, one of the best in the books. He once said, "I could have hit .600 if I'd been willing to hit singles. But I figured the people was paying to see me hit home runs."

If you let fear and greed direct your investing, you will be swinging very hard at the ball. You may knock it clean out of the park. Or you may strike out. The better strategy may be to go for "singles and doubles," so you don't get GIRFed or FIRGed.

An investor who started 1987 with $1,000 in the stock market and who didn't jump in or out during 1987's market gyrations ended the year with $1,052. In the face of one of the most severe stock market crashes in history, he or she made 5.2 percent for the year. That's what singles-and-doubles investing will get you.

HOW TO USE YOUR OUCH FACTOR TO SELECT A MIX

At the beginning of this section we referred to your "Ouch Factor." That refers to a game we play in some seminars. The game is called *Ouch*, and it is designed to help individuals get a handle on risk. Here is how Ouch is played.

The object of Ouch is to figure out how much you could lose in a year without losing your cool, and how long you could stand to be "under water" (in a loss position) before you would drown.

First, go back to Figure 5–1. This time, we will ignore the time frame. When we play Ouch, we look only at the low end of the 1-year range. That number represents about the worst that can happen to me over a 1-year period. For example, look at the low end of Portfolio F's 1-year range, –19.4 percent. Then ask yourself, "If I woke up 1 year from today and saw this return on my account statement, would I be so upset that I would seriously consider cutting my losses and pulling out of the market?"

Don't answer too quickly. It's easy to say, "I know the market will come back—I would certainly tough it out." But really *think* about it for a minute. Imagine yourself sitting at lunch with your coworkers. Every single one of them is talking about how he or she got out months ago, and just in the nick of time. Pity the poor slobs, they say, who didn't make it out in time.

Imagine sitting at home, channel surfing the evening news. It has been another bad day on Wall Street. All three major networks run lead stories about the carnage. They all interview financial experts who question seriously whether the market will *ever* come back. Now imagine that going on, day after day, for a year.

Now that you are in the proper frame of mind to play Ouch, take another look at the portfolios. At what point do you say ouch? Don't listen to your head; listen to your gut. The mix where you say

"Ouch" is the mix that is likely to get you into trouble. Go back to the previous mix; it may test you, but it probably won't break you.

THE STAR PORTFOLIOS

Part 2 of this book presents 11 different investment mixes you can use to set your asset allocation. The mixes are similar in concept to the simple mixes in Figure 5–1, with a couple of differences:

- They include all five of the major asset classes and subclasses we looked at in the last chapter.
- We didn't set the mixes by simply scaling percentages up or down. Instead, we used a computer program called an *efficient frontier* model to create the most highly diversified mixes we could. The details of how the portfolios were created are explained in Appendix A, "How the *Star* Portfolios Were Created."

REGULATE YOUR INVESTMENTS

We said earlier that your grandmother was the greatest investment advisor in history. So, who was the second best? It was John Wayne. He gave the Second Best Piece of Investment Advice Ever Given: "Don't make any sudden moves, Pilgrim!" He must have said it in a dozen movies.

The *r* in *Star* stands for regulate, as in "regulate your investments." It means, "don't make any sudden moves." Think about how a faucet regulates, or controls, the flow of water. That's what we're talking about. The way to regulate your investments is to do things gradually, over time. Any time you invest, do it gradually. And any time you change your investments, do that gradually, too. Experts call it *dollar cost averaging*.

We will talk more about regulating your investments later in the book. You will learn two key techniques for maintaining your portfolio: *rebalancing* and *step transfers*. For now let's look at how to regulate your investments "on the front end."

Let's say you have $1,000 to invest. To keep things simple, let's also say you were thinking of investing the money in stocks. You might wonder whether today is a good time to invest that $1,000:

- If you do and the market goes down, you are going to lose money right off the bat. Bummer.
- If you don't invest today because you are worried about the market falling and the market goes up instead, the stock you buy is going to be more expensive. Double bummer.

It's a classic rock-and-a-hard-place situation. You are doomed if you do and doomed if you don't.

As always, there is a simple solution. (Remember, "keep it simple"?) Invest a little now, the same amount next month and for the next few months after that. That way, if the market does go down, you didn't commit your entire $1,000 at the top of the market. On the other hand, if the market goes up, you will have bought at least some of your stock at the cheaper price. In short, you will be buying into the market at the average of its performance over the period. Figures 5–3 and 5–4 illustrate the point.

In Figure 5–3, market prices rise steadily throughout the period. The earlier purchases are made at lower prices than the later ones, and they have the effect of reducing the average cost of the investment. Figure 5–4 shows how dollar cost averaging works in a declining market. In this case, it's the later purchases that are made at lower

FIGURE 5–3

The Effects of Dollar Cost Averaging in a Rising Market

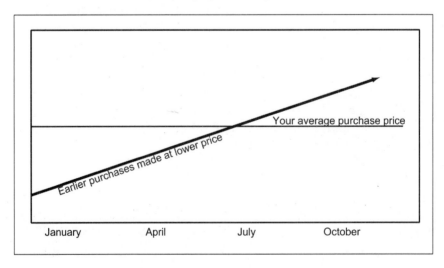

January   April   July   October

FIGURE 5–4

The Effects of Dollar Cost Averaging in a Falling Market

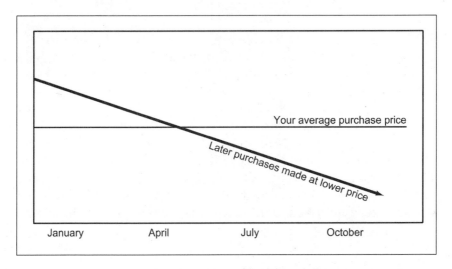

prices, reducing the average purchase price. But, in either event, making gradual purchases will reduce the risk that you will buy at the market's high point.

REGULATING ON AUTOPILOT

Right about now, you may be thinking, "That sounds nice, but it's awfully complicated." Well, actually, it's incredibly simple. Most of us don't invest $1,000. We invest $50 or $100 a week through our 401k plan. Well, if you are doing that, you are already putting in a little bit this month, the same amount next month, and the same amount each month after that—forever.

Suppose you don't participate in your company's 401k plan? Stop. Do not pass Go. Do not collect $200. Go straight to the personnel office and sign up. Here's why:

- Uncle Sam gives you a tax break for saving in a 401k plan. You don't have to pay income tax on the amounts you save until you withdraw them, down the road.
- Many employers match their employee's contributions. In many cases the match is 50 cents on the dollar up to the

first 6 percent of pay you contribute. In some cases it's
more. If your plan has a match and you don't participate,
you are literally leaving free money on the table.

Suppose you don't have a company savings plan? If you are self-
employed, Uncle Sam has several different ways for you to get a
tax break for saving. See your lawyer, accountant, or financial planner for information.

For your after-tax savings, nearly every mutual fund in the
country offers *periodic investment plans* (PIP). These plans allow
individuals to start investing in funds even if the investor doesn't
meet the fund company's minimum amounts to open a new account.
The investor commits to invest a specific amount on a regular basis
to the fund. These arrangements allow individuals to start investing
with smaller amounts, and the regular deposits give them the benefit
of dollar cost averaging.

LEARNING TO LOVE A MARKET CORRECTION

A market correction hardly sounds like good news, but it can actually work in your favor. That's because there is a little bit of magic
associated with dollar cost averaging. It can actually enable you to
buy an investment at a price *lower than its market average.* Here's how.

When the stock or bond market declines, someone who invests
a regular *amount* will end up buying more shares (or more bonds)
than they did before the market fell. For example, if I invest $100 a
month in a stock that trades at $10 per share, then I buy 10 shares per
month. If the stock's price falls to $8 per share, then I buy 12 shares
per month.

Figure 5–5 shows an example of the effect this can have on stock
purchases. Let's say I invest $100 per month in a stock that trades in
January for $10 per share. The price of the stock drops $1 per month
through May, when the stock rebounds. It continues to rise through
the end of the year, when it trades at $13 per share. The labels below
the line in Figure 5–5 show the number of shares I buy each month
with my $100 investment.

The average price per share for the year is $9.17. But when I add
up the number of shares I have at the end of the year and divide that
by my $1,200 investment, I find that my average cost per share was
$8.76. In other words, I bought my shares for 41 cents per share *less*

FIGURE 5–5

Buying a Stock for Less Than Its Average Price

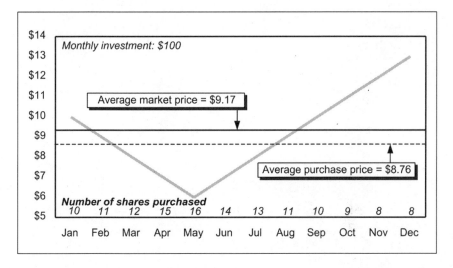

than their average price. The reason is that, as the price dropped, I bought more shares. The market correction actually worked in my favor!

PUTTING THE *STAR* STRATEGIES TO WORK

You now have everything you need to fix your mix. You know how to spread your savings, use time to protect yourself, understand your attitude, and regulate your investments. Without further ado, it's time to do exactly that. And that's where Part 2 of this book will take you.

6
CHAPTER

Using the *Star* Portfolios

Pick the Star portfolio that's right for you.

Up to this point, we have been explaining the ideas behind strategic investing and the tools you need to put it to work for you. Now it's time to roll up your sleeves and begin building your portfolio.

In this chapter, we are going to begin a three-step process to building an investment portfolio:

Step 1. Select the mix of basic asset classes that best fits your needs and preferences. The *Star* portfolios in Part 2 of the book will help you do that.

Step 2. Select investment funds to fill the slots in your portfolio. We will explain how to do that in Part 3 of the book.

Step 3. Periodically review the performance of your funds and make any needed midcourse corrections to your portfolio to keep it on track. This step amounts to checking your road map to see if you are still headed in the direction you want to go and making any midcourse corrections as needed.

These steps are shown in Figure 6–1. This approach might look like we are putting the cart before the horse. After all, how can we set

FIGURE 6-1

Steps to Build and Maintain a Portfolio

percentages without first picking our funds? The entire approach is built on the principle that *asset allocation*, the mix of the five basic investment types, determines over 90 percent of our investment performance. That's why the first step, fixing the mix, is by far the most important.

THE *STAR* PORTFOLIOS

The next 11 chapters cover the *Star* portfolios. In each chapter, we use the five basic types of investments we looked at in Chapter 4 to create a different investment mix. The mixes are arranged from the most conservative to the most aggressive. We have given each mix a name and a number (kind of like an old spy movie, if you think about it). For example, Portfolio 0, the most conservative, is *The Mattress,* and Portfolio 100, the most aggressive, is *The Sky Dive.*

HOW THE PORTFOLIOS ARE NUMBERED

Each portfolio has a number from 0 to 100. The numbers increase by 10 from portfolio to portfolio. For example, the first portfolio is 0, the second portfolio is 10, and so on. There is a method to this madness.

Imagine a risk scale that runs from 0 to 100. The rating 0 represents the most conservative mix you can make using the five basic asset classes, and the rating 100 represents the most aggressive mix you can make. By adjusting the mix, we can come up with portfolios with just the amount of risk we want. For example, we can create a portfolio that would fall at point 50 on the risk scale, halfway between *The Mattress* and *The Sky Dive*.

That's what we have done with the *Star* portfolios. The 11 portfolios run the length of our 0 to 100 risk scale, and they are evenly spaced at 10-point increments along the scale. Figure out where you want to be on the scale, and you will find a *Star* portfolio that falls at or near that point.

THE SUMMARY CHARTS

There is a summary chart at the beginning of each chapter. This chart shows the key information about each portfolio. The summary charts are similar to Figure 6–2.

FIGURE 6–2

A Sample Portfolio Summary Chart

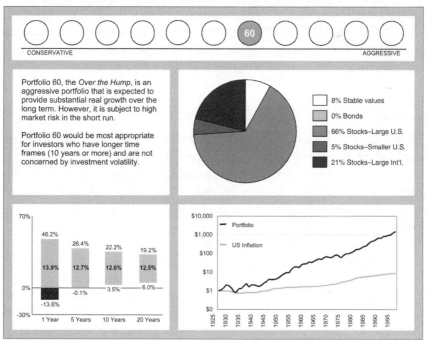

Portfolio 60, the *Over the Hump*, is an aggressive portfolio that is expected to provide substantial real growth over the long term. However, it is subject to high market risk in the short run.

Portfolio 60 would be most appropriate for investors who have longer time frames (10 years or more) and are not concerned by investment volatility.

- 8% Stable values
- 0% Bonds
- 66% Stocks–Large U.S.
- 5% Stocks–Smaller U.S.
- 21% Stocks–Large Int'l.

RISK SCALE

There are four sections in the chart. The top section shows the position of the portfolio along the risk scale which is numbered by 10s from 0 to 100. Figure 6–2 shows Portfolio 60, the *Over the Hump*. From points 0 to 70, the circle representing the portfolio is gray. Beyond point 70, the circle would be black. That's to remind you to be a bit more cautious with these mixes. Beyond point 70, you might need more than 20 years to realize the full return potential of the portfolio. (The portfolios beyond point 70 are so volatile that return actually *drops* as risk goes up when measured over a 20-year time frame. You can see the effect by comparing the return ranges for the *Star* portfolios. Beyond point 70, the low end of the range begins to widen, and the expected returns decline.) We will talk more about that in Portfolio 70, *The Deep End*.

INVESTMENT MIX

The middle right section of the chart shows the portfolio's investment mix. Each of the five basic asset classes is shown, along with the percentage of that asset class in the portfolio. The pie chart shows the portfolio's mix visually. The mixes were created using a type of computer program known as an *efficient frontier model*. The program does not try to find good mixes or eliminate bad mixes. It assumes there is no such thing as a good or bad mix, only mixes that are more or less efficient than others.

TALES FROM THE EFFICIENT FRONTIER

Here's how it works: We said there are two things to consider when evaluating an investment: risk and return. Let's look at two investments. Both pay exactly the same return, but one is riskier than the other. Which one would you choose? Most people say they would choose the less risky investment since it pays the same return as the riskier investment.

But wait a minute! Aren't we contradicting ourselves? We have been saying all along that return goes up as risk increases. Well, that's true, until we start mixing investment together. There are literally zillions of different ways we could combine the five asset classes. Some of those mixes will have the same expected returns. But of the mixes with the same return, some will be more diversified than others.

For example, a mix of large U.S. stocks and large international stocks is more diversified than large U.S. stocks alone. Depending on how you mix the two investments, you may be able to improve diversification, thereby reducing risk, without giving up return. In number-crunching jargon, the mix is more *efficient* than U.S. stocks. It squeezes more blood out of the turnip, as it were, by squeezing more return out of the risk taken.

The efficient frontier model lines up all the possible mixes of the five asset classes by risk. That's where the 0 to 100 scale comes in. Then it picks the mix at each level of return that has the highest expected return—the most efficient mix at that risk level. The result is a series of portfolios, each one notch riskier than the last, that is expected to earn the highest return for its level of risk. For this book, we simply used every 10th portfolio.

RETURN RANGES

The 1-, 5-, 10-, and 20-year return range estimates are shown in the middle left section of the chart. These estimates are *forward-looking*; they show what is expected to happen in the future over different time frames, based on what has happened in the past. The return ranges are shown on a chart that is similar to one you see in the newspaper or on television every day. The weather forecast is often accompanied by a chart that shows the high and low temperatures for the next several days. The top end of each bar represents the day's forecast high, and the low end represents the forecast low.

And so it is with the return range chart. Each bar shows the high and low end of a portfolio's return range for a different period. The estimated high and low returns are shown at the top and bottom of each bar. The expected return for the same period is shown in the middle of the bar.

HISTORICAL EARNINGS

The bottom section of the portfolio summary chart shows the historical earnings of the portfolio from 1926 through 1996. Again, these aren't the earnings of particular funds. The *Star* portfolios are made up of *asset classes,* the five basic investment types. We have used market indexes for each asset class to represent their performance.[1]

The earnings graph shows how $1 invested in the particular portfolio would have grown since 1926. The graph compares that growth to the increase in consumer prices since the same year. That inflation line will help you gauge the degree of inflation protection the portfolio provides. If the portfolio line is well above the inflation line, the portfolio can be expected to provide strong inflation protection. If the portfolio line and the inflation line run neck and neck, as they do at the conservative end of the range, then the portfolio can be expected to provide relatively little inflation protection.

The historical earnings graph will also help you get a feel for the market risk of a portfolio. If the line is smooth and steady, as is typical at the conservative end, then there is relatively little market risk associated with the portfolio. If the line is choppy, particularly in the 1930s or the 1970s, then the portfolio will provide a bumpier ride.

You can also get a feel for the risk and return of each portfolio in the historical earnings table that appears in each chapter. These tables show the high, low, and average earnings of each portfolio over each of the decades between 1926 and 1996.

FINDING YOUR MIX

Here is how to use the *Star* portfolios to find an investment mix that meets your needs and preferences. Pick a mix to start with. You can start with Portfolio 0 and work your way toward more aggressive portfolios, or you might start with Portfolio 50, the *Partly Cloudy,* and work your way in whatever direction you need to. I generally suggest that people start with Portfolio 30. It's relatively conservative but not extremely so.

Begin with your time frame, and look at the return range bar nearest to that time frame. Ask yourself these questions:

---

1   In some cases, we have used "derived" historical data to represent an asset class. For example, most types of stable values weren't around before the 1970s, and international stocks weren't widely followed before that time. A complete description of the process used to create the *Star* portfolios and the historical returns appears in Appendix A, "How the *Star* Portfolios Were Created."

- *Is the return estimate in the middle of the bar sufficient to meet my needs?* If you have decided you need to earn 10 percent on your investments and the portfolio is expected to earn 7.8 percent, it's probably too conservative.
- *Could I live with earning only the return shown in the pessimistic estimate below the bar?* The return shown below the bar is a worst-case estimate of your average annual earnings from the portfolio. (Actually, it's not quite the worst-case estimate since 5 percent of the time things could actually be worse.) It's what you might expect if everything went wrong with investment markets over your time frame. It's unlikely that things would ever get this bad, but then nobody expected the Great Depression either. If you couldn't live with this pessimistic result, then the portfolio is probably too aggressive.

Suppose you decide the expected return is too low *and* you can't live with the low end of the range. Then you need to rethink your investment requirements. The low end of the range is the potential price you pay for a higher return. Remember, the low end of the range is an unlikely event. But if you can't live with it, then you need to lower your return expectations and look at a more conservative portfolio.

TESTING YOUR OUCH FACTOR

Once you have found a mix that matches your time frame, test it against your Ouch Factor. We explained the game of Ouch in the last chapter. Ask yourself:

- *If I woke up 1 year from today and discovered I had earned (or more likely lost) the percentage shown on the low end of the 1-year range, would I be so upset that I would seriously consider cashing out immediately at that loss?* As we said in Chapter 5, if you truly can't stand the heat (and there is nothing wrong with that!), then it is best not to go in the kitchen in the first place.
- *If, after 5 years, my investments had recovered only to the return shown on the low end of the 5-year range, would I continue to stick with my plan, or would I sell out?* The low end of the

5-year range gives the best indication of how long a
portfolio might remain under water. So, this question
amounts to, "How long can I hold my breath before I
drown?"

Some of us have a tendency to overestimate our capacity for pain.
We think we should be able to handle the risk, even if we feel an
uneasiness in the pit of our stomach. If that's the quandary in which
you find yourself, listen to your feelings, not to what someone else
says you ought to do. That's the best way to avoid getting in over
your head.

WHAT RETURNS MEAN IN DOLLARS

It's pretty easy to see what rates of return mean over a 1-year period.
If I invest $1,000 today and earn a 8.9 percent rate of return over the
next year, then I will have earned $89, and I will have $1,089. But
how much will I have if I earn an average of 8.9 percent per year for
5 years? And, perhaps more to the point, how much will I have *left*
after 5 years if I *lose* an average of 8.9 percent per year?

Appendix B, "What a Return Will Earn," has a table that will
answer these questions. Each row of the table corresponds to a rate
of return, and each column shows a different time frame. Find the
rate of return, and read across the columns to your time frame, and
the table will tell you what each dollar you invest will grow (or
shrink) to.

ROLLING YOUR OWN PORTFOLIO

There really isn't anything magical about the 11 portfolios in the *Star*
series, and there is nothing to prevent you from putting together
your own mix. For example, you may not like international stocks.
Kick them out, and replace them with U.S. stocks. Or you may like
small-company stocks, although you don't like the very aggressive
portfolios. In that case, replace some of the stock in a more conservative portfolio with some small-company stock. Remember, the
Star portfolios aren't any "better" than other mixes. They are simply
calculated to be more efficient.

GETTING DOWN TO BUSINESS

You don't have to read all the *Star* portfolio chapters. Browse through them until you find one that interests you. Then read about that portfolio, and see if you feel comfortable with it. Once you have found your mix, skip ahead to Part 3 of the book, where we will show you how to select funds to fill the slots in your portfolio.

PORTFOLIOS FOR EVERY INVESTOR

7 CHAPTER

The Mattress

What's the safest place to stash your money? In a mattress. A very conservative portfolio for investors who want to avoid risk.

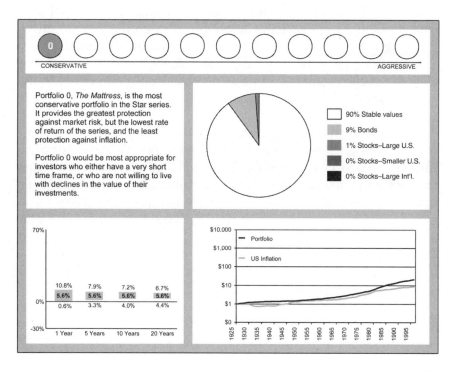

CONSERVATIVE   AGGRESSIVE

Portfolio 0, *The Mattress*, is the most conservative portfolio in the Star series. It provides the greatest protection against market risk, but the lowest rate of return of the series, and the least protection against inflation.

Portfolio 0 would be most appropriate for investors who either have a very short time frame, or who are not willing to live with declines in the value of their investments.

- 90% Stable values
- 9% Bonds
- 1% Stocks–Large U.S.
- 0% Stocks–Smaller U.S.
- 0% Stocks–Large Int'l.

	1 Year	5 Years	10 Years	20 Years
	10.8%	7.9%	7.2%	6.7%
	5.6%	5.6%	5.6%	5.6%
	0.6%	3.3%	4.0%	4.4%

- Portfolio
- US Inflation

What's the safest, most conservative place you can stash your money? We ask this question at investment seminars, and invariably someone calls out "In a mattress!" That's the first *Star* portfolio—the most conservative mix in the series. We call it *The Mattress*. It's not exactly like sticking your money in a mattress, but it comes about as close as you can get to doing so and still be investing.

That's not to say there is anything wrong with an ultraconservative investment. It will suit some people's needs quite well. If you have a very short time frame, this is probably a good place to put your money. If you absolutely cannot stand the thought of seeing any losses whatsoever on your account statement, even with a 20-year time frame, then this portfolio would probably meet your needs. There is no guarantee it will never lose money, but it comes about as close as possible without literally stashing your money in a mattress.

WHAT'S IN THE PORTFOLIO

The Mattress is heavily weighted toward stable values. "Heavily weighted?" you say. "If it's as conservative as you can get, shouldn't it be 100 percent stable value?" Good point. Remember the discussion of portfolio *efficiency* in Chapter 6? We said that certain mixes generate an expected return at lower risk because of diversification. This portfolio provides an example of that phenomenon. By adding a small bond component and a very small stock component to the stable values in this portfolio, we are able to increase expected return without increasing risk significantly.

It may seem odd to include even 1 percent stocks in the most conservative portfolio. For that matter, some people may be uncomfortable adding even 1 percent bonds! If that's how you feel, then follow your instincts, and invest 100 percent in stable values. At least in theory, you will give up some small amount of return and be no better protected against market risk. But you may sleep a *lot* better at night. And that's the most important thing, particularly for investors at this end of the spectrum.

RISK AND RETURN

The Mattress falls at position 0 on our risk scale. That doesn't mean it has zero risk. No investment is totally risk free. You could literally

TABLE 7–1

Dollar Ranges for Portfolio 0

	1 Year, $	5 Years, $	10 Years, $	20 Years, $
High	1,108	1,460	2,002	3,665
Average	1,056	1,312	1,720	2,957
Low	1,006	1,177	1,476	2,384

stuff your money in a mattress, and you would still be faced with the possibility that your house could burn down. Position 0 simply means that this is the most conservative portfolio in the *Star* series.

The Mattress is expected to grow at a fairly slow and steady pace. Table 7–1 shows how much a $1,000 investment would be expected to grow over time. The columns in the table correspond to the bars in the *Portfolio Summary* chart at the beginning of the chapter. For example, the high amount in the 1-year column shows how much your investment will grow if you earn the 10.8 percent return shown at the top of the 1-year bar in the *Portfolio Summary* chart. The average row shows estimates based on the expected return of Portfolio 0—the amounts in the center of the four bars. The portfolio growth will most likely fall somewhere around this number.

The average return expected from the portfolio is 5.6 percent. The return range for the portfolio is relatively narrow, even at 1 year. The high and low estimated returns vary by only 5 percent from the average. That may seem like a lot, but remember that the high and low estimates are for extreme cases. And we will see later that, for more aggressive portfolios, the ranges can be many times wider.

The Mattress is the only portfolio that doesn't show a loss as the low end of its 1-year range. (Again, that doesn't mean the portfolio could not lose money. But it is highly unlikely to do so.) In a bad year, your investment would still be expected to grow, but only by 0.6 percent. As Table 7–1 shows, if you start with $1,000, you would end the year with $1,006.

In short, *The Mattress* is a relatively predictable portfolio. Over 5 years, you can expect a $1,000 investment to grow to somewhere between $1,200 and $1,500, most likely in the neighborhood of

TABLE 7-2

Portfolio 0, Decade by Decade

Decade	High, %	Average, %	Low, %	No. Loss Years
1926–1929	4.8	4.3	4.0	0
1930–1939	2.6	1.4	0.1	0
1940–1949	2.1	1.1	0.4	0
1950–1959	3.7	2.5	2.0	0
1960–1969	5.6	4.2	3.0	0
1970–1979	9.8	6.6	4.8	0
1980–1989	14.4	10.0	5.5	0
1990–1996	8.1	5.7	3.1	0

$1,300. Over 20 years, you can expect the same investment to grow to somewhere between $2,400 to $3,700, and probably close to $3,000.

LONG-TERM PERFORMANCE

Table 7–2 shows how *The Mattress* has performed over the long term. (As we said before, the historical performance is based on the performance of the five basic asset classes, not specific funds. But, given that 90 percent of long-term performance is driven by the percentages allocated to these asset classes, and given that funds tend to look more and more like their asset classes over time, the asset class performance fairly represents the performance we would expect from specific funds over the long term.)

THE GREAT BULL MARKET

Let's start with the 1920s, the period of one of the greatest bull markets in history. We begin in 1926, the first year for which we have reliable data. *The Mattress* was largely left out of the party. While stock investors enjoyed double-digit returns approaching 20 percent, stable value investors (who were relegated to savings accounts and treasury bills at the time) received only 4 percent or so on their investments.

The party ended with the Wall Street Crash of 1929. By that time, *Mattress* investors probably weren't feeling quite so left out in the cold. Every portfolio, except this one and Portfolio 10, lost money that year. But despite their losses in the closing year of the decade, more aggressive investors were still well ahead of *The Mattress*.

THE GREAT DEPRESSION

The conservatism of *Mattress* investors was vindicated in the 1930s, when the Crash of 1929 led into the Great Depression, which lasted the entire decade. While more aggressive investors saw catastrophic years when the value of their investments dropped by 40 percent or more, *Mattress* investors never saw anything worse than a break-even investment. (We are assuming, of course, that even *Mattress* investors were properly diversified. There are many stories about conservative investors who put their savings in financial institutions that failed and weren't completely reimbursed, even with the arrival of federal deposit insurance.) Portfolio 0 was the only portfolio that did not experience loss years during the 1930s. Every other portfolio saw at least 3 years of losses, and most saw 4 or 5.

But curiously, *Mattress* investors did not end even this decade any better off than those more aggressive than themselves. For the decade, *The Mattress* earned an average of 1.4 percent per year. Investors in portfolios all the way up to Portfolio 50 did better than that, despite their years of losses. Even those who were just a bit more aggressive (Portfolios 10 and 20) doubled the return of *The Mattress*.

WAR AND RECOVERY

The 1940s were slow, but safe, for *Mattress* investors. As in the 1930s, Portfolio 0 was the only one that didn't experience losses during the decade. Every other portfolio in the series suffered exactly 3 years of losses.

But in some respects, the 1940s were worse for *Mattress* investors than the 1930s. The portfolio earned only an average of 1.1 percent per year during the decade, while other portfolios had begun to recover to average returns in the 5 to 10 percent range. But *Mattress* investors did have the security of not seeing their investment values drop in any year during the decade—they always made *something*, even if it wasn't a lot.

THE NIFTY FIFTIES

The 1950s were very good to *Mattress* investors—they more than doubled their return over the previous decade. Of course, everyone pretty much doubled his or her return over the 1940s. The investment markets during the 1950s were truly the rising tides that lifted all boats, both conservative and aggressive.

Not that even the 1950s were without pain for more aggressive investors. From Portfolio 20 on, every portfolio suffered 1 or 2 years of losses, and in some cases the worst annual loss ran to 10 percent or more. *Mattress* investors were spared this pain. But the cost was a lower long-term return. For the decade, Portfolio 0 earned an average of 2.5 percent per year, compared to 6.7 percent for Portfolio 10, the next portfolio in the series. And, like Portfolio 0, Portfolio 10 didn't lose money in the 1950s.

THE GO-GO YEARS

The Mattress did better than its neighbors during the turbulent 1960s. It earned an average of 4.2 percent per year, while Portfolio 10's return actually dropped to an average of 5.1 percent. Portfolios 20 through 50 all earned an average of between 6.0 and 7.5 percent, so they certainly didn't outpace *The Mattress* by a wide margin.

The Mattress provided about the same degree of loss protection in the 1960s as it did during the 1950s. Only this portfolio and Portfolio 10 escaped the decade without any loss years. All the others suffered through 3 or 4 loss years during the decade. Their losses in those years were about the same magnitude as they experienced in the 1950s. But their good years weren't as good as the 1950s, which resulted in lower average returns. By the end of the decade, *Mattress* investors probably felt better than they did at the beginning.

THE DISCO DECADE

Mattress investors came into their own during the 1970s. The U.S. stock market slid into a Crash That Nobody Heard.[1] It's not that there were more loss years than the 1960s; it was just that the

---

1   Wall Street turned in one of its worst performances in history during this decade. Between 1973 and 1975, the stock market lost over one-third of its value, and its performance during the rest of the decade was lackluster, at best.

bad years were so much worse. The portfolios up to Portfolio 50 actually had fewer loss years than in the 1960s, and most managed to improve average performance over the 1960s. But in their worst year, most portfolios lost more than twice as much as in their worst year in the 1960s.

As always, *The Mattress* was spared this pain. In most decades, the tradeoff for this security is a return well below that of other portfolios. But historically high interest rates in the 1970s drove up the return on stable values relative to other investments. For the decade, stables earned an average of 6.6 percent, higher than any previous decade's average return. In fact, the average 1970s annual return topped the *highest* annual return in any previous decade since the 1920s.

THE ME DECADE

The 1980s were good to everyone, including *Mattress* investors. Portfolio 0 earned an *average* annual return of 10 percent per year over the course of the decade, once again beating its highest single year in any previous decade. Portfolios across the board sprang to new heights during the 1980s. It's the only decade in which every portfolio in the series turned in a double-digit return.

Losses were almost unheard of during the 1980s. Of the 11 portfolios (including 2 of the most aggressive), 7 made it through the decade without a single loss year. And only Portfolio 100 had more than 1 loss year. It had 2, but its worst loss was only 1 percent. It was almost impossible to lose money in the 1980s, no matter how hard you tried.

THE RECENT PAST

The 1990s haven't been as spectacular for *Mattress* investors as were the 1980s. Unfortunately, it's no longer possible to earn double-digit returns by figuratively stashing your money in a mattress. So far in the 1990s, one would have to invest in Portfolio 40 or better to earn in the double digits. That's more consistent with longer-term investment history.

As in prior decades, Portfolio 0 provides a high level of protection against investment risk. Its return in this decade hasn't fallen below 3 percent. And *The Mattress* has been relatively predictable, as well. Its return hasn't risen above roughly 8 percent.

INFLATION PROTECTION

The earnings graph at the bottom of the *Portfolio Summary* chart shows what we have been talking about. Portfolio 0's growth line is smooth and steady, without any of the choppiness we see in more aggressive portfolios. But the tradeoff is equally visible in the earnings graph. Portfolio 0's growth line barely rises above the inflation growth line, which moves upward just about as smoothly and as steadily as Portfolio 0.

In other words, *The Mattress* has managed to keep pace with inflation, but it hasn't moved ahead of it. *Mattress* investors can expect most of their earnings to be eaten away by inflation, leaving them with a real, or inflation-adjusted, return near 0 percent.

EVALUATING *THE MATTRESS*

As we said at the beginning of the chapter, Portfolio 0 works well for two different types of people:

- Those with very short time frames, say, a year or less
- Those who simply cannot tolerate any decline in the value of their investments

8

CHAPTER

Belt and Suspenders

Figuratively speaking, a portfolio for investors who wear a belt and suspenders to bed so their pajamas won't fall down. For those who don't like surprises.

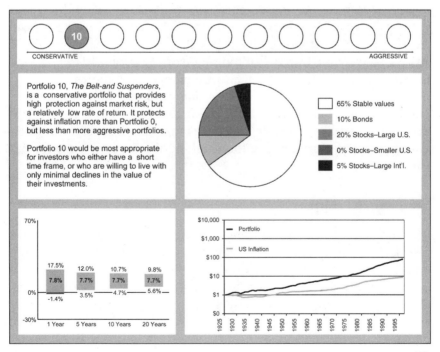

10

CONSERVATIVE

AGGRESSIVE

Portfolio 10, *The Belt-and Suspenders*, is a conservative portfolio that provides high protection against market risk, but a relatively low rate of return. It protects against inflation more than Portfolio 0, but less than more aggressive portfolios.

Portfolio 10 would be most appropriate for investors who either have a short time frame, or who are willing to live with only minimal declines in the value of their investments.

- 65% Stable values
- 10% Bonds
- 20% Stocks–Large U.S.
- 0% Stocks–Smaller U.S.
- 5% Stocks–Large Int'l.

70%

17.5%   12.0%   10.7%   9.8%

7.8%   7.7%   7.7%   7.7%

0%

-1.4%   3.5%   -4.7%   5.6%

-30%

1 Year   5 Years   10 Years   20 Years

$10,000

Portfolio

$1,000

US Inflation

$100

$10

$1

$0

1925 1930 1935 1940 1945 1950 1955 1960 1965 1970 1975 1980 1985 1990 1995

There is an old joke about very conservative investors. They are so conservative, it is said, that they wear a belt and suspenders to bed so their pajamas don't fall down! Well, it may be that there is nothing at all wrong with being that conservative. We will see in this chapter that *Belt and Suspenders* investors have looked pretty smart over the years.

WHAT'S IN THE PORTFOLIO

The Belt and Suspenders allocates the majority of its investments to stable values. In that regard, it resembles Portfolio 0, *The Mattress*. But this portfolio, which falls at position 10 on our risk scale, cuts the percentage of stable values from 90 percent of the portfolio to 65 percent. The difference is made by increased allocation to stocks and bonds. That change has a significant impact on the performance of the portfolio.

We said in Chapter 6 that some portfolios are more *efficient* than others. They manage to squeeze more return out of each unit of risk. As we move through the *Star* portfolios, we will discover something amazing. While return does go up with risk, it doesn't go up at the same pace as risk.

As we move to more aggressive portfolios, we will see that return increases less with each move. For example, moving from Portfolio 0 to Portfolio 10 "buys" us 2.2 percent in expected return over a 1-year time frame. But moving from Portfolio 10 to Portfolio 20 buys us only 1.4 percent in additional expected return.

The pie graph in the *Portfolio Summary* chart shows the percentage of each asset class in *The Belt and Suspenders*. As we will see below, adding even 25 percent stocks, as this portfolio does, can increase performance without taking the investor very far out on a limb.

RISK AND RETURN

As we noted above, *The Belt and Suspenders* falls at point 10 on our risk scale. That makes it a relatively conservative portfolio, although not as conservative as Portfolio 0. Table 8–1 shows how much a $1,000 investment can be expected to grow in Portfolio 10 over time. As we noted with Portfolio 0, the high, average, and low figures for each time frame correspond to the returns shown in the middle of

TABLE 8–1

Dollar Ranges for Portfolio 10

	1 Year, $	5 Years, $	10 Years, $	20 Years, $
High	1,175	1,761	2,764	6,487
Average	1,078	1,449	2,098	4,392
Low	986	1,189	1,586	2,962

and below the bars in the return range chart that appears in the *Portfolio Summary* chart at the beginning of this chapter. For example, $1,000 invested at an average rate of return of 12.0 percent per year over 5 years (the high return estimate for that time frame) will grow to $1,761.

The average return and dollar figures are the most likely returns over each time frame. A portfolio will rarely, if ever, earn exactly this amount, but in most years, the return and dollar growth should fall somewhere around these figures.

We said earlier that Portfolio 10's expected return is 2.2 percent higher than that of Portfolio 0. That's the largest return jump in the series. An investor can expect the greatest incremental reward for taking the first step away from *The Mattress*.

As we have said all along, there is no free lunch in the investment world. That's the case here, as well. Portfolio 10 takes the investor where *The Mattress* didn't go—into loss territory. Over any 1-year period, Portfolio 10 could lose 1.4 percent. If you invest $1,000 today, you could find yourself left with $986 at the end of the year.

The picture brightens over longer periods of time, particularly with respect to Portfolio 0. Portfolio 10's low return estimate over 5 years is 3.5 percent. That's just a bit higher than Portfolio 0's low estimate of 3.3 percent. The same trend continues over longer time frames. As one goes to longer time frames, the low return estimate for Portfolio 10 becomes progressively higher than the same estimate for Portfolio 0.

In other words, if you can stand the prospect of very modest losses over a 1-year time frame, Portfolio 10 actually becomes less risky, at least on the down side, than Portfolio 0. The reason is that Portfolio 10's increased earnings power outweighs its increase in

T A B L E   8–2

Portfolio 10, Decade by Decade

Decade	High, %	Average, %	Low, %	No. Loss Years
1926–1929	13.9	8.4	1.7	0
1930–1939	13.5	2.8	−11.1	3
1940–1949	10.4	3.2	−2.2	3
1950–1959	14.2	6.7	0.1	0
1960–1969	8.6	5.1	0.1	0
1970–1979	15.2	6.9	−0.4	1
1980–1989	18.2	12.4	7.5	0
1990–1996	14.3	7.5	2.7	0

market risk. Even with the increased market risk thrown in, it still comes out ahead of Portfolio 0 for time frames of 5 years or more.

LONG-TERM PERFORMANCE

Table 8–2 shows how *The Belt and Suspenders* has performed since 1926.[1]

THE GREAT BULL MARKET

Even *Belt and Suspenders* investors joined the party during the 1920s. And, as we will see in a minute, they suffered from a hangover in the 1930s, too. From 1926 to 1929, *Belt and Suspenders* investors earned an average of 8.4 percent per year on their investments. Now, that may not seem like a lot, but it's more than double what Portfolio 0 investors earned during the same period. And like *Mattress* investors, they didn't suffer a loss in the Crash of 1929. In fact, they made it through the decade with no losses at all. One can imagine the *Belt and Suspenders* investor feeling pretty smug at the close of the decade.

---

1   As we have noted, the historical performance of the *Star* portfolios is based on the historical returns of the five basic asset classes, as represented by various market indexes. A complete explanation appears in Appendix A, "How the *Star* Portfolios Were Created."

THE GREAT DEPRESSION

Reality caught up with *Belt and Suspenders* investors in the 1930s. *We're in the Money,* a popular anthem of the age, was definitely not the theme song of these, or any other, investors more aggressive than *The Mattress.*

Portfolio 10 lost money 3 years out of 10 in the 1930s. That's the same number of loss years as Portfolios 20 and 30, both of which are more aggressive. Certainly the bad news for *Belt and Suspenders* investors wasn't as bad as the news for investors in those more aggressive portfolios, but it was bad enough. In its worst year in the 1930s, Portfolio 10 lost just over 11 percent of its value. That's enough to make a lot of investors cry Ouch! And we are still in the realm of relatively conservative portfolios.

That's not to say the news was all bad during the 1930s. In its best year in the decade, Portfolio 10 earned 13.5 percent. That's not as spectacular as what some of the more aggressive portfolios earned the same year, but *Belt and Suspenders* investors didn't have to live with quite the same magnitude of pain in the bad years either.

Belt and Suspenders investors made it through the decade with a tradeoff. They doubled the average annual return of *Mattress* investors (2.8 percent per year, as opposed to 1.4 percent), but they earned less than either Portfolios 20 or 30. They could take some consolation in the fact that their losses in the bad years weren't quite as bad as those more aggressive portfolios. But that's like banging up your car in a fender-bender: It looks good only in comparison to a major car wreck.

WAR AND RECOVERY

The 1940s was another bumpy decade for *Belt and Suspenders* investors, although they weren't nearly as traumatic as the 1930s. Portfolio 10 lost money in 3 years, as did every other portfolio with the exception of Portfolio 0. But Portfolio 10 lost only 2.2 percent in its worst year in the decade, a far cry from its 11 percent loss in the 1930s.

All in all, the 1940s were a little better than the prior decade for *Belt and Suspenders* investors. They earned an average annual return of 3.2 percent, compared to 2.8 percent in the 1930s. In their best year, they earned over 10 percent, a bit less than the previous decade's high. For *Belt and Suspenders* investors, the 1940s were better than the 1930s, but still not a decade to write home about.

THE NIFTY FIFTIES

The *Belt and Suspenders* crowd did better in the 1950s. They more than doubled their 1940s return, earning an average of 6.7 percent per year during the decade. That's not bad, particularly compared to the 2.5 percent per year earned during the decade by *Mattress* investors. And Portfolio 10 earned its return without a single loss year. It is the only portfolio, other than Portfolio 0, that can make that claim.

The best years of the 1950s were quite good to *Belt and Suspenders* investors. In its best year during the decade, Portfolio 10 earned 14.2 percent. That's pretty good, particularly considering the total absence of loss years during the decade. In short, Portfolio 10 did pretty well in the 1950s, particularly for a portfolio with two-thirds of its assets allocated to stable values.

THE GO-GO YEARS

Portfolio 10 looked rather lackluster during the Go-Go Years of the 1960s. Its average return of 5.1 percent per year was actually lower than its average during the prior decade. That trend continues with all the *Star* portfolios through Portfolio 100. *The Belt and Suspenders* could manage no better than 8.6 percent during its best year of the decade, well below its 14.2 percent best year for the 1940s. It made *some* money even in its worst year, although at 0.1 percent it was little more than pocket change. Still, that year was no worse than its worst year of the 1950s.

The Belt and Suspenders provided just about the same degree of loss protection in the 1930s as *The Mattress*. And that points out the relative strength of Portfolio 10. It will outperform Portfolio 0 in good years and provide just about the same degree of loss protection in marginal years. It is only in a pretty bad year that Portfolio 10's stable value base proves insufficient to ward off losses.

THE DISCO DECADE

The 1970s provide an example of what we were just talking about. Most portfolios suffered 2 or 3 years of losses during this decade—

Portfolio 0 was the only one to escape without any loss years at all. Portfolio 10 almost made it, however. It suffered only 1 year of losses, and during that year it only lost 0.4 percent. That's about as close to a break-even as you can get.

At the same time, Portfolio 10 didn't really outperform *The Mattress* the way it had in previous decades. On average, Portfolio 10 earned 6.9 percent per year, while Portfolio 0 earned 6.6 percent. That's a little disappointing for investors who might have expected more of an earnings boost from *The Belt and Suspenders'* 25 percent stock component. But stocks performed poorly for much of the first half of the decade, and their performance during the second half was less than stellar. In short, there was little boost to be had.

THE ME DECADE

We said in connection with *The Mattress* that the 1980s were good to almost everybody. *Belt and Suspenders* investors received their share of good news throughout the decade. Portfolio 10 earned an average of 12.4 percent per year during the decade, thanks in part to high stable value returns and a stock market that showed unprecedented strength for much of the decade.

As we pointed out in the last chapter, about the only way to lose money in the 1980s was to really work at it. The decade was a fluke in at least one respect: Most experts would agree we are unlikely to again see 12 percent returns in the near future from a portfolio composed primarily of stable value investments.

THE RECENT PAST

Things seemed to have settled back down to normal for Portfolio 10 over the course of the 1990s. From 1990 to 1996, the portfolio earned an average of about 7.5 percent per year. That's right in line with the 7.7 percent average return estimate shown in the return range chart. It's also more in line with the long-term investment history.

Portfolio 10 continues to provide relatively strong protection against loss. So far in the 1990s, it hasn't suffered a loss year. But keep in mind that we have not suffered through any really bad years in this decade. In fact, none of the portfolios through Portfolio 20 have experienced annual losses. And even the most aggressive portfolios have seen only 2 loss years. The earnings range suggests we could see modest losses in Portfolio 10 in a fairly bad year.

INFLATION PROTECTION

The real advantage of *The Belt and Suspenders* is the degree of inflation protection it provides, particularly when compared to *The Mattress*. We said in the last chapter that *The Mattress* is expected to do little more than keep pace with inflation over the long term. *The Belt and Suspenders* is expected to do better than that, as one can see in the earnings graph at the bottom of the *Portfolio Summary* chart for Portfolio 10.

Like *The Mattress*, *The Belt and Suspenders'* earnings line is smooth and steady. But it maintains a constant spread over inflation throughout its 71-year history. Granted, it's not much of a spread, particularly when compared to some of the more aggressive portfolios. Inflation will remain an issue for the *Belt and Suspenders* investor, but it will be less of an issue that it is for *Mattress* investors.

EVALUATING *THE BELT AND SUSPENDERS*

Portfolio 10 works well for those who aren't so conservative that they would stash their savings in a mattress but who aren't comfortable with the risks of portfolios with major stock and bond investments. *The Belt and Suspenders* can provide a good compromise for these investors. It affords more inflation protection than *The Mattress*, yet it still provides nearly as much protection against market risk.

9
CHAPTER

The Shallow End

Enough water to swim, but not enough to drown. A safe portfolio that provides a modest and consistent return.

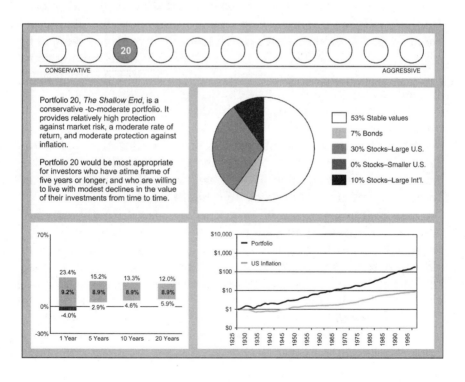

CONSERVATIVE   AGGRESSIVE

Portfolio 20, *The Shallow End*, is a conservative -to-moderate portfolio. It provides relatively high protection against market risk, a moderate rate of return, and moderate protection against inflation.

Portfolio 20 would be most appropriate for investors who have atime frame of five years or longer, and who are willing to live with modest declines in the value of their investments from time to time.

- 53% Stable values
- 7% Bonds
- 30% Stocks–Large U.S.
- 0% Stocks–Smaller U.S.
- 10% Stocks–Large Int'l.

When you go to a pool in the summertime, what kind of swimmer are you? Some people like to dive into the deep end. Others prefer the shallow end, where the water is waist-deep. Swimming in water up to your waist pretty well describes Portfolio 20, *The Shallow End*. Mind you, this portfolio isn't the baby pool. We're not talking about just putting a toe in the water. If you are looking for a portfolio with just a little exposure to stocks, you might like Portfolio 10 better.

Portfolio 20 is a conservative to moderate portfolio. It moves a bit more deeply into stocks, but the water doesn't generally come up past your belt line. This portfolio has more market risk (or volatility) than the two previous portfolios we looked at, but its downside is beneath most people's Ouch Factor. It is also a broadly diversified portfolio. It includes four of the five basic asset classes, and its asset allocation is fairly well balanced between them. At the same time, the portfolio remains firmly anchored in stable values, which tends to reduce its volatility.

WHAT'S IN THE PORTFOLIO

The pie graph in the *Portfolio Summary* chart shows the asset allocation of Portfolio 20. *The Shallow End* allocates about half its investments to stable values. That's down from the two-thirds we saw in Portfolio 10 and the 90 percent in Portfolio 0. We are moving from conservative to moderate portfolios, and we are doing so by replacing increasing amounts of stable values with stocks.

We are also increasing the relative size of our international stock allocation. We first used international stocks in Portfolio 10, where they made up one-fifth of the total stock allocation. In Portfolio 20, they increase to one-fourth of the total stock allocation. As we move to more aggressive allocations, we will begin to shift an increasing amount of our stock investment overseas.

As we move into moderate portfolios, we are slowly reducing our relatively modest allocation to bonds, as well. Bonds tend to be crowded out of the *Star* portfolios by stable values. Stable values often pay returns near what bonds will pay. Since stables don't rise and fall with investment markets, the computer model used to create the portfolios views stables as more efficient than bonds. In real life, the effect is particularly noticeable in 401k plans, where GIC funds often pay returns on par with bond funds. That's one reason why relatively few 401k plans have bond funds.

RISK AND RETURN

As we have discussed, *The Shallow End* is a conservative to moderate portfolio, which falls at position 20 on our risk scale. The expected return ranges are shown on the bar graph in the middle left section of the *Portfolio Summary* chart. Table 9–1 shows the expected growth of a $1,000 investment in Portfolio 20 over different time frames. As with the other portfolios in the *Star* series, the amounts in Table 9–1 correspond to the returns shown on the bar graph in the *Portfolio Summary* chart. For example, if the portfolio earns an average of 8.9 percent per year for 10 years (the average return estimate for a 10-year time frame), a $1,000 investment would grow to $2,346.

As we noted for the other portfolios, the returns shown in the average row of Table 9–1 and the center of the bars in the *Portfolio Summary* chart are the most likely returns from Portfolio 20 over different time frames. It is unlikely that the portfolio would ever earn exactly this return, but in most years its return should fall somewhere around this return. The high and low estimates are optimistic and pessimistic estimates of the return. They represent what the portfolio might be expected to earn in very good or very bad years.

In our discussion of *The Belt and Suspenders*, we talked about how an investor gets paid the most for taking the first steps into market risk. When we moved from Portfolio 0 to Portfolio 10, our expected return over 1 year increased by 2.2 percent. As we move from Portfolio 10 to Portfolio 20, we are paid slightly less; our expected return increases only by 1.4 percent. Still, that is a larger payoff for taking on an additional unit of market risk than we will see in later portfolios in the series.

Since our return increases with the move to Portfolio 20, it should come as no surprise that market risk goes up as well. In a bad

TABLE 9–1

Dollar Ranges for Portfolio 20

	1 Year, $	5 Years, $	10 Years, $	20 Years, $
High	1,234	2,025	3,480	9,595
Average	1,092	1,534	2,346	5,482
Low	960	1,155	1,572	3,118

year, *Shallow End* investors can expect to see the value of their investments decline by 4.0 percent. That's higher than the 1.4 percent drop we saw in Portfolio 10, but still modest. A $1,000 investment would drop to $960 if that loss were realized.

The prospects of loss diminish with longer time frames. Over 5 years, Portfolio 20's low estimated return is 2.9 percent, which means that a $1,000 investment could still be expected to grow to $1,155 even over a bad 5-year market. What is more likely is that the portfolio would earn 9.2 percent, which would grow the $1,000 to $1,534.

In short, the trend that began in Portfolio 10 continues in Portfolio 20. To the extent that you are willing to live with market risk, you can increase the expected return from your investments.

LONG-TERM PERFORMANCE

Table 9–2 shows how *The Shallow End* has performed since 1926. (As always, the historical performance is based on the five major asset classes, not specific funds. There is a more complete explanation in Appendix A, "How the *Star* Portfolios Were Created.")

THE GREAT BULL MARKET

We said in previous chapters that *Mattress* investors and *Belt and Suspenders* investors were left out of the wild party that went on in

TABLE 9–2

Portfolio 20, Decade by Decade

Decade	High,%	Average, %	Low, %	No Loss Years
1926–1929	20.0	10.8	−0.3	1
1930–1939	26.6	3.3	−16.6	3
1940–1949	15.3	4.7	−3.9	3
1950–1959	21.5	9.3	−2.1	1
1960–1969	12.2	5.8	−1.9	3
1970–1979	18.9	7.5	−5.2	2
1980–1989	21.8	14.0	6.8	0
1990–1996	16.8	8.3	1.0	0

the investment markets of the 1920s. *Shallow End* investors weren't left out of the party. Instead, you might think of them as the guests who had only a couple of drinks. They woke up the next morning with a hangover, but theirs was less severe than those who partied the hardest.

Shallow End investors didn't make it through the decade without loss. The Crash of 1929 caused their portfolios to decline by 0.3 percent. That isn't much of a loss, particularly when compared to the losses suffered by more aggressive investors.

THE GREAT DEPRESSION

The Crash of 1929 got all the headlines, but it was merely a harbinger of what was to come in the 1930s. At the time, market pundits thought is was simply a correction, the market's way of shaking off the excesses of the 1920s. "The business of America is fundamentally sound," announced President Hoover. That pronouncement reflected the sentiment of many investors. But instead of a correction, the Crash ushered in the worst and most prolonged bear market in history.

If *Belt and Suspenders* investors suffered a broken leg in the 1930s, *Shallow End* investors suffered a compound fracture. That's the price one pays for a higher return, even in *The Shallow End*. Portfolio 20 actually did the best of all the *Star* portfolios during the 1930s. It earned an average of 3.3 percent per year. That return is not only higher than the more conservative portfolios in the series, it's also higher than the return earned by the more aggressive portfolios. So, at least for the 1930s, *The Shallow End* was the smartest place to be.

That's not to say that *Shallow End* investors didn't experience their share of pain. In 1931, the worst year of the decade, they saw the value of their portfolios drop by 16.6 percent. That's well beyond the –4.0 percent return estimate at the low end of this portfolio's return range. [The 1931 loss points out that portfolios can lose more than the return at the low end of the estimated range. The low end represents what would be expected 95 percent of the time. In an extreme case (and the Great Depression was about as extreme as they come), losses can be worse than estimated by the range.] It's also beyond the threshold of pain for many investors. Still, it pales in comparison with the losses suffered in the same year by those who were more aggressive. *Shallow End* investors suffered through 3 years of losses in the 1930s, about the same number as other moderate investors.

WAR AND RECOVERY

We have said before that the 1940s were mediocre for most investors, although they outperformed the disastrous 1930s by a wide margin. *Shallow End* investors fell into this pattern with most other investors. They earned an average of 4.7 percent per year over the decade, above the more conservative portfolios but less than more aggressive portfolios. That is just what one would expect.

Portfolio 20 experienced 3 loss years in the 1940s, the same as every other portfolio except Portfolio 0. In 1941, the worst year, the portfolio lost 3.9 percent. That's in line with the low-end expected return for the portfolio. It's also a far cry from the 16.6 percent loss suffered in 1931, and it is less than the losses suffered in 1941 by more aggressive portfolios. The 1940s were certainly an improvement over the 1930s for *Shallow End* investors, but still nothing to shout about.

THE NIFTY FIFTIES

Like most other investors, *Shallow End* investors more than doubled their return during the 1950s. They earned an average of 9.3 percent per year for the decade, which is slightly above the average return estimated by the return ranges in the *Portfolio Summary* chart.

Shallow End investors lost money only once in the decade, in 1957. Their loss wasn't too painful—it amounted to only 2.1 percent. The best years of the 1950s were quite good to *Shallow End* investors, as they were to others. In 1954, the best year of the decade, Portfolio 10 earned a return of 21.5 percent. *Shallow End* investors earned double-digit returns in 5 years of the decade. Those kinds of returns, from a portfolio with half its assets in stable values, go a long way toward easing the pain of the occasional loss year.

THE GO-GO YEARS

Portfolio 20 might have been called the *Just As You Would Expect*. In every decade other than the 1930s, Portfolio 20's return falls right into line—higher than the more conservative portfolios and lower than the more aggressive ones. The 1960s were no exception. *Shallow End* investors earned an average return of 5.8 percent per year. That's not great; it's certainly less than the 1950s. Portfolio 20 earned double-digit returns in only 3 years during the decade. In its best year, 1961, it managed to eke out a 12.2 percent return.

On the other hand, *Shallow End* investors were spared some of the misery that other investors experienced in the 1960s. In its worst year, 1962, Portfolio 20 lost only 1.9 percent. Aggressive investors lost nearly 10 percent that year. *Shallow End* investors had the same number of loss years as more aggressive investors, but their losses were smaller, and less painful.

THE DISCO DECADE

Shallow End investors were in the same boat as other moderate investors during the 1970s. They lost money during 2 years out of the decade, but they managed to end it with an average return of 7.5 percent per year, better than their 1960s performance.

In fact, *Shallow End* investors fared about the best of any investors during the decade. Moderate investors in general (Portfolios 20 through 50) earned about 7.5 percent per year. But Portfolio 20 earned the return with less volatility. In its worst year, the portfolio lost 5.2 percent, while other moderate portfolios with the same average return lost 15 percent or more. As was the case with the 1930s, *The Shallow End* was a good place to be in the 1970s.

THE ME DECADE

We have said before that the 1980s were almost too good to be true. It seemed that no matter where you put your money, it grew like crazy. And *The Shallow End* was no exception. How often in a single lifetime would one expect to see a portfolio with over half invested in stable values earn an *average return* of 14 percent? That's higher than the highest rates earned by the portfolio in some prior decades!

And that's one of the problems with the 1980s. Many people who came of age in that decade or later somehow assume that what went on in those 10 years was normal. The extraordinary performance seen in the 1980s was anything but normal. It was as singular in its own way as the Great Depression. Both were once-in-a-lifetime events that are unlikely to be repeated any time soon. (And any time a market pundit says that to you, remind yourself of this: Just because something is *unlikely* to happen, that doesn't mean it *can't* happen. We could experience another boom or bust at any time.)

Portfolio 20, along with the other moderate portfolios in the *Star* series, coasted through the 1980s. It earned double-digit returns in 7 years during the decade and capped its performance with a stellar 21.8 percent return in 1985. That wouldn't be so unusual for a stock portfolio, but it's almost unheard of in one anchored by stable values.

THE RECENT PAST

Investment markets seemed to have returned to normal in the 1990s. Fortunately, they appear to have done so without the trauma we saw in the 1930s. Portfolio 20 has earned an average of 8.3 percent per year so far in this decade, just slightly below the average rate shown on the return range graph in the *Portfolio Summary* chart. Portfolio 20 has not lost money so far in the 1990s, and it is the only moderate portfolio that can make that claim.

INFLATION PROTECTION

Like other moderate portfolios, Portfolio 20 provides a reasonable amount of protection against inflation. *Shallow End* investors can expect to see modest real (or inflation-adjusted) growth in their investments, in the neighborhood of 5.6 percent or so. Portfolio 20, like other moderate portfolios, strikes a balance between market risk and inflation.

EVALUATING *THE SHALLOW END*

Portfolio 20 is well suited for investors who prefer a middle-of-the-road approach but who want to maintain a conservative slant in their investing. It provides a fair degree of protection against inflation, but at the same time it keeps market risk in check under all but extreme circumstances. It would be a bit risky for investors with short time frames, but for moderate investors with a time frame of 5 years or more, *The Shallow End* can provide an opportunity to jump into the water without getting in over their head.

10
CHAPTER

The Jogger

A slow and steady portfolio that earns a decent return, although there may be a bump or two along the way.

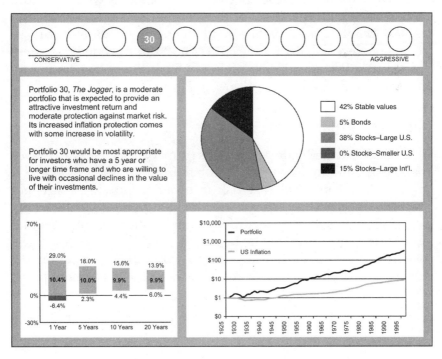

CONSERVATIVE   30   AGGRESSIVE

Portfolio 30, *The Jogger*, is a moderate portfolio that is expected to provide an attractive investment return and moderate protection against market risk. Its increased inflation protection comes with some increase in volatility.

Portfolio 30 would be most appropriate for investors who have a 5 year or longer time frame and who are willing to live with occasional declines in the value of their investments.

- 42% Stable values
- 5% Bonds
- 38% Stocks–Large U.S.
- 0% Stocks–Smaller U.S.
- 15% Stocks–Large Int'l.

The *American Heritage Dictionary*[1] gives the following definitions for *jogging:*

- To move by shoving, bumping, or jerking; jar: *a rough wagon ride that jogged the passengers.*
- To run or ride at a steady slow trot: *jogged out to their positions on the playing field.*

That's a pretty fair description of the next portfolio in the *Star* series, *The Jogger.* Investors in this portfolio have by and large seen their savings grow at a steady or slow trot. But they have also seen occasional bumps in the road that have shaken things up a bit.

WHAT'S IN THE PORTFOLIO

Portfolio 30 continues the trend toward smaller allocations to stable values and bonds and larger allocations to stocks. For the first time, allocations to stocks (53 percent) are larger than allocations to bonds and stable values (47 percent). This portfolio also continues the trend of increasing allocations to international stocks. Here, they make up slightly more than one-quarter of the total stock allocation.

We continue to reduce our bond allocation as we move from more conservative to middle-of-the-road portfolios. As we noted in the last chapter, stable values tend to crowd bonds out of these portfolios since stables provide returns near those of bonds, with less market risk. Portfolio 30 allocates only 5 percent of its total investments to bonds.

RISK AND RETURN

Portfolio 30 is a moderate portfolio. Its primary objective is to balance market risk and inflation risk. It differs from Portfolio 20 in that it takes on a bit more market risk in order to provide a stronger measure of protection against inflation. Table 10–1 shows the expected growth of $1,000 over different time frames. As with the other portfolios in the series, the high, average, and low dollar estimates correspond to the return estimates shown at the top, middle, and bottom of the bars in the *Portfolio Summary* chart. For example, if

---

1   *American Heritage Dictionary of the English Language,* 3rd ed., Houghton Mifflin, Boston, 1992.

TABLE 10-1

Dollar Ranges for Portfolio 30

	1 Year, $	5 Years, $	10 Years, $	20 Years, $
High	1,290	2,290	4,251	13,433
Average	1,104	1,608	2,573	6,582
Low	936	1,118	1,543	3,201

Portfolio 30 earns its high estimate of 15.6 percent per year for 10 years, a $1,000 investment will grow to $4,251.

There is another trend that continues with Portfolio 30. When we moved from Portfolio 0 to 10, we saw an increase of 2.2 percent in our expected return. Our move from Portfolio 10 to 20 increased our expected return by 1.4 percent. Now, as we move from Portfolio 20 to 30, we increase our expected return by only 1.2 percent. We haven't given up much compared to our last move, but we have given up something. We will see the same increase as we move through the moderate portfolios up to Portfolio 60. Beyond that point, we will see our incremental return drop sharply.

As always, we have to live with incremental risk if we want incremental return. With Portfolio 30, we step over the –5 percent loss point. Over a 1-year time frame, *Joggers* can expect to see the value of their portfolio drop as much as 6.4 percent.[2]

LONG-TERM PERFORMANCE

Table 10–2 shows *The Jogger*'s performance since 1926. (As we have noted with previous portfolios in the *Star* series, the historical performance is taken from market indexes that represent the five basic asset classes. We are looking at *market* performance, not individual fund performance.)

---

2 As we will see in the decade-by-decade review of *The Jogger's* performance, the portfolio has lost more than this amount four times; three times in the 1930s, and once in the 1970s. Again, the return ranges forecast what will *probably* happen, but they can't predict the future.

TABLE 10–2

Portfolio 30, Decade by Decade

Decade	High, %	Average, %	Low, %	No. Loss Years
1926–1929	25.2	12.8	−2.1	1
1930–1939	33.7	3.2	−22.3	3
1940–1949	19.9	5.7	−5.5	3
1950–1959	27.4	11.5	−4.4	1
1960–1969	15.6	6.2	−3.4	3
1970–1979	22.9	7.5	−9.6	2
1980–1989	25.4	15.3	5.0	0
1990–1996	19.3	8.9	−1.6	1

THE GREAT BULL MARKET

If the decade of the 1920s was a wild investment party, then *Joggers* stayed at the party a little longer than more conservative investors. The years 1927 and 1928 were double-digit years for these investors, and the Crash of 1929 didn't hurt them too badly. *Joggers* only lost 2.1 percent in the 1929 market crash. Most of us could probably shrug off a loss like that.

THE GREAT DEPRESSION

Things went downhill for *Joggers* in the 1930s. Like other moderate investors, they took a shellacking in what turned out to be the most prolonged bear market in history. They earned an average return of only 3.2 percent. That's actually *less* than Portfolio 20 investors earned for the decade. Of course, it's also *better* than more aggressive investors earned during the same period. From Portfolio 30 on, average returns during the 1930s get worse and worse.

That's not to say there weren't some bright spots. In 1933, *Joggers* earned almost 34 percent on their investments, and they also earned double-digit returns in 1925 and 1936. But these banner years were largely offset by 3 disastrous years in which *Joggers* suffered losses well into the double digits.

That brings up a point we made in an earlier chapter. No matter how good a forecasting system may be, it can't predict the future. The return ranges at the beginning of the chapter are based on the best statistical methods that number crunchers have at their disposal. Even so, the low end of the 1-year range for Portfolio 30 is –6.4 percent. That's far short of the 22.3 percent loss experienced by the portfolio in 1931, at the depth of the Depression.

So, does that mean our return ranges are unreliable? Not according to the number crunchers. The ranges forecast what is *likely* to happen 95 percent of the time. Five years out of a hundred, the number crunchers tell us, a portfolio could do worse than the low end of the range. In this case, a lot worse.

WAR AND RECOVERY

Things returned a little closer to normal for *Joggers* in the 1940s. Their average annual return for the decade, 5.7 percent, was little more than half the 9.9 percent we would expect for a 10-year period. In fact, it was at the low end of the 10-year range. *Joggers* suffered through 3 loss years, 2 at the beginning of the decade and 1 just after the war ended. But the worst loss was only 5.5 percent, a minor inconvenience compared to the 20 percent losses experienced in the 1930s.

The decade wasn't really as bad as it looks. *Joggers* did manage to earn double-digit returns in 5 years during the decade; it was the remaining years that dragged the return down. For *Joggers*, like most other investors, the 1940s were a decade investors would just as soon forget about. Most were simply thankful it wasn't as bad as the 1930s.

THE NIFTY FIFTIES

Things brightened considerably for *Joggers* in the 1950s. Their larger allocation to stocks allowed them greater participation than more conservative investors in the stock market's gains during the decade. *Joggers'* average annual return increased to 11.5 percent per year, and *Joggers* earned double-digit returns in 6 years during the decade. In 2 years, 1954 and 1958, their returns exceeded 20 percent.

Losses weren't much of an issue for *Joggers* during this decade. Portfolio 30 experienced only 1 loss year (1957), and that loss only amounted to 4.4 percent. That's well within the 6.4 percent range of expected losses.

THE GO-GO YEARS

The 1960s looked a lot like the 1940s. There was a war that lasted half the decade, and most investments failed to perform up to expectations. *Joggers* earned an average return of 6.2 percent per year, quite a bit less than 9.9 percent expected from this portfolio. The 1960s certainly had their moments, though. *Joggers* saw double-digit returns in 4 years during the decade, including 2 years in a row, 1963 and 1964. But like the 1940s, the rest of the decade dragged down returns to mediocre levels, including modest losses in 3 years.

The losses in the 1960s, unlike the losses in the 1930s, did not exceed the low end of the return range. The worst loss of the decade was a 3.4 percent loss in 1966. That's more typical of the losses a *Jogger* might expect to see under normal market conditions.

THE DISCO DECADE

The 1970s began with a burst of optimism, but they soon sank into the Crash That Nobody Heard. The U.S. stock market lost nearly 40 percent of its value during 1973 and 1974, during the height and the climax of the Watergate scandal. A $1,000 investment in stocks made at the beginning of 1973 sank to $627 by the close of 1974. That kind of performance rivals the worst of the Great Depression. But it isn't as legendary as the 1929 Crash, or even the 1987 crash, because it didn't happen all at once. Instead, investors received unrelenting bad news, day after day, for 2 years. The market crashed 30 points at a time.

Joggers weren't spared their share of pain during this decade. In 1974, the portfolio lost 9.6 percent, the first time since the 1930s the portfolio suffered a loss greater than the low end of its earnings range. And that came on the heels of a 4.9 percent loss the year before. Fortunately, those were the only 2 loss years experienced by *Joggers* during the decade. The rest of the decade wasn't too bad; Portfolio 30 earned double-digit returns in 6 out of the 10 years. Those good years offset the performance of 1973 to 1974 and helped the portfolio end the decade with an average return of 7.5 percent per year. That return was better than the average return of the 1960s but still below the 9.9 percent expected from the portfolio over a 10-year period.

THE ME DECADE

The 1980s were almost enough to make one believe in Santa Claus. In *Wall Street*, one of the decade's most popular movies, the rapacious financier Gordon Gekko announces, "Greed is good! Greed works!" He might well have added, "Risk is good! Risk works!" Investors were richly rewarded for taking risks in the 1980s. The more risk you took, the more money you made. And, at least if you were a moderate investor, you never had to deal with loss years.

That was pretty much the picture for *Joggers* during the 1980s. They made an average return of 15.3 percent per year on their investments, and in 1985 they made over 25 percent. They earned double-digit returns in 7 years during the decade, and they exceeded 20 percent annual returns three times.

If you are a *Jogger* who began investing in the 1980s, we caution you again. It was great; it was wonderful. But you can't count on it happening again any time soon.

THE RECENT PAST

The 1990s are more representative of what *Joggers* might expect. For the first 7 years of the decade, Portfolio 30 earned an average return of 8.9 percent, which is fairly close to the 10.0 percent annual return expected over 5 years. The portfolio has experienced only 1 loss year so far in this decade. That was in 1990, when the portfolio lost 1.6 percent. That's not the sort of loss that will cause many people to lose sleep.

INFLATION PROTECTION

You can see from the *Portfolio Summary* chart that *Joggers* have historically maintained a fairly wide margin over inflation. On an inflation-adjusted basis, Portfolio 30 should provide an average of about 7 percent real growth per year. As with the other moderate portfolios in the *Star* series, *The Jogger* balances market risk against inflation protection. But we are now entering the realm where we take on additional market risk to increase returns over and above what is needed to protect ourselves against inflation. This portfolio, and the ones that follow it, are more focused on providing *real growth*, or inflation-adjusted growth.

EVALUATING *THE JOGGER*

Portfolio 30 fits the needs of moderate investors who demand a well-diversified portfolio and who are willing to take on market risk beyond what is strictly necessary to protect against inflation. Portfolio 30 is expected to provide moderate real growth over the long term, and its short-term losses are expected to be relatively small.

11

CHAPTER

The Center Line

The perfect portfolio for the middle-of-the-road investor. But remember, traffic can hit you from both sides.

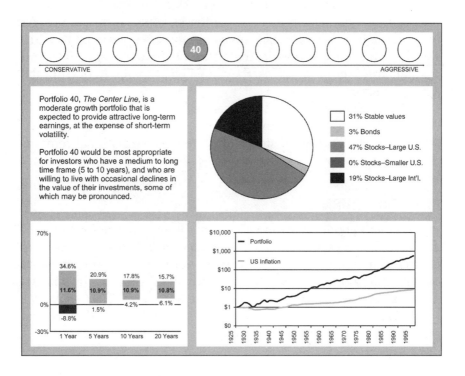

CONSERVATIVE   40   AGGRESSIVE

Portfolio 40, *The Center Line*, is a moderate growth portfolio that is expected to provide attractive long-term earnings, at the expense of short-term volatility.

Portfolio 40 would be most appropriate for investors who have a medium to long time frame (5 to 10 years), and who are willing to live with occasional declines in the value of their investments, some of which may be pronounced.

- 31% Stable values
- 3% Bonds
- 47% Stocks–Large U.S.
- 0% Stocks–Smaller U.S.
- 19% Stocks–Large Int'l.

70% / 0% / -30%

	1 Year	5 Years	10 Years	20 Years
	34.6%	20.9%	17.8%	15.7%
	11.6%	10.9%	10.9%	10.8%
	-8.8%	1.5%	-4.2%	6.1%

$10,000 / $1,000 / $100 / $10 / $1 / $0

- Portfolio
- US Inflation

1925 1930 1935 1940 1945 1950 1955 1960 1965 1970 1975 1980 1985 1990 1995

Portfolio 40 is called *The Center Line* because it is a good fit for middle-of-the-road investors. But if you consider yourself a *Center Line* investor, remember what sometimes happens to those in the middle of the road. Oncoming traffic can hit you from both directions.

That's what life can be like for *Center Line* investors. Most of the time the portfolio behaves as one would expect from a moderate portfolio. But in extremely volatile markets, like those we experienced in the 1930s and the 1970s, the portfolio can take you for a ride that's scarier than a roller coaster.

WHAT'S IN THE PORTFOLIO

The basic mix of *The Center Line* is two-thirds stocks, one-third stable values and bonds. That's fairly close to the classic 60 percent stock–40 percent bond "trustee's mix" used by many balanced funds. (It is called the *trustee's mix* because many banks and trust companies used this mix as the asset allocation for nearly all their clients. It was, and still is, considered to provide a good balance between growth and protection against undue market risk.) But that doesn't mean the portfolio is a magic bullet answer to risk versus return issues. As we will see below, *Center Line* investors must be prepared to withstand significant declines in the value of their investments. And under extreme circumstances, they must be prepared to ride out the storm for several years.

Portfolio 40 allocates 19 percent of its assets to international stocks, which comes out to just over a quarter of its total stock allocation. The portion of stocks allocated to international remains the same as for Portfolio 30.

RISK AND RETURN

As we noted above, Portfolio 40 is a moderate, middle-of-the-road portfolio, but it carries its share of market risk. It may be too risky for investors who consider themselves very conservative investors or who may not be willing to live with significant declines in the value of their investments. But over the long term, *The Center Line* has rewarded investors with higher average returns and more real growth. As with previous portfolios in the *Star* series, Table 11–1

TABLE 11–1

Dollar Ranges for Portfolio 40

	1 Year, $	5 Years, $	10 Years, $	20 Years, $
High	1,346	2,580	5,159	18,543
Average	1,116	1,681	2,804	7,805
Low	912	1,079	1,503	3,244

shows the expected future growth of $1,000 invested in Portfolio 40 today. The dollar ranges in the table correspond to the return ranges shown in the *Portfolio Summary* chart.

Portfolio 40 is the first portfolio to take us into a double-digit expected return. Over any given 1-year period, the portfolio is expected to earn an 11.6 percent return. As we have said before, the portfolio probably won't earn that particular return in any particular year, but its returns should fall somewhere around that figure, and over time they should average out to that return.

Over longer periods, the average expected return declines to 10.9 percent, and eventually to 10.8 percent. That's due to the volatility of the portfolio.[1] The fact that the portfolio probably won't earn exactly 11.6 percent in any particular year brings the averages down just a bit. The effect is more noticeable as our portfolios get more aggressive.

In a 1-year period, Portfolio 40 can lose as much as 8.8 percent of its value. (As we saw in the two previous portfolios, the low end of the range covers what is expected to happen 95 years out of 100. The Depression years and the 1930s show what can happen in the other 5.) Unless you are prepared to withstand a drop in value of that magnitude, investing in *The Center Line* may amount to stepping out into traffic. And in extreme cases, you may have to wait several years to recover the value of your investments. We will see more about that as we look at *The Center Line*'s history.

---

1 It also has a lot to do with how number crunchers calculate averages and the difference between "arithmetic" and "geometric" averages. If you want to know more, there is an article on this topic on the www.veeneman.com Web site.

TABLE 11–2

Portfolio 40, Decade by Decade

Decade	High, %	Average, %	Low, %	No. Loss Years
1926–1929	30.4	14.7	–3.8	1
1930–1939	40.2	2.7	–28.0	4
1940–1949	24.5	6.9	–7.1	3
1950–1959	34.8	13.9	–6.3	1
1960–1969	18.9	6.9	–5.7	3
1970–1979	26.8	7.6	–13.9	2
1980–1989	29.2	16.4	2.7	0
1990–1996	22.0	9.7	–3.6	1

LONG-TERM PERFORMANCE

Table 11–2 summarizes the performance of *The Center Line* since 1926. (As always, the portfolio's performance is based on market indexes that represent the five basic asset classes. The portfolio illustrates *market* performance, not individual fund performance.)

THE GREAT BULL MARKET

As our portfolios move more toward the aggressive end of the series, their performance in the 1920s looks like New Year's Eve revelers. Those who partied the hardest had the worst hangovers the next day.

Center Line investors didn't do too badly in the 1920s. They earned an average return of almost 15 percent per year between 1926 and 1929, and they only lost 3.8 percent in the Crash of 1929. One can almost imagine them as looking at more aggressive investors and shaking their heads. The market would catch up with them in the 1930s.

THE GREAT DEPRESSION

The contrast between the Crash of 1929 and the Great Depression that followed it points out one of the key characteristics of the moderate portfolios (Portfolios 20 to 50) in the *Star* series. A short-term crisis, like the Crash, isn't terribly traumatic for moderate investors. But a prolonged bear market, such as the one experienced in the 1930s, can cause considerable pain.

Center Line investors didn't do quite as well as their more conservative colleagues in the 1930s. They earned an average return of 2.7 percent per year for the decade, slightly under the 3.3 percent earned by the more conservative Portfolio 20. It was a tumultuous decade for *Center Line* investors, with returns ranging from a low of –28.0 percent in 1931 to a high of 40.2 percent in 1933. (The 1931 return shows that losses can far exceed the low end of the expected return range in isolated instances. The number crunchers tell us it shouldn't happen more than 5 years out of 100, but when it does happen, you have to be willing to ride out the storm.) Portfolio 40 earned double-digit returns in 3 years out of the decade, and it suffered double-digit losses in another 3.

Nowadays, the conventional wisdom is that, even if the market crashes, it will recover in a few months. The 1987 crash seems to bear that out. That may be true most of the time, but it isn't necessarily true *all* of the time. For example, *Center Line* investors had to wait until 1935 for the value of Portfolio 40 to return to its pre-Crash levels. As we will see later, the same thing happened to a lesser extent in the 1970s.

THE WAR YEARS

Like other investors, the *Center Line* crowd recovered from the Great Depression during the 1940s. Investment markets returned to some semblance of normalcy, although returns for the decade fell below their long-term averages. For the decade, Portfolio 40 earned an average of 6.9 percent, well below its 10.9 percent expected return.

Portfolio 40 investors experienced losses in 3 years during the decade. They didn't suffer any double-digit losses, and all their losses were less than the low end of the return range. During the decade, *Center Line* investors never had to wait more than 3 years to recover losses (1940 to 1942). Even with a world war, the 1940s were still a better decade for investors than the Depression years.

THE NIFTY FIFTIES

Things really brightened up for *Center Line* investors in the 1950s. Portfolio 40 earned an average of 13.9 percent per year for the decade, thanks to its substantial stock allocation. Like other moderate portfolios, *The Center Line* suffered only 1 loss year, in 1957, when it lost 6.3 percent. It recovered that loss the following year.

But the decade was dominated by good news. Portfolio 40 earned double-digit returns in 7 years of the decade, topped by earnings of 34.8 percent in 1954. It was around this time that the 60 percent stock–40 percent bond mix became a nearly universal favorite among investors. It's not hard to understand why, given the generous returns and relatively controlled volatility shown by Portfolio 40 during the 1950s.

THE GO-GO YEARS

We have previously talked about the fact that a portfolio probably won't ever hit its expected return on the nose. The 1950s and the 1960s offer a prime example of what is more likely. We saw earlier that Portfolio 40's expected return is 10.9 percent per year. In fact, it didn't earn that return in any year during the two decades. It didn't even earn that rate as an average annual return for either of them. In the 1950s, Portfolio 40 earned an average of 13.9 percent per year. In the 1960s, it earned an average of 6.9 percent per year. An average of the two comes closer to the expected return that either does alone. That's what we mean when we say that the actual return will fall "somewhere around" the expected return.

The 1960s were generally subpar years for *Center Line* investors, as they were for most other investors. Portfolio 40 experienced 3 loss years, the worst being a 5.7 percent loss in 1966. That's well within the 1-year return range for Portfolio 40. And during the decade, *Center Line* investors never had to wait longer than 1 year to recover their losses.

THE DISCO DECADE

The 1970s presented a different picture for *Center Line* investors. It was during this decade than investment professionals began to question the one-size-fits-all philosophy of the trustee's mix.

It's not that the decade was worse than the 1960s. It was simply much more volatile. Returns during the decade ranged from a low of –13.9 percent in 1974 to a high of 26.8 percent the next year. (The 1974 loss shows once again how actual losses can, on occasion, exceed the return ranges. The number crunchers give us some comfort by assuring us that while it does happen, it should happen only in extreme circumstances.) At times, the 1970s seemed like a wild roller coaster ride to even moderate investors. But *Center Line* investors earned an average 7.6 percent per year for the decade, higher than the 6.9 percent they earned during the 1960s.

The volatility of the 1970s had a noticeable impact on how long *Center Line* investors had to wait to recover losses, as well. During the Crash That Nobody Heard, Portfolio 40 took 3 years (1972 to 1975) to recover its losses. (See this same section in Chapter 10.)

THE ME DECADE

The 1980s provided a welcome relief for *Center Line* investors. For the decade, they earned an average return of 16.4 percent, well above the average expected return. Like other moderate investors, the *Center Line* crowd coasted through the decade without a single loss year, and in their best year (1985), they earned a return of almost 30 percent. They earned double-digit returns 7 out of 10 years and returns over 20 percent in 3 of them. In short, the 1980s were just about as good as the 1930s were bad.

Decades like the 1980s make up for ones like the two that preceded it. These returns point out again that a portfolio can underperform its expected return for years, as Portfolio 30 (and most other portfolios) did in the 1960s and 1970s. Even 10-year returns can be misleading, particularly for a 10-year period like the 1980s. That's the strongest reason for looking further into the past when considering investment mixes.

THE RECENT PAST

As is the case with the other portfolios in the *Star* series, the 1990s look more "normal" than any other recent decade. *The Center Line*'s average annual return of 9.7 percent is more in line with its expected return, and both the actual high and low returns are more in line with the ends of the return range. There have been relatively few surprises for *Center Line* investors in the years since 1990.

INFLATION PROTECTION AND REAL GROWTH

We have moved well beyond mere inflation protection and into the realm of real, or inflation-adjusted, growth. Over the long term, Portfolio 40 should provide average annual growth of about 7.6 percent after inflation, assuming the inflation rate continues at its current average of 3.1 percent per year. As we said earlier, the tradeoff for this expected real growth is increased market risk. An investor who prefers to minimize market risk while still providing inflation protection might find Portfolios 10 or 20 better suited to his or her needs.

EVALUATING *THE CENTER LINE*

Although Portfolio 40 is a moderate portfolio, it inches ever closer to the realm of aggressive investing. If you think you might be a *Center Line* investor, ask yourself the following questions:

- Would I be willing to live with double-digit losses under extreme circumstances?
- Would I be willing to wait several years for my investments to recover their losses, even as my friends and family question my sanity for not bailing out?

12 CHAPTER

Partly Cloudy

The sun may be out in the morning, but it may storm in the afternoon. A portfolio for investors who want a good return and can tolerate occasional setbacks.

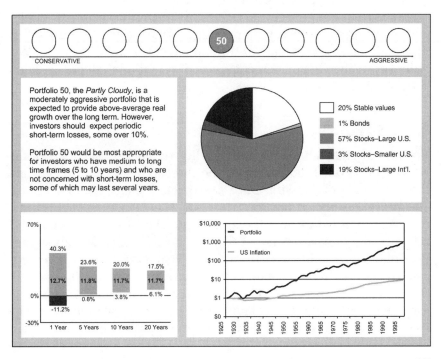

CONSERVATIVE | 50 | AGGRESSIVE

Portfolio 50, the *Partly Cloudy*, is a moderately aggressive portfolio that is expected to provide above-average real growth over the long term. However, investors should expect periodic short-term losses, some over 10%.

Portfolio 50 would be most appropriate for investors who have medium to long time frames (5 to 10 years) and who are not concerned with short-term losses, some of which may last several years.

- 20% Stable values
- 1% Bonds
- 57% Stocks–Large U.S.
- 3% Stocks–Smaller U.S.
- 19% Stocks–Large Int'l.

Bar chart (1 Year, 5 Years, 10 Years, 20 Years):
- 1 Year: 40.3%, 12.7%, -11.2%
- 5 Years: 23.6%, 11.8%, 0.8%
- 10 Years: 20.0%, 11.7%, -3.8%
- 20 Years: 17.5%, 11.7%, -6.1%

Line chart: Portfolio, US Inflation (1925–1995)

Portfolio 50 is named the *Partly Cloudy* for a couple of reasons. First, it behaves a lot like a partly cloudy day. The sun may be out in the morning, and it may storm in the afternoon. Second, lightning can strike, even on a partly cloudy day. *Partly Cloudy* investors should keep those points in mind before leaving the house without an umbrella.

The past 71 years have been a mixed bag for Portfolio 50. Its average return for the period tops 10 percent per year, and it has earned as much as 44 percent in a single year. But it has also seen its share of rainy days. In 1931, it lost more than one-third of its value, and in 1974 it lost 18 percent. Portfolio 50 stands as strong evidence of the investment maxim that you don't earn a higher long-term return without living with increased short-term volatility.

WHAT'S IN THE PORTFOLIO

Portfolio 50 is the midpoint in the *Star* series, but it is the most aggressive of the *Star* series' moderate portfolios. Stable values and bonds make up only 21 percent of the portfolio; the remainder is composed of stocks. Portfolio 50 is the first to include smaller U.S. stocks; 3 percent of the portfolio is allocated to this asset class.

The remaining stock allocation is split among large U.S. stocks and international stocks, with the largest share going to U.S. stocks. International stocks remain at the same level as in Portfolio 40. We will see an increasing percentage of international stocks in later portfolios in the series.

RISK AND RETURN

We have already alluded to the volatility, or market risk, of Portfolio 50. With this portfolio, we cross the threshold where double-digit losses are not only possible but also expected. That's the price for its 12.7 percent expected return.

As we move toward the aggressive end of the risk scale, the return ranges, particularly at 1 year, become increasingly wide. Portfolio 50 is no exception. In any given year, *Partly Cloudy* investors can expect their return to run anywhere from a high of 40.3 percent to a low of –11.2 percent. That's just about 5 times as wide as the range for Portfolio 0. The volatility of the portfolio also shows up in its dollar ranges (Table 12–1). As with previous portfolios, the dollar

TABLE 12-1

Dollar Ranges for Portfolio 50

	1 Year, $	5 Years, $	10 Years, $	20 Years, $
High	1,403	2,887	6,176	24,992
Average	1,127	1,748	3,029	9,077
Low	888	1,039	1,456	3,238

amounts shown in the table correspond to the return ranges shown on the bar graph in the *Portfolio Summary* chart. The table shows the value of $1,000 invested in Portfolio 50 over various time frames. For example, if Portfolio 50 earns the 40.3 percent return at the high end of its 1-year range, a *Partly Cloudy* investor will end the year with just over $1,400. But if it loses the 11.2 percent return at the low end of its 1-year range, the investor will have only $888.

Earlier in the book, we talked about the second law of investing: Risk goes down over time. With other portfolios, the element of time wasn't quite so important. Risk wasn't all that high to begin with, and it moderated pretty quickly. Relatively few years were about the most it took to withstand all but the most catastrophic losses.

As we move into really aggressive portfolios, the element of time becomes even more important, if for no other reason than that it takes a lot more of it to recover from the losses this portfolio is bound to rack up when the stock market turns ugly. We will see the impact of these losses, and the time required to recover from them, in Portfolio 50's performance in the 1930s and the 1970s.

The return ranges for Portfolio 50 suggest the impact of these losses. The loss at the low end of the range turns barely positive at 5 years, and the high end of the range narrows to about 23 percent. The range continues to narrow over 10- and 20-year time frames. As we said earlier, you need to allow increasingly long time frames as you become more aggressive in your investing.

LONG-TERM PERFORMANCE

Table 12–2 summarizes Portfolio 50's performance since 1926.

TABLE 12–2

Portfolio 50, Decade by Decade

Decade	High, %	Average, %	Low, %	No. Loss Years
1926–1929	35.2	15.9	−6.6	1
1930–1939	44.4	2.2	−34.0	5
1940–1949	30.5	8.2	−8.9	3
1950–1959	42.1	16.1	−8.2	2
1960–1969	22.0	7.5	−7.0	3
1970–1979	32.0	7.3	−17.5	3
1980–1989	31.9	17.4	−0.1	1
1990–1996	26.6	10.7	−6.1	1

THE GREAT BULL MARKET

Partly Cloudy investors have four-fifths of their investments allocated to stocks of different types, so they reaped the benefits of the stock market's boom years between 1926 and 1928. In 1928, they earned 35.2 percent, close to their record high for the 71-year period.

But they also felt some of the pain of the stock market's crash in 1929. In that year, *Partly Cloudy* investors lost 6.6 percent. That loss exceeds some investors' 5 percent threshold of pain, but it was most likely well within the tolerance of knowledgeable investors with an 80 percent stock allocation.

The problem with the 1920s was that most of the investors in the market, including a fair number of *Partly Cloudy* investors, were not very knowledgeable. The ones who got chased out of the market just after the crash were probably the lucky ones.

THE GREAT DEPRESSION

The 1930s began with unremitting bad news for *Partly Cloudy* investors. The 6.6 percent loss of 1929 was followed by a 19.3 percent loss in 1930 and a 34.0 percent loss in 1931. Losses of that magnitude are well beyond the low end of Portfolio 50's return range. Once again, it points out that the return ranges can estimate only what will happen *most* of the time. A catastrophic market meltdown, like the one that occurred from late 1929 through 1932, breaks all the rules, even those laid down by number crunchers.

It's not just that the losses of the 1930s were so severe. They were also prolonged. It took Portfolio 50 seven years to recover its melt-down losses. It didn't return to its 1928 level until the end of 1935. And that's despite a 44.4 percent return, the highest it ever earned, in 1933.

THE WAR YEARS

Portfolio 50 earned a respectable 8.2 percent average return during the 1940s. Even so, it underperformed its 11.7 percent expected 10-year return by a significant margin. But *Partly Cloudy* investors probably weren't complaining. More likely, they were incredibly relieved to be rid of the 1930s.

The interesting thing about the 1940s is that *Partly Cloudy* investors earned double-digit returns in 5 years and topped 20 percent in 2 of them. Double-digit returns should be no real surprise to *Partly Cloudy* investors. That's what they're after. But losses in 3 years, and mediocre returns in the other 2, dragged the portfolio's average return back to the single digits.

THE NIFTY FIFTIES

The 1950s were an above-average decade for *Partly Cloudy* investors, as they were for nearly all moderate and aggressive investors. Port-folio 50 earned a 16.1 percent average return, well above its 11.7 percent expected average return. *Partly Cloudy* investors earned double-digit returns 7 out of 10 years, and their return topped 20 percent four times during the decade.

Portfolio 50's heavy allocation to stocks boosted its returns during the good years of the 1950s. And while most years in the decade were good, Portfolio 50 also felt the pain of the couple of years that weren't as good. It suffered an 8.2 percent loss, its worst of the decade, in 1957. Every other moderate portfolio lost money in 1957 as well, but Portfolio 50 also lost money in 1953. It was the only moderate portfolio to do so.

THE GO-GO YEARS

The 1960s was a disappointing decade for *Partly Cloudy* investors. They earned an average return of 7.5 percent, well below their 1950s return, and significantly below the 11.7 percent annual return expected for Portfolio 50 over 10 years.

The sun shined brightly twice in the decade—the portfolio earned 21.9 percent returns in both 1961 and 1967. It earned double-digit returns 6 out of the 10 years, and it topped 20 percent twice. But it suffered losses in the same 3 years as the other moderate portfolios we looked at previously, and these losses dragged its average return for the decade below what would be expected of it.

THE DISCO DECADE

As we have progressed from conservative to moderate portfolios, we have seen the 1970s take an increasingly heavy toll on our portfolios. That's because they have allocated an increasing percentage of their assets to stocks, and stocks took it on the chin in the 1970s. More conservative portfolios in the *Star* series actually performed better in the 1970s than they did in the 1960s. Not so Portfolio 50. It earned an average annual return of 7.3 percent in the 1970s, which falls just short of the 7.5 percent it earned in the 1960s. That's not true of all portfolios on the aggressive side of the risk scale. More aggressive portfolios, which allocate more of their assets to international stocks, managed to improve their performance in the 1970s. It's only moderate portfolios such as Portfolio 50, which maintained relatively higher allocations to large U.S. stocks, that showed a decline in performance.

The decade started out well enough for *Partly Cloudy* investors. After a minor loss of 0.3 percent in 1970, Portfolio 50 earned 15.0 percent and 18.7 percent returns in the following 2 years. Then the slide began, and by the end of 1974, Portfolio 50 had lost 27 percent of its value. It wouldn't recover to its 1972 levels until 1976. And had it not been for its 35.5 percent return in 1975, its highest of the decade, it could have taken even longer. Portfolio 50 is also the only moderate portfolio to suffer a loss in 1970. That loss is attributable to its relatively heavy concentration in stocks.

The second half of the decade was kinder than the first to *Partly Cloudy* investors. Portfolio 50 exceeded its expected return in 4 out of 5 years. Those returns helped bring Portfolio 50 out of the doldrums and turn in a respectable, if below-average, perform-ance for the decade.

THE ME DECADE

The concentration in stocks that hurt *Partly Cloudy* investors in the 1970s paid off in the 1980s. Portfolio 50 turned in a record-breaking return of 18.4 percent per year. It earned double-digit returns in 7 out of the 10 years, and it earned over 20 percent in 5 of them.

Unlike the more conservative portfolios in the *Star* series, Port-folio 50 did not make it through the decade entirely unscathed. It lost 0.1 percent in 1981, when both large U.S. and international stocks lost ground. But Portfolio 50's losses were almost unnoticeable, and they didn't dampen the exuberance of an otherwise remarkable decade.

As we have said with other portfolios, an investor is naturally tempted to extrapolate the performance of the 1980s into the future. Many of the 10-year return figures we see for mutual funds reflect the performance of this decade. For example, a 10-year performance history for Portfolio 50 as of the end of 1996, similar to the history presented in investment fund marketing materials, would look like Table 12–3. If Table 12–2 were all we had to go on, Portfolio 50 would look like a no-lose proposition. In the past decade, it appears to have never earned less than 12 percent. We know from the longer history that in less generous market environments, Portfolio 50 can lose a considerable portion of its value. It has happened on at least two occasions.

We could repeat the same exercise with even more aggressive portfolios and reach the same conclusion. In fact, the less diversified the portfolio, the better the picture. That is one of the factors that has led so many investors to invest all their savings in stocks, without

TABLE 12–3

10-Year Return History for Portfolio 50

Time Frame, Years	Return, %
1	16.1
3	14.8
5	12.1
10	12.2

regard for the potential market risk. And as we have seen, that risk can be considerable, even with a relatively moderate portfolio like Portfolio 50.

THE RECENT PAST

Portfolio 50's performance in the 1990s has mirrored that of the other moderate portfolios in the *Star* series. Its average return is close to its 5-year expected return, and its highs and lows have generally remained within the expected range. The only time lightning struck the portfolio was in 1990, when it lost 6.1 percent, which is well within the low end of Portfolio 50's 1-year range. Its high return for the decade, a 26.6 percent return in 1995, is likewise well within the expected range.

INFLATION PROTECTION AND REAL GROWTH

Like the other portfolios in the middle of our risk scale, Portfolio 50 provides substantial real, or inflation-adjusted, growth. Over a 10-year time frame, *Partly Cloudy* investors should expect to see real growth in the neighborhood of 8.3 percent. Of course, the tradeoff for this level of real growth is increased volatility. As we saw earlier, Portfolio 50 can underperform its expected return by a substantial margin for extended periods of time.

EVALUATING THE *PARTLY CLOUDY*

The price for a higher return is higher volatility. We can't say it enough. And the way to balance the return against the volatility is to make sure you allow plenty of time for the portfolio to realize its full earnings potential. Portfolio 50 underperformed its expected return during both the 1960s and the 1970s. An investor from that era who was counting on a 12.7 percent return from the portfolio would have been sorely disappointed—for 20 years running. By the same token, a 1980s-era investor would have been delighted at its results.

So, if you consider yourself a *Partly Cloudy* investor, be prepared for a prolonged thunderstorm. You may have to sit in a shelter for a long time before the rain stops. Or you may open your front door to find a bright, sunny day. With this portfolio, you have to be prepared for either eventuality.

Over the Hump

*We're taking on more risk now,
but the returns are better too.*

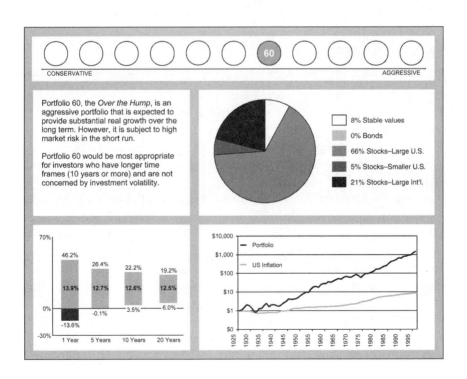

CONSERVATIVE   60   AGGRESSIVE

Portfolio 60, the *Over the Hump*, is an aggressive portfolio that is expected to provide substantial real growth over the long term. However, it is subject to high market risk in the short run.

Portfolio 60 would be most appropriate for investors who have longer time frames (10 years or more) and are not concerned by investment volatility.

- 8% Stable values
- 0% Bonds
- 66% Stocks–Large U.S.
- 5% Stocks–Smaller U.S.
- 21% Stocks–Large Int'l.

	1 Year	5 Years	10 Years	20 Years
High	46.2%	26.4%	22.2%	19.2%
Mid	13.9%	12.7%	12.6%	12.5%
Low	-13.6%	-0.1%	3.5%	6.0%

Portfolio

US Inflation

In offices and shops all across America, Wednesday is "hump day." The toughest part of the week behind them, workers around the country cruise toward Friday. And when the toughest part of a job or a project is done, many people say they are *"over the hump."*

Well, we're going to use *over the hump* just a bit differently. We began with a couple of conservative portfolios (Portfolios 0 and 10), and then we looked at four moderate portfolios (Portfolios 20 through 50). Those moderate portfolios were the large hump in the middle of the *Star* series. We're *over the hump* now; we're past the middle, moderate portfolios. Investing in portfolios from Portfolio 60 on is definitely not for the faint of heart. You can get a sense of Portfolio 60's volatility by the choppiness of its line in the *Portfolio Summary* chart.

But if you are willing to live with the roller-coaster ride that goes with being an *Over the Hump* investor, you can expect to earn an attractive return over the long term. Your biggest question may be "How long is long?" It could take 20 years for an *Over the Hump* portfolio to perform to its expected return. And you should plan on allowing nearly 10 years for the portfolio to recover from extreme, once-in-a-century losses.

WHAT'S IN THE PORTFOLIO

What sets Portfolio 60 apart from the moderate portfolios that preceded it is its relative lack of diversification. 92 percent of the portfolio is invested in stocks; only 8 percent remains in stable values, and nothing is allocated to bonds. Stable value investments and bonds could soar to new heights, and it would have a negligible effect on Portfolio 60. *Over the Hump* investors put nearly all their eggs in one basket—stocks.

We aren't saying Portfolio 60 is totally undiversified. It spreads its investments among large U.S. stocks (50 percent), smaller U.S. stocks (10 percent), and large international stocks (40 percent). As we saw in Chapter 4, there is enough difference between U.S. and international stocks that most experts consider them separate asset classes. And as long as the investor fills each slot in the portfolio with funds that invest in a number of different stocks, the portfolio is diversified within each asset class, as well.

But we are saying Portfolio 60 is less diversified than the moderate portfolios that preceded it. Those portfolios allocated higher percentages of their investments to stable values and bonds, which differ more from stocks than various types of stocks differ from each other.

RISK AND RETURN

That's one of the reasons Portfolio 60 is expected to earn more than the diversified portfolios that preceded it. As we have said all along, risk and return go hand in hand. We are now at the part of our risk spectrum where we need to reduce diversification to increase return. When we begin doing that, we move from moderate investing to aggressive investing. (Using that same test, one could argue that Portfolio 50, or even Portfolio 40, is an aggressive portfolio. However, those portfolios maintain a significant allocation to bonds and stable values, whereas Portfolio 60 has only a small allocation. In the end, there is no sharp dividing line between moderate and aggressive investing, only a progression from one to the other.)

As with the other portfolios in the *Star* series, Table 13–1 shows the value of a $1,000 investment at the end of various time frames, assuming Portfolio 60 earns the return ranges on the bar graph in the *Portfolio Summary* chart. For example, if Portfolio 60 earns the low end of the 5-year range, –0.1 percent, a $1,000 investment at the beginning of the 5-year period would be worth $998 at the end. On the other hand, if Portfolio 60 performs to its expected return, a $1,000 investment will grow to over $10,000 over a 20-year time frame.

Portfolio 60 is expected to earn an average return of 13.9 percent per year. However, when one begins averaging likely good and bad years, the expected return drops to 12.7 percent per year

T A B L E   13–1

Dollar Ranges for Portfolio 60

	1 Year, $	5 Years, $	10 Years, $	20 Years, $
High	1,462	3,230	7,395	33,650
Average	1,139	1,818	3,265	10,526
Low	864	998	1,404	3,207

for a 5-year period. That drop is attributable to the volatility of this portfolio. We saw similar drops in the moderate portfolios in the series, but they grow larger as we move into the aggressive end of the risk scale.

In any single year, Portfolio 60 can earn as much as 46.2 percent, or it could lose as much as 13.6 percent.[1] As was the case with prior portfolios, the return range narrows markedly with the passage of time. Over 5 years, the range is –0.1 to 26.4 percent, and over 10 years it is 3.5 to 22.2 percent. But as portfolios become more aggressive, it takes longer for the narrowing to occur. The low end of Portfolio 10's range narrows to 3.5 percent in 5 years; for Portfolio 60, it takes 10.

LONG-TERM PERFORMANCE

Portfolio 60's performance since 1926 is summarized in Table 13–2.

THE GREAT BULL MARKET

Over the Hump investors did pretty well between 1926 and 1929. They earned an average return of 17.3 percent, the second best of any *Star* portfolio. But when the crash came in 1929, they lost nearly 10

T A B L E 13–2

Portfolio 60, Decade by Decade

Decade	High, %	Average, %	Low, %	No. Loss Years
1926–1929	41.2	17.3	–9.5	1
1930–1939	55.3	1.0	–40.4	5
1940–1949	35.8	9.5	–10.6	3
1950–1959	48.8	18.4	–10.3	2
1960–1969	26.6	8.3	–9.0	3
1970–1979	35.5	7.5	–22.0	3
1980–1989	35.4	18.4	–1.4	1
1990–1996	29.3	11.8	–7.5	1

---

1   As we will see in Portfolio 60's history, it lost considerably more in the 1930s than the low end of the return range suggests.

percent of the value of their investments. And that was just in 1929, before the Great Depression settled in for a long run.

THE GREAT DEPRESSION

Over the Hump investors took a beating in the 1930s. Of course, all investors were a bit beaten up by the Depression-era markets. But the beating dished out to Portfolio 60 would have put *Over the Hump* investors in the hospital.

1930 was a disaster. Portfolio 60 lost almost a quarter of its value. The decade's worst loss came in 1931, when *Over the Hump* investors lost another 40 percent. By the end of 1932, when the initial bloodbath was over, Portfolio 60 had lost over half its 1928 value. Even a 55 percent gain in 1933 couldn't bring the portfolio back to its pre-Crash levels. It wouldn't see its 1928 value again until the beginning of 1936.

Over the Hump investors must have felt the worst was over by that point. But they weren't out of the woods yet. After strong showings in 1935 and 1936, the portfolio suffered a 34.8 percent loss in 1937 that threw it back below its pre-Crash value. Eight years after the Crash, it still had not fully recovered from its effects. Portfolio 40's value was still below its 1928 level at the close of the decade.

WAR AND RECOVERY

Other investors began the 1940s ahead of where they were when the Crash occurred. *Over the Hump* investors started out behind. In fact, Portfolio 60 wouldn't surpass its 1928 value until early 1943. At that point, *Over the Hump* investors were finally *Over the Hump*.

Portfolio 60 earned an average of 9.5 percent per year during the decade. Like other portfolios (both moderate and aggressive), it underperformed its expected return. Portfolio 60 earned double-digit returns in 5 years, but that isn't the great news it would be for more conservative portfolios. After all, we expect a portfolio as aggressive as Portfolio 60 to turn in a double-digit performance. That's the only way it can perform to its expected return.

THE NIFTY FIFTIES

The 1950s are an example of what we have just been talking about. Portfolio 60 outperformed its expected return in this decade, as did the other moderate and aggressive portfolios in the *Star* series. [The conservative portfolios (Portfolios 10 and 20) actually underperformed their expected returns during the 1950s. It was a strong era for stock markets, but stable values and bonds were lackluster.] As we said early on, a rising tide lifts all boats. For *Over the Hump* investors, the 1950s was a high-tide decade, and it lifted their boat to an 18.4 percent average return per year.

Over the Hump investors earned that return without experiencing any extraordinary losses or gains. Like Portfolio 50 investors, they lost money twice in the decade, but neither loss was surprising. The worst loss, of 10.3 percent in 1957, was well within the low end of Portfolio 60's 1-year return range. So it shouldn't test the stamina of *Over the Hump* investors, who expect declines of that magnitude.

THE GO-GO YEARS

The 1960s treated *Over the Hump* investors much the same as other moderate and aggressive investors. Portfolio 60 turned in a fair performance, but it underperformed its expected return.

As we have noted in connection with other portfolios, the 1960s was an inconsistent decade. It earned its nickname as a result of the performance of U.S. stocks, particularly smaller-company stocks, in the middle of the decade. In 1967 alone, small stocks earned a return of over 80 percent (83.6 percent, as measured by the Ibbotson Associates Small Stock Index). Those returns helped boost the earnings of Portfolio 60, but its allocation of 5 percent to small stocks was too small for the boost to have a significant impact on its overall return.

Portfolio 60 had its best year of the decade in 1967, when it earned 26.6 percent. Its worst year was in 1969, when it lost 8.2 percent. It experienced only 3 loss years during the decade, which put it squarely in line with other moderate and aggressive portfolios.

THE DISCO DECADE

The 1970s were no kinder to *Over the Hump* investors than they were to others. In fact, since *Over the Hump* investors, in search of higher returns, take on more risk than more moderate investors, the decade was more harsh on the *Over the Hump* crowd.

Like other moderate and aggressive portfolios, Portfolio 60 underperformed its expected return in the 1960s for the second decade in a row. As we pointed out with previous portfolios in the *Star* series, a portfolio can underperform its average for extended periods. As we move to more aggressive portfolios, however, the extent to which they underperform their averages grows larger.

Portfolio 60 began the decade with reasonably strong growth. Then in 1972, it fell into a long slide, along with the domestic and international stock markets. The slide didn't stop until the end of 1974, by which time Portfolio 60 had lost about one-third of its 1972 value. Like the immediately preceding *Star* portfolios, Portfolio 60 recovered a bit over a year later, and it closed 1976 comfortably ahead of where it had been in 1972.

THE ME DECADE

The 1980s were good to all investors. Stable value and bond investors profited from a decline in interest rates that boosted their returns to historically high levels. At the same time, the stock markets turned in record-breaking performances. And while *Over the Hump* investors had nothing to complain about, their overall return for the decade only matched their performance of the 1950s. The bull markets of the 1980s certainly rewarded risk takers, but they also rewarded diversification in a way the 1950s did not.

Over the Hump investors earned an average of 18.4 percent per year during the 1980s, a return well above the expected return for Portfolio 60. They didn't earn that return with a few spectacular years. Instead, the return was based on solid performance throughout the decade. The decade's highest return, 35.4 percent, was well within the 46.2 percent at the top end of the portfolio's 1-year range. And the decade's worst return, a loss of 1.4 percent, was nearly inconsequential.

THE RECENT PAST

Things returned to some semblance of normality in the first half of the 1990s. Portfolio 60 earned an average of 11.8 percent per year, reasonably close to its 12.7 percent expected return for a 5-year period. Its 1990s high return of 29.3 percent and its low return of –7.5 percent are well within the high and low one would expect from this portfolio. If Portfolio 60 finishes the decade in the same fashion, there should be no surprises for *Over the Hump* investors.

REAL GROWTH

As you can see from the line graph in the *Portfolio Summary* chart, inflation is not the issue for *Over the Hump* investors. There is a large spread between Portfolio 60's earnings and the rate of inflation. Assuming inflation remains at its recent levels of about 3 percent per year, Portfolio 60 would be expected to grow at a real (inflation-adjusted) rate of about 10.4 percent per year.

EVALUATING THE *OVER THE HUMP*

We said at the beginning of this chapter that aggressive portfolios are not for the faint of heart. During the Depression, *Over the Hump* investors lost nearly half their investments, and they had to wait almost 15 years to finally recover from the 1929 stock market crash. In the 1970s, they saw almost one-third of their investments disappear in a slide that lasted almost 2 years. And it took them over a year after the slide stopped to recover.

If you consider yourself an *Over the Hump* investor, make sure you have the stomach for the wild ride you will undoubtedly experience at some point in the future. And make sure your time frame is long enough for you to be able to ride out a market downturn. Portfolios as aggressive as this tend to lose their value quickly, then take a long time to recover. Bailing out after the initial drop is a nearly sure prescription for maximizing your losses.

14
CHAPTER

The Sports Car

You can hit top speeds, but watch out for road conditions. For long-term investors who don't mind a few down years.

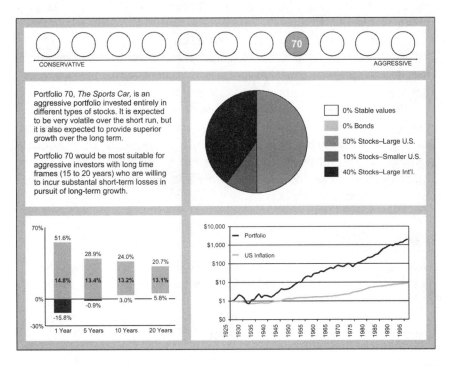

CONSERVATIVE   70   AGGRESSIVE

Portfolio 70, *The Sports Car,* is an aggressive portfolio invested entirely in different types of stocks. It is expected to be very volatile over the short run, but it is also expected to provide superior growth over the long term.

Portfolio 70 would be most suitable for aggressive investors with long time frames (15 to 20 years) who are willing to incur substantial short-term losses in pursuit of long-term growth.

- 0% Stable values
- 0% Bonds
- 50% Stocks–Large U.S.
- 10% Stocks–Smaller U.S.
- 40% Stocks–Large Int'l.

1 Year: 51.6%, 14.8%, -15.8%
5 Years: 28.9%, 13.4%, -0.9%
10 Years: 24.0%, 13.2%, 3.0%
20 Years: 20.7%, 13.1%, 5.8%

Portfolio
US Inflation

Imagine a shiny red sports car in your driveway. We aren't talking about some cute two-seater you might buy for your daughter. No, we are talking about a mean, hungry, performance vehicle. A Corvette, or a Porsche. A car with a cockpit that looks like the inside of a fighter jet. A car that means business.

Some people (okay, mainly guys) get excited at an image like that. It appeals to their sense of adventure. They know they could get killed driving a high-performance car, but they just can't help it. These brave few (or the foolhardy, depending on one's point of view) are *Sports Car* investors.

But the funny thing is, there are a lot of investors out there who think they are driving a family sedan with a set of fancy hubcaps or maybe a racing stripe down the side. They don't know it, but they are behind the wheel of a *Sports Car* portfolio. And if the market takes a nosedive, they could find themselves in the middle of a car wreck.

WHAT'S IN THE PORTFOLIO

Stocks, and nothing but stocks. If investing were cable TV, you would be tuned to the stock channel. (Of course, if you watch CNBC, you already *are* tuned to the stock channel.) Portfolio 70 is the first in the *Star* series to allocate absolutely nothing to stable values or bonds. Half the portfolio is invested in large U.S. stocks; 10 percent is invested in small U.S. stocks, and the remaining 40 percent is invested in large international stocks. We will see in just a minute that this asset allocation can be very volatile.

Many people allocate their investments in mixes that look very much like Portfolio 70, all in stocks. In fact, many investors are actually *more* aggressive than Portfolio 70 because they allocate nothing to international stocks. As we saw in Chapter 4, large international stocks can provide some level of diversification when combined with U.S. stocks.

RISK AND RETURN

There is nothing in the world wrong with investing this aggressively as long as investors understand the level of market risk involved. But many investors haven't experienced a bear market firsthand, and they aren't familiar with how long an aggressive portfolio can stay underwater when markets head south.

TABLE 14–1

Dollar Ranges for Portfolio 70

	1 Year, $	5 Years, $	10 Years, $	20 Years, $
High	1,516	3,556	8,601	42,925
Average	1,148	1,873	3,452	11,729
Low	843	956	1,343	3,106

Table 14–1 illustrates the point. It shows the value of a $1,000 investment over different periods of time, assuming Portfolio 70 earns the high, average, or low expected returns shown on the bars in the *Portfolio Summary* chart. In an unfavorable stock market, Portfolio 70 could lose the 15.8 percent shown at the low end of the 1-year range. (We will see that under extreme circumstances, such as those experienced during the Great Depression, it can, if fact, lose substantially more. The number crunchers tell us only that the return probably won't fall below the low end of the 1-year return range in 95 years out of 100. That means that in the other 5 years, it probably *will*.) If that happens, the investor will be left with $843.

In a prolonged bear market, Portfolio 70 can stay underwater for over 5 years. If that happens and the portfolio loses the 0.9 percent per year shown at the low end of the 5-year range, then the original $1,000 investment would be worth only $956 at the end of the 5-year period. In other words, *Sports Car* investors have to be prepared to wait quite a long while to recover losses, even in a bear market that falls short of a calamity on the scale of the Great Depression. We will see evidence of that in Portfolio 70's performance during the 1970s.

So why is it that all-stock portfolios don't *look* all that frightening? In most cases, we view them from the perspective of only the last 10 years. Table 14–2 shows Portfolio 70's 10-year return history. The returns in Table 14–2 make all-stock investing look very attractive. Consistent, double-digit returns and no losses. But compare those returns to the return and dollar ranges we talked about before. What's missing from the 10-year performance table is the level of market risk taken on to generate those returns. When *The Sports Car* hits a bump in the road, it can be bone-jarring, and there are times when it can feel like it is spinning out of control.

TABLE 14–2

10-Year Return History for Portfolio 70

Time Frame, Years	Annual Return, %
1	16.1
3	15.1
5	13.1
10	12.8

LONG-TERM PERFORMANCE

Table 14–3 summarizes the performance of Portfolio 70 since 1926. (As we have noted with prior portfolios in the *Star* series, the performance history is calculated from market performance, not individual fund performance.)

THE GREAT BULL MARKET

Sports Car investors were richly rewarded for their aggressiveness during the period between 1926 and 1929. In 1928 alone, the value

TABLE 14–3

Portfolio 70, Decade by Decade

Decade	High, %	Average, %	Low, %	No. Loss Years
1926–1929	43.4	17.5	−11.7	1
1930–1939	61.0	0.4	−43.8	5
1940–1949	40.3	10.4	−11.3	3
1950–1959	53.4	19.2	−11.0	2
1960–1969	30.5	8.8	−10.5	3
1970–1979	38.7	8.4	−24.3	3
1980–1989	40.5	20.1	−1.5	1
1990–1996	25.9	10.6	−12.6	1

of their portfolio grew by 43.4 percent. And even after the Crash of 1929, in which they lost 11.7 percent, *Sports Car* investors finished the decade with an average return of 17.5 percent, the second highest of any *Star* portfolio. If *Sports Car* investors ended the decade believing that American business was fundamentally sound, as President Hoover proclaimed, then the future must have seemed bright indeed. Unfortunately, they had just hit a major pothole that would cause the wheels to fall off their car.

THE GREAT DEPRESSION

Stock investors were damaged seriously during the Great Depression, and it took a long time for them to recover. Between 1929 and 1932, Portfolio 70 lost two-thirds of its value. It didn't recover to its pre-Crash levels until 1943. That's the same amount of time it took Portfolio 60 investors to recover. The difference was that *Sports Car* investors fell further in the 4-year slide.

The high volatility of Portfolio 70 was apparent during the 1930s. In 1931, it lost 43.8 percent; 2 years later it made 61.0 percent. Both the gain and the loss were outside the expected return range for the portfolio. When all was said and done, *Sports Car* investors had pretty much broken even for the decade—they earned a paltry 0.4 percent. But their portfolios still hadn't regained their pre-Crash levels of 1928. For that they would have to wait 3 more years.

WAR AND RECOVERY

Portfolio 70 returned to double-digit returns in the 1940s, but just barely. Its average return of 10.4 percent fell short of its expected return of 13.2 percent, but *Sports Car* investors probably didn't notice. The best comparison they had available was the 0.4 percent they had earned the previous decade. Next to that, 10.4 percent looked pretty good.

The best news of the decade was that its volatility returned to more tolerable levels. Both the decades' high return (40.3 percent in 1945) and its low return (−11.3 percent in 1941) were within the 1-year return range for the portfolio. It suffered 3 loss years during the decade, as did every other *Star* portfolio, with the exception of Portfolio 0.

THE NIFTY FIFTIES

Like its namesake, Portfolio 70 shifted into high gear and made up for lost ground in the 1950s. Its total allocation to stocks, which had worked against it in the 1930s, turned in its favor in this decade. It earned an *average* of 19.2 percent per year, which came close to Portfolio 20's *high* return for the decade. Once again, aggressiveness was rewarded, as it had been in the 1920s.

Sports Car investors experienced two losses during the decade. The worst came in 1957, when the portfolio lost 11.0 percent. That loss might seem large to some of us, but it shouldn't shake up *Sports Car* investors, who expect to lose as much as 15.8 percent in a bad year. And the best year was truly spectacular. In 1953, the portfolio earned 53.4 percent. That return is at the top end of its 1-year return range.

THE GO-GO YEARS

After the exuberance of the 1950s, it is not surprising that the stock market would settle back into a decade of mediocre performance. The decade certainly had its moments, and *Sports Car* investors profited from all of them. It saw a 3-year run of double-digit returns from 1963 through 1965, and it earned a decade-high 30.5 percent return in 1967.

But it seemed as if the decade could never get up a sufficient head of steam to repeat the performance of the 1950s. A recession in 1962 knocked the props from under the market. In 1966 it happened again, when the U.S. government kicked up its spending on both the war in Vietnam and the domestic War on Poverty. And the market closed the decade with another losing year, which brought *The Sports Car*'s average return to a mediocre 8.8 percent.

THE DISCO DECADE

The 1970s gave birth to bad music and bad investment performance. By the end of the decade, Portfolio 70 had earned a return of 8.4 percent, which just about equaled its performance in the 1960s. Nonetheless, after the fabulous 1950s, Portfolio 70 failed to perform up to its expected return for the second decade in a row. Many aggressive investors openly wondered if the U.S. and international stock markets had finally run out of gas.

Like other moderate and aggressive portfolios, Portfolio 70 grew at a respectable rate until 1972, when stock markets began the long slide some call The Crash That Nobody Heard. Portfolio 70 lost just over one-third of its value, much like Portfolio 60 did. But it took *Sports Car* investors several months longer to recover; it wasn't until relatively late in 1976 that they finally regained their 1972 levels.

THE ME DECADE

Those who lost faith in aggressive investing after two decades of subpar performance left the party just a bit too soon. In the 1980s, *Sports Car* investors earned an average return of 20.1 percent per year over the decade. Even the 1987 stock market crash didn't hurt *Sports Car* investors. Thanks largely to its international diversification, Portfolio 70 earned 11.7 percent in 1987.

As it had in the 1950s, Portfolio 70 hit the gas and made up for lost ground. In the decade's first year, *Sports Car* investors earned 30.4 percent. Then came the incredible bull run of 1985 to 1986. In 1985 Portfolio 70 earned 40.5 percent; the next year it earned 38.6 percent. In 2 years, *Sports Car* investors nearly doubled the value of their investments.

It's tempting to look at the spectacular results of those 2 years and invest very aggressively. But don't forget the preceding two decades of underperformance. *Sports Car* investors sometimes spend a long time with the car in the shop before they get moving again.

THE RECENT PAST

In the first 6 years of the 1990s, Portfolio 70 has shifted back into second gear. Its average return of 10.6 percent per year is somewhat under the 13.4 percent one would expect over a 5-year period. The portfolio's volatility is up compared to the 1980s; in 1990 it lost 12.6 percent, due largely to losses in the international markets. Portfolio 70 may suddenly shift into high gear again, or it may cruise along in second; only time will tell.

REAL GROWTH

Sports cars weren't made for trips to the grocery store. A Ferrari will take you to the corner store, but you can get their more cheaply (and perhaps more safely) in a station wagon. By the same token, Portfolio 70 isn't intended to simply protect against inflation. Over the long haul, its double-digit expected return leaves inflation in the dust. But it is a volatile portfolio, and it can remain under water for a long time.

Portfolio 70 is designed to provide a high level of real (inflation-adjusted) growth over the long run. That's what makes *Sports Car* investors willing to live with its volatility in the short run. Assuming inflation continues at its current level of 3.1 percent per year, Portfolio 70 can be expected to grow at an inflation-adjusted rate of 11.3 percent per year.

The point is that you don't need to invest *all* your money in stocks to fend off inflation. That's a much riskier strategy than is required. We saw earlier than any of the moderate portfolios in the *Star* series (Portfolios 20 through 50) will do an adequate job of providing a shield against inflation.

EVALUATING *THE SPORTS CAR*

Sports cars can be a lot of fun to drive. They can also be dangerous. We have seen that an all-stock portfolio carries substantial market risk. Double-digit gains and losses aren't unusual—for this portfolio they are the norm.

If you have allocated your investments to one or two stock funds, you are taking on about the same degree of risk as *Sports Car* investors. Again, there's nothing wrong with that, *as long as you are aware of the risk.* But the 10-year performance record (Table 14–2) seduces too many investors, who expect double-digit returns to continue indefinitely. If we can learn anything from market history, we can learn that double-digit returns will probably not be the case indefinitely. And that's why we have emphasized that looking at risk and looking at the longer history are the two of the best self-defense measures an investor can take.

15

CHAPTER

The Deep End

For investors who thrive on risk and are looking for big returns.

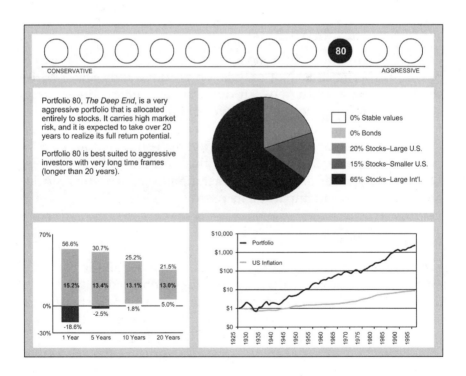

CONSERVATIVE   AGGRESSIVE

Portfolio 80, *The Deep End*, is a very aggressive portfolio that is allocated entirely to stocks. It carries high market risk, and it is expected to take over 20 years to realize its full return potential.

Portfolio 80 is best suited to aggressive investors with very long time frames (longer than 20 years).

- 0% Stable values
- 0% Bonds
- 20% Stocks–Large U.S.
- 15% Stocks–Smaller U.S.
- 65% Stocks–Large Int'l.

In Chapter 9, we looked at Portfolio 20, *The Shallow End*. We are now at the same point on the opposite end of the risk spectrum, so we have named Portfolio 80 *The Deep End*. This portfolio is for aggressive investors who are not only willing to live with risk but who thrive on it. To many of us, these investors may appear to have gone *off* the deep end, but they can be richly rewarded for their willingness to take risk.

As we have said all along, risk has two sides; Portfolio 80 provides a stark illustration of what can happen to aggressive investors in a stormy market. Portfolio 80 has spent more time underwater during the past 71 years than any portfolio we have seen so far. But at just about the time the most stalwart investor would give up on the portfolio, it has a knack for bursting through its previous high and roaring on to record returns.

To be a successful *Deep End* investor, you have to count on one of two things: a lot of luck or a lot of time. Investors who jumped in at the beginning of the 1980s got rich relatively quickly. The less lucky investors who dove in at the beginning of the 1960s had to wait almost 30 years for their investment to really pan out.

WHAT'S IN THE PORTFOLIO

Portfolio 80 continues the trend away from diversification in search of ever-higher returns. Not only is the portfolio fully allocated to stocks but the balance between domestic and international large stocks is also tipped squarely in favor of international stocks. Portfolio 80 also continues the trend of increasing allocations to smaller U.S. stocks. The *Star* series "tops out" its small-stock allocation at 15 percent, the percentage allocated in this portfolio. We will see in Portfolio 80's performance history that the allocation to small stocks has had a significant impact on its returns.

RISK AND RETURN

We first see an unusual effect in Portfolio 80 that we alluded to early on. In Chapter 9, we said that as portfolios become more aggressive, the *incremental return* one receives for moving to the next step grows smaller and smaller. Now, for the first time, we see a drop in a portfolio's expected return from that of its predecessor.

Table 15–1 shows average expected returns for the aggressive portfolios in the *Star* series over 5-, 10-, and 20-year time frames. As

TABLE 15–1

Average Expected Returns for Aggressive Portfolios

	5 Years, $	10 Years, $	20 Years, $
Portfolio 70	13.4	13.2	13.1
Portfolio 80	13.4	13.1	13.0
Portfolio 90	13.2	12.9	12.8
Portfolio 100	13.0	12.7	12.5

we move to successively more aggressive portfolios, the expected return actually *drops*. For example, Portfolio 80 is expected to earn *less* than Portfolio 70 over both 10- and 20-year time frames.

At first glance, that result seems to contradict the first law, that risk goes up with return. Portfolio 80 is clearly riskier than Portfolio 70—a comparison of the return ranges shows that they get wider and wider as we move from Portfolio 70 through 100. So, what's going on?

The answer can be found in our time frames. We have limited them to a maximum of 20 years. (We limited our maximum time frame to 20 years because that's as far as we felt an individual can look ahead in planning for the future. Over time frames longer than 20 years, enough can change to make forecasting of questionable value.) Portfolios 80 to 100 are so volatile that they are expected to take more than 20 years to realize their full return potential. (How long will it take them to do so? The number crunchers tell us it could take Portfolio 100 as long as a century! But they are also quick to point out that this is all very theoretical.) For that reason, we have marked Portfolio 80's position on the risk scale with a black circle, instead of a gray one. We did so to remind you that it may take longer than 20 years for risk to go up with return, at least for this portfolio.

Obviously, the investor should not underestimate Portfolio 80's risk, or the risk of the two remaining portfolios in the *Star* series. These mixes are best suited for adventurers who can afford to either lose money or wait a lifetime to reach their goals. Table 15–2 shows the dollar ranges for Portfolio 80. Each amount in the table corresponds to a high, average, or low expected return on the bar graph in the *Portfolio Summary* chart. The dollar range is very wide at the longer time frames; for example, over a 20-year period, the portfolio

T A B L E   15–2

Dollar Ranges for Portfolio 80

	1 Year, $	5 Years, $	10 Years, $	20 Years, $
High	1,566	3,817	9,486	49,069
Average	1,152	1,873	3,437	11,584
Low	814	883	1,198	2,628

could earn anywhere from roughly $2,600 to $49,000. It all depends on whether Portfolio 80 earns near the high or the low end of its earning range over 20 years.

LONG-TERM PERFORMANCE

Portfolio 80's investment performance since 1926 is summarized in Table 15–3.

THE GREAT BULL MARKET

Deep End investors didn't do quite as well during the late 1920s as Portfolio 70 investors, but they did well enough. From 1926 through

T A B L E   15–3

Portfolio 80, Decade by Decade

Decade	High, %	Average, %	Low, %	No. Loss Years
1926–1929	43.4	16.1	−15.0	1
1930–1939	66.5	0.7	−44.1	5
1940–1949	43.0	11.5	−11.0	3
1950–1959	53.7	19.3	−11.0	2
1960–1969	32.9	9.3	−11.5	4
1970–1979	40.4	9.5	−22.8	3
1980–1989	49.8	21.2	0.5	0
1990–1996	26.2	7.9	−18.7	2

1929, Portfolio 80 earned an average return of 16.1 percent per year, under the 17.5 percent return earned by investors in Portfolio 70. *Deep End*ers did about as well during the up years, but they were hurt more by the Crash in 1929. They lost 15.0 percent in 1929, the worst loss suffered by any *Star* portfolio.

The increased exposure to small stocks is what hurt Portfolio 80 the most. Small stocks actually bore the brunt of the Crash; they lost 51.4 percent of their value in 1929, while large U.S. stocks lost only 8.4 percent of theirs. Portfolio 80, with the maximum small-stock exposure of any *Star* portfolio, was hit the hardest.

THE GREAT DEPRESSION

Deep End investors actually did a bit better than most other aggressive investors during the 1930s. They earned an average of 0.7 percent per year, better than Portfolio 70's 0.4 percent annual return and Portfolio 100's 0.2 percent annual return. Nonetheless, the first part of the decade was disastrous for *Deep End* investors, as it was for most other investors.

Portfolio 80 lost a total of 68 percent of its value between the end of 1928 and the market low in 1932. It saw a brief recovery in 1937, but it slipped back underwater shortly after that and didn't break the surface for good until 1943. *Deep End* investors, like other aggressive investors, spent the entire decade in water up over their heads.

By now, the return pattern of the 1930s should be familiar. Portfolio 80's losses during the decade exceeded the low end of its return range in 3 separate years, and its gain exceeded the high end of the range in 1933. As we have said in connection with prior portfolios, the return ranges show what will probably happen most of the time. They can't predict what will happen all of the time.

WAR AND RECOVERY

The 1940s provided a measure of recovery for *Deep End* investors. Despite World War II and its aftermath, or perhaps *because* of it, Portfolio 80 returned to double-digit performance. Its annual return of 11.5 percent wasn't up to the level of the 13.1 percent expected of it over 10 years, but it was a vast improvement over the paltry 0.7 percent per year earned in the 1930s.

The gains and losses experienced by the portfolio fell back into line with expectations. The decade-high return of 43.0 percent in 1945 and the decade-low return of –11.0 percent in 1941 were both within the expected 1-year range of –18.6 to 56.6 percent. Wile the 1940s may not have been a great decade for *Deep End* investors, Portfolio 80's performance probably helped to restore their faith in aggressive investing, which had been severely tested by the debacle of the 1930s.

THE NIFTY FIFTIES

In the 1950s we see a pattern that we have seen with other aggressive portfolios and that we will continue to see as we complete the *Star* series. After living with downright lousy performance for 10 years, and another 10 years of average performance after that, Portfolio 80 finally shot up into the stratosphere like the early rockets that captured the public's imagination during the decade. Portfolio 80 couldn't have done much better if it had tail fins.

Deep End investors earned an average of 19.3 percent per year in the 1950s. They wouldn't see performance on that level again for another 30 years. In 1954, Portfolio 80 grew by 53.7 percent. And that growth didn't come on the heels of a big loss, as it had in the 1930s. The year before, Portfolio 80 had lost just 1.4 percent, one of only 2 loss years in the entire decade. The other loss occurred in 1957, when the portfolio lost 11.0 percent. That's not so much, considering that one would expect Portfolio 80 to lose as much as 18.6 percent in a bad year.

THE GO-GO YEARS

After the spectacular growth of the 1950s, Portfolio 80 settled back down for another 20 years of so-so growth. It's not that *Deep End* returns weren't attractive; the 9.4 percent per year return was about equal to what *Shallow End* investors (Portfolio 20) earned during the 1950s. Portfolio 80's return during the 1960s was simply below the average one would expect from a portfolio this risky.

Portfolio 80 wasn't much more volatile in the 1960s than it had been the decade before. It suffered 4 loss years instead of 2, but its worst loss was only 11.5 percent in 1969. That compares to its decade-low return of –11.0 percent in the 1950s. But as we noted in connection with Portfolio 70, the investment markets couldn't seem to sustain any momentum for more than a couple of years.

Portfolio 80's small-stock exposure helped it in a couple of key years during the decade. Small stocks earned 83.6 percent in 1967, compared to large U.S. stock earnings of 24.0 percent during the same year. Small stocks followed up that gain with a return of 36.0 percent the following year, when large stocks earned only 11.0 percent. But small stocks gave back some of these gains at the close of the decade; they lost 25.1 percent in 1969, when large U.S. stocks lost only 8.5 percent.

THE DISCO DECADE

Portfolio 80 earned about the same average return in the 1970s (9.5 percent) that it had earned in the 1960s (9.3 percent). But *Deep End* investors went through much more of a roller-coaster ride to get there in the 1970s then in the decade before. Portfolio 80 lost a decade-low 22.8 percent in 1973 and earned a decade-high return of 40.4 percent in the following year. It went through 3 loss years and 4 years of returns over 20 percent.

The long market slide of the early 1970s put *Deep End* investors through much the same experience as other aggressive investors. Portfolio 80 lost 35 percent of its value during the slide, which was comparable to the losses experienced by investors in Portfolio 70. And like Portfolio 70 investors, *Deep End* had to wait until well into 1976 before the value of their investments again reached their 1972 levels. The decade is a good example of what to expect from an aggressive portfolio in a weak, but not disastrous, decade.

THE ME DECADE

After languishing below its expected return for another 20 years, *Deep End* investors might have suspected they were due for a shot in the arm. They would have been right. The 1980s ushered in stock returns that hadn't been seen since the 1950s. Portfolio 80 broke 20 percent five times during the decade and 40 percent twice (1985 and 1986), on its way to an average return of 21.2 percent per year.

Portfolio 80 made it through the decade without a single loss year, and that sets it apart from other aggressive portfolios. Most suffered small losses in 1981, when large U.S. stocks lost about 5 percent. But smaller U.S. stocks made about 13.9 percent in the same year; Portfolio 80's larger allocation to this asset class enabled it to end the year with a 0.5 percent gain.

THE RECENT PAST

After a home-run decade, Portfolio 80 seems to have settled down for a long winter's sleep. Its returns in the first half of the 1990s have been well below what is expected of it, and it has underperformed every other moderate and aggressive portfolio (including *The Shallow End*) in the *Star* series. Smaller U.S. stocks have spent much of the decade in the doldrums, and international stocks have not performed as well as U.S. stocks. We may have to wait until the 2010s for another spectacular performance from Portfolio 80. Then again, it *could* happen tomorrow.

One disturbing note for *Deep End* investors came in 1990, when Portfolio 80 lost 18.7 percent. That loss is sharply higher than the 12.6 percent loss sustained by Portfolio 70 in the same year. The reason for the loss is Portfolio 80's increased exposure to smaller U.S. stocks and international stocks. In 1990, small stocks lost 21.6 percent, and international stocks lost 23.2 percent. On the other hand, large U.S. stocks lost only 3.2 percent. As a result, aggressive investors with concentrated holdings in small U.S. and international stocks were hit the hardest by the market decline of 1990.

REAL GROWTH

We have said in connection with other aggressive portfolios that adequate inflation protection is provided by less aggressive portfolios. Portfolios at this end of the risk scale are designed to provide high, inflation-adjusted growth over the long term. If inflation remains at its current level of 3.1 percent per year, Portfolio 80 could be expected to provide average real (inflation-adjusted) growth of 11.7 percent per year.

EVALUATING *THE DEEP END*

The black circle we use to mark Portfolio 80's position on the risk scale captures its key characteristic. *The Deep End* is a very aggressive portfolio, and it can be expected to provide among the highest average returns in the *Star* portfolio series. At the same time, it is difficult to say how long it could take the portfolio to realize its full earnings potential. Investors considering the *Deep End* portfolio should give a great deal of thought to their willingness to withstand losses and their ability to remain underwater for long periods of time, before they jump into this end of the investing pool.

16

CHAPTER

The Black Diamond

For experts only. Heavy exposure to international stocks means constant volatility, but the returns can be huge.

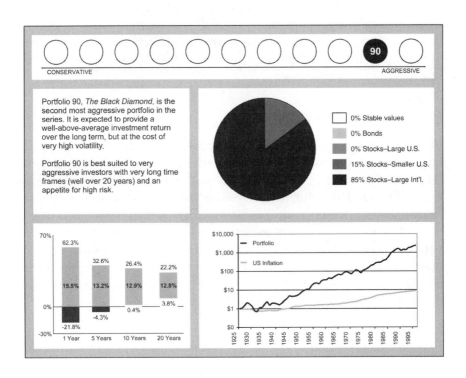

CONSERVATIVE — 90 — AGGRESSIVE

Portfolio 90, *The Black Diamond*, is the second most aggressive portfolio in the series. It is expected to provide a well-above-average investment return over the long term, but at the cost of very high volatility.

Portfolio 90 is best suited to very aggressive investors with very long time frames (well over 20 years) and an appetite for high risk.

- 0% Stable values
- 0% Bonds
- 0% Stocks–Large U.S.
- 15% Stocks–Smaller U.S.
- 85% Stocks–Large Int'l.

Bar chart (returns):
- 1 Year: 62.3%, 15.5%, -21.8%
- 5 Years: 32.6%, 13.2%, -4.3%
- 10 Years: 26.4%, 12.9%, 0.4%
- 20 Years: 22.2%, 12.8%, 3.8%

Line chart: Portfolio vs. US Inflation, 1925–1995

Skiers are familiar with "degree of difficulty" signs that are posted at the top of most ski trails. Each sign has a symbol and a legend that indicates the type of skier for whom the trail is considered most suitable. Green circle signs mark beginner trails, and blue square signs indicate intermediate slopes. Signs with a black diamond mark the most difficult trails. The legend below the sign reads EXPERTS ONLY.

There is a certain prestige in being able to ski a black diamond slope. Most skiers, at one time or another, venture onto a black diamond to see if they can handle it. Most of us find that we can't. The worst thing about blundering onto a black diamond trail is that one cannot easily blunder off. Once on the trail, you have to see it through to the end. For most of us, that means inching down the slope as carefully as we can until we can get off the darned thing. An unfortunate few are oblivious to the potential danger involved. They end up cartwheeling through the air like a rag doll that some temperamental child has cast aside.

That's why we have named Portfolio 90 *The Black Diamond.* If you are an experienced investor and if you have a strong sense of your personal tolerance for unrelenting bad news, you can make a lot of money with this portfolio. But if you are new to the sport or even if you are an intermediate investor, take heed of the sign posted at the top of this trail. Its centerpiece is a large black diamond. You know what the words say.

WHAT'S IN THE PORTFOLIO

Portfolio 90 is an easy portfolio to describe. It is made up of 85 percent large international stocks, 15 percent small U.S. stocks. There are no large U.S. stocks in the portfolio. As we have done for the past few portfolios, we are reducing diversification in pursuit of the highest returns we can find.

This portfolio's lack of exposure to large U.S. stocks causes it to behave somewhat differently than other aggressive portfolios. It outperforms them at times when foreign markets are strong and U.S. markets are weak. The portfolio underperforms other aggressive portfolios when that situation is reversed.

RISK AND RETURN

We saw in our look at Portfolio 80 that return actually drops as risk goes up at this end of the risk spectrum. At least that's the case over 20 years. Portfolio 90, like its predecessor, is expected to take longer than 20 years to realize its full return potential. It could take much longer to do so. As a reminder of the longer time frame, we have used a black circle, rather than a gray one, to mark this portfolio's position on the risk scale.

Over the 20-year time frame included in the bars in the *Portfolio Summary* chart, *Black Diamond* investors can expect to see an average return in the neighborhood of 12.8 percent per year. In any given year, the return could be expected to run as high as 62.3 percent or as low as –21.8 percent. The dollar ranges that correspond to Portfolio 90's return ranges are shown in Table 16–1. As always, each figure in the table shows the value of $1,000 invested in the portfolio over different time frames, assuming it earns the high, average, or low expected return shown on the bars in the *Portfolio Summary* chart at the beginning of this chapter.

Portfolio 90 is essentially a clone of Portfolio 80, except that Portfolio 90 shifts the remaining large U.S. stock allocation into international stocks. International investing did not really come into its own until about 1970. Before then, there were no widely adopted international indexes we could use to measure the performance of international stocks. To account for that situation, we assume that the international allocation of each *Star* portfolio was invested in large U.S. stocks until 1969. (We adjusted the large-stock returns used from 1926 through 1969 for the international allocations to account for differences in the returns of international stocks. We made the adjustment by calculating the average spread

T A B L E   16–1

Dollar Ranges for Portfolio 90

	1 Year, $	5 Years, $	10 Years, $	20 Years, $
High	1,623	4,106	10,443	55,406
Average	1,155	1,859	3,371	11,083
Low	782	801	1,036	2,108

between U.S. and international large-stock returns, and then we added this spread to the large-stock returns used for international allocations prior to 1970.) In 1970, that allocation is switched over to the international sector.

Since our model uses essentially the same returns for large U.S. stocks and large international stocks prior to 1970, the returns for Portfolios 80 and 90 will mirror each other from 1926 through 1969. The period since then is the most important for comparing the two portfolios.

LONG-TERM PERFORMANCE

Table 16–2 summarizes Portfolio 90's performance history from 1926 through 1996.

THE GREAT BULL MARKET

Portfolio 90 fared about the same as other aggressive portfolios during the late 1920s. From 1926 through 1929, it earned an average return of 16.2 percent per year, a return lower than those earned by investors in Portfolios 60 and 70. Portfolio 90 was dragged down in 1929 by the same factor that weighted down Portfolio 80's performance—

TABLE 16–2

Portfolio 90, Decade by Decade

Decade	High, %	Average, %	Low, %	No. Loss Years
1926–1929	43.4	16.2	−14.9	1
1930–1939	66.6	0.8	−44.1	5
1940–1949	43.1	11.5	−11.0	3
1950–1959	53.8	19.4	−11.0	2
1960–1969	32.9	9.4	−11.4	3
1970–1979	39.6	10.2	−21.8	3
1980–1989	61.7	22.3	1.3	0
1990–1996	30.8	5.5	−23.0	2

the bottom fell out of small stocks in the 1929 Crash. They lost 51.4 percent of their value in 1929 alone, and Portfolio 90 allocates the same 15 percent to this asset class as Portfolio 80.

THE GREAT DEPRESSION

Portfolio 90 took the same shellacking that other aggressive portfolios received in the 1930s. Once again, its performance paralleled that of Portfolio 80. Portfolio 90 earned an average of 0.8 percent per year during the decade. That return was second best of the aggressive *Star* portfolios, surpassed only by Portfolio 60's 1.0 percent average return. Of course, when the highs and lows are separated by less than 1 percent, and when the highest return *is* 1 percent, the difference may not really matter.

Portfolio 90 was buoyed by its small-stock investments during parts of the decade and dragged down by them during others. In 1933, smaller U.S. stocks earned an astounding 142.9 percent return, the highest annual return earned by any asset class in the entire 71-year period. But that return followed 4 consecutive years of losses, in which small stocks lost 86 percent of their value. Even after the record-high returns of 1933, small-stock values were still only 35 percent of their 1928 highs.

WAR AND RECOVERY

After 10 years of misery mixed with euphoria, when 30 percent losses were routinely followed by 30 percent gains, *Black Diamond* investors hunkered down for slow but steady growth. They finished the decade with an average return of 11.5 percent, one of the two best among the *Star* portfolios. One other portfolio earned the same average return during the 1940s; it should come as no surprise that it was Portfolio 80.

Even though Portfolio 90's performance improved dramatically over the 1930s, it still fell somewhat short of the 12.9 percent expected of it over a 10-year period. We see something very unusual at this end of the risk spectrum. Even though Portfolios 80 and 90 earned the same average return during the 1940s, the decade was a little better for Portfolio 90. The reason is that we expect a little less of Portfolio 90 over a 10-year period. Its expected return is 12.9

percent, while Portfolio 80's expected return is 13.2 percent. So while both portfolios fell just a bit shy of their marks, Portfolio 90 actually came a little bit closer to hitting its target.

THE NIFTY FIFTIES

Black diamond slopes can be treacherous. They can be narrow and steep, with bumps and gullies at every turn. Then, suddenly, they can open up into wide runs that even intermediate skiers can handle. But that usually doesn't last very long. Before you know it, you're back on the steep, deep, and twisty trail. That's why a lot of intermediate skiers take the opportunity to bail out of a black diamond if one presents itself.

The 1950s resembled a wide stretch on a black diamond run. Portfolio 90 ran fast and straight the entire decade, like a racer down a groomed slope. *Black Diamond* investors earned an average of 19.4 percent per year for the decade, a record that topped their 1920s performance, and one that wouldn't be matched until the 1980s. Portfolio 90 earned over 30 percent per year 4 times during the decade, and it earned over 40 percent twice. It experienced only 2 years of losses, the worst being a 11.0 percent drop in 1957.

Much of Portfolio 90's tremendous performance in the 1950s can be attributed to its allocations to small U.S. stocks. Small stocks performed well throughout the decade. They only lost money in 2 years during the decade, and they grew by over 60 percent per year in 2 others. Portfolio 80, which has the same 15 percent allocation to small stocks as this portfolio, experienced similar gains.

THE GO-GO YEARS

Growth can only be sustained for so long. After the explosive returns of the 1950s, it was probably inevitable that the 1960s performance of the stock markets would fall back to more realistic levels.

No investors managed to match, or even approach, their performance of the 1950s. But for aggressive investors, and for some moderate investors, it was a particularly disappointing decade. During the 1960s, Portfolios 0 through 40 managed to equal or better their 1940s track record. Portfolios 50 through 100 failed to do so, and the shortfall was particularly noticeable in Portfolios 80 and 90.

Once again, the culprit was the small-stock exposure of the two portfolios. During the 1960s, small stocks grew at a healthy rate of 15.6 percent per year. But during the 1940s, they had grown at an even healthier 20.7 percent. So, while the 1960s were certainly good years for *Black Diamond* investors, their average return fell below what they had earned over the prior two decades.

That doesn't mean the 1960s weren't kind to Portfolio 90. Its average return of 9.4 percent was highest of any *Star* portfolio during the decade. It suffered 3 loss years during the decade, one less than Portfolio 80, and its worst loss of the decade was no worse than 11.4 percent, which it sustained in 1969. And finally, both risk and return fell well within the expected range. If the 1960s weren't a banner decade for *Black Diamond* investors, they were at least a respectable decade.

THE DISCO DECADE

As we discussed earlier in the chapter, the performance of Portfolios 80 and 90 mirror each other through the 1960s. They begin to diverge in the 1970s because we have actual historical data for the performance of the international allocation.

Portfolio 90 earned an average of 10.2 percent per year during the decade, somewhat higher than the 9.5 percent earned by Portfolio 80. Both portfolios sustained 3 years of losses during the decade. But Portfolio 90's worst loss, 21.8 percent in 1974, wasn't quite as bad as the 22.8 percent loss experienced by Portfolio 80 in the same year.

Portfolio 90 took about the same amount of time as other aggressive portfolios to recover from the market slide of 1973 to 1974. By the end of 1976, Portfolio 90 had regained its 1972 highs, although just barely. By the close of the decade, Portfolio 90 had improved its average return over its 1960s average, but it had still not topped its performance of the 1950s, or even that of the 1940s.

THE ME DECADE

If Portfolio 90 spent the 1960s and 1970s catching its breath, then it took off at a dead run during the 1980s. And like the bunny in the battery commercial, it just kept going and going. Portfolio 90 broke all records during the 1980s. It earned its highest return of any decade since 1926, easily surpassing its previous record from the 1950s. It sailed through the decade without a single loss, and its 1986 61.7 percent was the second highest earned by any of the *Star* portfolios during the 1980s.

  Black Diamond investors earned an average of 22.3 percent during the 1980s. Their returns were buoyed throughout the decade by the performance of international stocks, which consistently outperformed large U.S. stocks throughout most of the decade. The strength of the overall performance is indicated by the fact that the portfolio earned an annual return over 50 percent twice in the decade, during the peak years of 1985 and 1986.

THE RECENT PAST

Portfolio 90 has had a checkered history during the 1990s. It began the decade with a 23.0 percent loss, caused by a very bad year in both small U.S. and international stock markets. Moderate portfolios with major allocations to large U.S. stocks fared better; those stocks lost only 3.2 percent in 1990.

  Portfolio 90 has rebounded since its 1990 loss, but its performance continues to be dragged down by a lackluster showing in international stocks. It has managed to outperform Portfolio 80 only once, in 1983. Its average return of 5.5 percent for 1990 through 1996 is well below Portfolio 80's return of 7.9 percent for the same period.

REAL GROWTH

We have said on a number of occasions that aggressive investing is for adventurous investors in pursuit of high growth after inflation. Portfolio 90 is expected to provide real (inflation-adjusted) growth of 12.0 percent per year, assuming inflation sticks to its current average of 3.1 percent per year. Those who are most concerned about keeping pace with inflation or maintaining a reasonable lead over it can do so at far less risk by investing in one of the moderate portfolios in the *Star* series.

EVALUATING *THE BLACK DIAMOND*

As we said at the beginning, *The Black Diamond* sacrifices diversification for the prospect of a higher return. At times, that strategy has paid off handsomely; the 1980s show how international returns can boost portfolio performance. But the strategy is a two-edged sword; as recently as 1990 we saw how it can push a portfolio into steep decline at a time when better-diversified portfolios experience only modest losses.

As one aggressive investor said after a particularly bad day, "What the heck. The lows are lower, but the highs are higher." If you have the stomach for that sort of volatility and plenty of time, you may like skiing on a black diamond run.

17 CHAPTER

The Sky Dive

For thrill-seekers. Requires unshakable faith, endurance, and a touch of wild abandon.

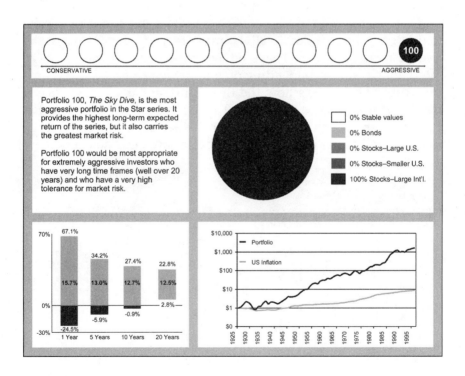

CONSERVATIVE   AGGRESSIVE

Portfolio 100, *The Sky Dive*, is the most aggressive portfolio in the Star series. It provides the highest long-term expected return of the series, but it also carries the greatest market risk.

Portfolio 100 would be most appropriate for extremely aggressive investors who have very long time frames (well over 20 years) and who have a very high tolerance for market risk.

- 0% Stable values
- 0% Bonds
- 0% Stocks–Large U.S.
- 0% Stocks–Smaller U.S.
- 100% Stocks–Large Int'l.

We have arrived at the far end of the risk scale. Portfolio 100 is named *The Sky Dive*. It's for people who find black diamond skiing not quite as challenging as they would like. This portfolio is almost guaranteed to challenge the investor from time to time. Unless you are a real thrill-seeker, it's more likely to scare you to death!

People who jump out of perfectly good airplanes for sport say they do it for the thrill. There is an unequaled exhilaration, they say, in a free fall from several miles up. The key, according to many experienced parachutists, is to have confidence in your equipment.

That pretty much describes the temperament needed to be an investment *Sky Diver*. Portfolio 100 is the least diversified, most volatile portfolio in the series. As long as the investor has an unshakable faith in the long-term power of the international stock markets and is willing to wait a very long time, Portfolio 100 should provide the highest average return of any *Star* portfolio.

WHAT'S IN THE PORTFOLIO

Portfolio 100 is invested exclusively in large international stocks. The portfolio is designed to anchor the aggressive end of our risk scale; to do that, it has to allocate all its investments to the riskiest of the five basic asset classes. That's either smaller U.S. stocks, or large international stocks, depending on whom we talk to.

Table 17–1 shows how the three different stock asset classes have performed since 1970. Small U.S. stocks have provided the highest average return per year over the period, followed by large international stocks and, close on its heels, large U.S. stocks.

T A B L E   1 7 – 1

Stock Performance Since 1970

	Large U.S. Stocks, %	Large Int'l. Stocks, %	Small U.S. Stocks, %
Highest	37.4	69.9	57.4
Average	12.3	12.9	14.2
Lowest	−26.5	−23.2	−30.9

But there are two problems with relying solely on the historical data since 1970:

- The period is dominated by the unprecedented stock market gains experienced worldwide since 1982.
- It includes the extraordinary period from 1975 through 1983, when smaller U.S. stocks outperformed their large counterparts by a wide margin. Without those years, some argue,[1] small-stock performance over the past 71 years is no better than large-stock performance.

The longer view suggests that large international stocks can be expected to be just a bit riskier than smaller U.S. stocks.[2] For that reason, we have used large international stocks to anchor the aggressive end of the risk spectrum.

RISK AND RETURN

As we said earlier, Portfolio 100 is the most aggressive mix in the *Star* series. Its expected return ranges are shown on the bars in the *Portfolio Summary* chart at the beginning of the chapter. The dollar ranges that correspond to these returns are shown in Table 17–2. The dollar values shown in Table 17–2 show the potential value of a $1,000 investment in Portfolio 100. For example, in the unlikely event that

TABLE 17–2

Dollar Ranges for Portfolio 100

	1 Year, $	5 Years, $	10 Years, $	20 Years, $
High	1,671	4,349	11,246	60,611
Average	1,157	1,842	3,297	10,564
Low	755	737	913	1,737

1 Most notably, Jeremy Siegel in *Stocks for the Long Run*, Richard D. Irwin, Homewood, Ill., 1994, pp. 79–86. See Chapter 4 of this book for a discussion of Professor Siegel's argument.

2 In this book, we use the "building blocks" approach developed by Ibbotson and Siegel and used by Ibbotson Associates in the "optimizer inputs" they publish quarterly.

Portfolio 100 earned an average of 22.8 percent per year over 20 years (the high end of its expected earnings range for 20 years), then $1,000 would be worth $60,611 by the end of the period. In the more likely event that it earned 12.5 percent per year over that time period (the middle of the range), the $1,000 investment would be worth $10,564.

Portfolio 100's expected returns for 5, 10, and 20 years are actually *lower* than those of Portfolios 70 through 90. That's because Portfolio 100's risk is so high that it is not expected to realize its full return potential in a period as short as 20 years. Theoretically, it could take as long as a century for this portfolio to meet its expectations. The *Portfolio Summary* chart shows Portfolio 100's position on the risk scale with a black circle, rather than a gray one, as a reminder.

LONG-TERM PERFORMANCE

Portfolio 100's performance history is summarized in Table 17–3. Keep in mind that international stock investing really did not come into its own until the 1960s. The first widely used international stock index came into use only in 1970. For the period 1926 to 1969, we assume Portfolio 100 was invested in large U.S. stocks.

THE GREAT BULL MARKET

Sky Divers earned the highest return of any *Star* investors during the late 1920s. Between 1926 and 1929, Portfolio 100 earned an

T A B L E   17–3

Portfolio 100, Decade by Decade

Decade	High, %	Average, %	Low, %	No. Loss Years
1926–1929	43.9	19.5	–8.2	1
1930–1939	54.4	0.2	–43.2	6
1940–1949	36.8	9.4	–11.4	3
1950–1959	53.0	19.6	–10.6	2
1960–1969	27.2	8.1	–9.9	3
1970–1979	37.6	9.4	–22.2	3
1980–1989	69.9	22.8	–1.0	2
1990–1996	32.9	3.8	–23.2	2

average return of 19.5 percent per year. And it didn't get hit as hard by the 1929 stock market crash since it had no exposure to small U.S. stocks. Small stocks lost over 50 percent of their value in 1929, while large U.S. stocks lost less than 10 percent of theirs. As a result, Portfolio 100 lost only 8.2 percent in 1929; Portfolio 90 lost 14.9 percent.

THE GREAT DEPRESSION

If *Sky Divers* came away from the 1920s with any smug sense of satisfaction, the 1930s wiped the grins off their faces. Portfolio 100 had the worst return of all the *Star* portfolios, with a return of 0.2 percent. Other investors may have made very little in the 1930s, but large-stock investors made almost nothing at all.

Between the end of 1928 and the end of 1932, *Sky Divers* lost 42 percent of their value. That's not quite as bad as Portfolio 90's loss—its exposure to small stocks cost it dearly during the 1930s. Like other aggressive investors, *Sky Divers* had to wait until 1943 for their investments to finally surpass their 1928 levels once and for all.

There was just enough good news in the 1930s to get an investor's hopes up, before the next market debacle dashed them. At times, it seemed as if large stocks had turned the corner. They earned 54.4 percent in 1933 and 48.0 percent in 1935. Other than a 34.9 percent loss in 1937, the second half of the decade wasn't too bad. But they weren't good enough to outweigh the disastrous first half of the decade.

WAR AND RECOVERY

The good news for Portfolio 100 investors in the 1940s was that their average annual return was 47 times higher in this decade than it had been in the last. The bad news was that it still came out to only 9.4 percent per year. Portfolio 100 didn't do quite as well as other aggressive portfolios (Portfolios 60 through 90) in the 1940s because it had no exposure to small stocks. Their recovery in the 1940s, particularly their 88.4 percent return in 1943, helped boost most of these portfolios into the double digits for the decade.

Still, the decade marked a substantial improvement in performance over the Depression years. The worst loss experienced by Portfolio 100 was 11.4 percent in 1941. It lost money in only

3 years during the 1940s, compared with 6 the decade before. If its average return was well below the 12.8 percent expected of it over 10 years, at least it was well above the 0.2 percent it had earned in the 1950s.

THE NIFTY FIFTIES

After a decade of gloom and doom, and another decade of ho-hum performance, *Sky Divers* got their due in the 1950s. Like other aggressive investors, they reaped big rewards when the baby boom hit and the stock markets took off. For once, the absence of smaller U.S. stocks didn't hurt Portfolio 100. It earned an average return of 19.6 percent per year, just a shade higher than the 19.4 percent earned by Portfolio 90.

The 1950s were a decade of records for aggressive investors, and *Sky Divers* led the way. Its decade-high return of 53.0 percent in 1954 was just slightly below the returns earned by Portfolios 70 to 90, which were buoyed by small-stock returns. But for most of the decade, the large company was king, and Portfolio 100 rode large U.S. stocks to the largest return of any *Star* portfolio in over 30 years.

THE GO-GO YEARS

We have seen in all the aggressive portfolios how the stock markets charged ahead during the 1920s, stumbled in the 1930s, plodded in the 1940s, and charged ahead again in the 1950s. In the 1960s, the last decade where we rely on large U.S. stock data, large stocks plodded along.

Portfolio 100 grew the least of any of the aggressive *Star* portfolios during the 1960s. Its average return of 8.1 percent was below the average return earned by Portfolios 60 through 90. As in prior decades, the shortfall was caused by a zero allocation to smaller company stocks.

Portfolio 100 sustained 3 loss years during the 1960s; the worst loss was 9.9 percent in 1966. It also lost money in 1969, but it lost less than other aggressive portfolios. In that year, its avoidance of small-company stocks actually helped it. But Portfolio 100's reliance on large stocks wasn't enough to carry it to the top, and it turned in its weakest 10-year performance since the 1930s.

THE DISCO DECADE

An absence of small stocks hurt Portfolio 100 again in the 1970s. This is the first decade for which we have international stock data. And it is another lackluster decade for Portfolio 100. It earned an average return of 9.4 percent per year, almost a full percentage point less than the 10.2 percent earned by Portfolio 90, and less than the 9.5 percent earned by Portfolio 80. As in prior decades, Portfolio 100 was held back by the absence of any smaller U.S. company stock in the mix.

Like other aggressive portfolios, Portfolio 100 took its lumps in the worldwide stock market slide of 1973 to 1974. It didn't lose as much as some other aggressive portfolios; it suffered only a 5 percent loss in the slide. But it took longer than other portfolios to recover from its modest loss. It didn't return to its 1972 level until early 1977.

THE ME DECADE

Portfolio 100 did exactly what one would expect of it in the 1980s— it performed just above the level of Portfolio 90. It earned an average return of 22.8 percent for the decade, which is the highest return earned by any of the *Star* portfolios over any decade. After another 20 years of disappointments, *Sky Divers* were once more king of the hill.

The reason, of course, was the unprecedented performance of international stocks. As well as the U.S. stock markets performed in the 1980s, the international stock markets performed even better. Large U.S. stocks earned an average return of 17.5 percent for the decade, and smaller U.S. stocks earned 15.8 percent per year. But large international stocks earned an average of 22.8 percent per year. In 1987, the year the U.S. stock market experienced its worst crash since 1929, large U.S. stocks earned 5.2 percent. In the same year, international stocks earned 24.9 percent. The following year they earned another 28.6 percent. Returns like that caught the attention of a lot of investors who had not previously given serious consideration to international investing.

THE RECENT PAST

Of course, the crowd moved in just as the international market turned soft. Between 1990 and 1996, international stocks earned just 3.8 percent per year. That's the worst performance of any *Star* portfolio in the 1990s; even Portfolio 0 earned a higher return. The well-publicized woes of the Japanese economy have had a lot to do with Portfolio 100's poor showing in this decade. In 1990 alone, international stocks lost about a quarter of their value. *Sky Divers* may be in for another long dry spell before Portfolio 100 takes off again.

REAL GROWTH

Obviously, the extreme aggressiveness of Portfolio 100 is not suitable for conservative or moderate investors searching for protection against inflation. An adequate defense against rising prices can be found at far less risk in Portfolios 20 through 50.

Sky Divers want to earn a return well in excess of inflation, and they are willing to take considerable risk for that return. Over the long run, Portfolio 100 should provide an inflation-adjusted (real) return in the neighborhood of 12.22 percent.

EVALUATING *THE SKY DIVE*

The easiest way to decide whether *The Sky Dive* might be suitable for you is to ask yourself the following question: Would I be willing to jump out of an airplane for fun? If you aren't sure, give it a try. If you find parachute jumping to be a great experience, then you might like investing this aggressively. If, like most of us, you wouldn't jump out of an airplane unless it was on fire, then *The Sky Dive* may be a bit too extreme for your tastes. You would probably sleep better with a less aggressive portfolio. And, over a 20-year period, you will probably make more money.

PART THREE

THE CARE AND FEEDING OF YOUR PORTFOLIO

18
CHAPTER

Animal Crackers

Shopping for mutual funds is like shopping for animal crackers: the contents are mostly the same—the differences are in flavor, price, and packaging.

So far, we have talked about how to set the mix of different asset classes that will ultimately determine over 90 percent of your investment performance. But we haven't talked about how to pick the funds that will fill each of the slots in that mix. For some investors, the choice will be fairly straightforward. Others will find a dizzying array of choices, with a cacophony of competing claims from the sellers of different products.

In this chapter we are going to begin to sift through the noise to help you pick the right funds for your portfolio. We will explain the different packages funds come in and how to find the right one for you. In the next chapter, we will show you a step-by-step procedure for selecting funds that meet your needs and your goals.

FUNDS ARE LIKE ANIMAL CRACKERS

I once attended a client meeting where the subject of employee communications was on the agenda. The company needed to explain its 401k plan to employees, and it had hired a communications consultant to help it prepare its materials.

When we arrived at the meeting room, we discovered a small box of animal crackers at each place at the table. They weren't all the same brand, and the boxes were different shapes and sizes. After the communications consultant was introduced, she began the meeting by inviting each of us to open the box of animal crackers in front of us and sharing some with others at the table.

"How much difference is there between the animal crackers?" she asked us. We all agreed they were pretty much alike. Animal crackers are animal crackers, after all.

"So how do the companies that make animal crackers compete for your business?" she asked us. We discussed the question for a few minutes and concluded that they differentiated themselves by the design of their box. And that was her point.

There are more stock funds than there are stocks. There are hundreds of bond funds to choose from. There are thousands of stable value vehicles. How does one sort them all out? Here's one way to do it:

- Start with the premise that animal crackers are animal crackers. About the only difference between them is that they come in five flavors: stable values, bonds, and three different types of stock.
- Mutual funds, variable annuities, and other investment vehicles are simply the containers. Inside, the investor will find one of the five basic flavors of animal crackers. (The five asset classes we described in Chapter 4 are the ones most commonly encountered by investors. Obviously, there are exotic investments, such as commodities and futures, that fall outside these groups. But those investments are used by relatively few investors, and most investment professionals recommend them only to experienced, very sophisticated investors.)

If you start from there, you can shop for funds the same way you would shop for animal crackers:

Step 1: What flavor of animal cracker am I looking for: stable values, bonds, or one of the three kinds of stock? That's the asset allocation question. It will eliminate four-fifths of the choices right off the bat.

Step 2: Do the various brands provide about the same quality? If some brands of animal crackers are clearly inferior to others, we can eliminate them as well. That will leave us with several comparable brands of animal crackers.

Step 3: How important is the brand name to me? For some of us, the brand name is very important. There are certain names we prefer to buy, even if a lesser brand would provide comparable quality. Others don't feel a strong brand loyalty. As long as a reputable manufacturer sells the animal crackers, they are fine. If brand name is important to you, then eliminate the brands you don't like.

Step 4: Which box of animal crackers is the least expensive?

The only differences between buying animal crackers and selecting funds is that investment funds don't go on sale and you don't have to go back to the grocery store every few days if your kids get hooked on them.

A NOTE FOR 401k INVESTORS

If you invest in a 401k plan, your decision is really pretty easy. Your employer typically offers five brands of animal crackers, one in each flavor. Most employers have screened the animal cracker companies to find those that provide animal crackers of reasonable quality at a reasonable expense.

If you have decided on a *Star* portfolio or if you have come up with your own asset allocation percentages, then your job is pretty easy. You simply need to determine which fund matches which asset class and allocate the corresponding percentage of your 401k account to that fund. The fund materials most companies provide to their employees show which asset class each fund falls into. For example, the fund description for your 401k plan's "Fixed Fund" may tell you it is a stable value fund. Or the fund description for the "Growth Fund" may tell you it invests in large U.S. stocks. If you aren't sure about a particular fund, call the toll-free number for your 401k plan or ask your benefits administrator.

What if your 401k plan offers more than one fund in a particular asset class? For example, it's not unusual these days for plans to offer more than one large U.S. stock fund. Remember, animal crackers are animal crackers, at least when they are the same flavor. You can split your allocation evenly between the funds, or you can use the suggestions in the remainder of this chapter to choose among them.

THE KINDS OF BOXES ANIMAL CRACKERS COME IN

As an individual investor, you are likely to come across three investment packages:

- Mutual funds
- Variable annuities
- Common funds

Let's take a look at each kind of fund and where they might make sense for you.

MUTUAL FUNDS

It's not unusual to hear investment seminar participants ask, "Should I invest my money in stocks, bonds, or in a mutual fund?" That's a good question to ask. A mutual fund isn't a *kind* of investment; it's a way of investing. A mutual fund is no more than one type of box the five different flavors of animal crackers come in.

Mutual funds generally stick with one type of investment. For example, some mutual funds invest in large U.S. stocks, while others invest in bonds. Relatively few funds invest in more than one asset class.[1] And most mutual funds stick to their "style." If they invest in large U.S. stocks, they stick with that asset class over the long haul—they don't jump to different asset classes.

Most individual investors will probably be familiar with mutual funds from their company savings plan. In the past few years, most companies have added brand-name and other mutual funds to

---

1   A notable exception is a *balanced fund,* which invests in both stocks and bonds. These funds generally divide their investments equally between stocks and bonds. See *balanced fund* in the glossary for more information. See also *asset allocation fund* and *lifestyle fund* in the glossary for information about variations of lifestyle funds.

their 401k plans and to other savings and retirement plans where employees direct the investments.

Mutual funds existed long before company savings plans. They have been around since the 1920s, and they were wildly popular for a time in the 1950s and 1960s. Nowadays, company savings plans make up the largest portion of many mutual fund companies' business. But for over 50 years, they were sold to individual investors from street-corner offices, in the retail market.

SO, WHICH INVESTMENTS IN THE FUND ARE MINE?

Mutual fund companies typically offer a number of different funds; most offer several funds in each of the five major asset classes. Each fund is managed by a portfolio manager or by a team of portfolio managers.

Every once in a while, a participant in an investment seminar will ask, "If a mutual fund owns 100 different stocks or bonds, which ones are mine?" The answer is, "All of them." Figure 18–1 illustrates how it works.

FIGURE 18–1

How a Mutual Fund Works

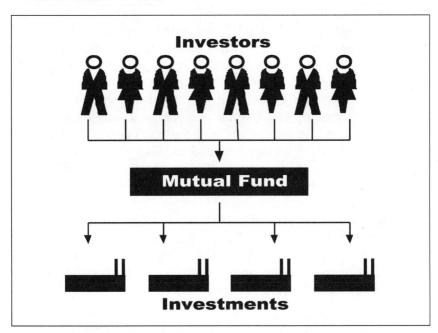

A mutual fund is what's called an *investment company*. That's a company that owns shares of other companies' stock, or bonds, or other types of investments. When you invest with a mutual fund, you become a shareholder of the fund. And that makes you part-owner of every investment made by the mutual fund. In other words, a mutual fund is a lemonade stand that sells animal crackers.

HOW MUTUAL FUNDS ARE SOLD

Mutual funds are sold to the public through investment brokers, by a sales force employed by the mutual fund company, or directly to the public over the phone and the Internet. Anyone who has sold animal crackers at retail for over 50 years has become very good at differentiating their product, or they wouldn't be able to stay in business.

Needless to say, mutual fund companies have mastered the art of turning the five basic asset classes into a mind-numbing variety of funds, all in the name of persuading you to turn your investing dollars over to them. There is no conspiracy. It's just that we sometimes forget that, after all, they do have a product to sell. And they are very good at their jobs.

Investment brokers are generally compensated for their services by commissions. When an investor buys a fund from a broker, he or she generally pays the commission through what is known as a *front-end load*. A *load* is a sales charge that is deducted from the amount invested. If I invest $100 in a fund with a 5 percent front-end load, $95 is actually invested and $5 pays for commissions and selling expenses.

Some other funds use what are called *back-end loads*. There is no sales charge up-front, but a percentage of any *withdrawal* is charged to cover commissions and selling expenses. Back-end loads typically decline over time. For example, a fund might charge a 5 percent load on any withdrawals during the first year, 4 percent on withdrawals in the second year, 3 percent in the third year, and so on.

There is another type of mutual fund, known as a *no-load fund*. No-load funds don't charge sales commissions on either the front or the back end. In most cases, these funds are marketed to the public by phone or by the Internet, and the fund company does not employ a sales force or a brokerage network.

WHICH ARE BETTER: LOADED FUNDS OR NO-LOADS?

We are back to angels dancing on the head of a pin. For years, there has been a fierce debate over the relative merits of loaded versus no-load funds. There is more smoke than fire to this particular debate, for the following reasons:

- Load versus no-load funds are just different boxes. The animal crackers inside are fundamentally the same. A loaded large U.S. stock fund invests in the same flavor animal crackers as does a no-load large U.S. stock fund.
- The mutual fund company doesn't receive the load. It goes to sales commissions and expenses. So there is no credible evidence that loaded funds can afford to hire better managers.

In that case, an intelligent investor would never buy a loaded fund, right? Not so fast. If a load is a sales commission paid to a broker, then the better question is, "When does it make sense for me to pay a sales commission?" It turns out that there are a number of occasions when it makes perfect sense to do so.

WHICH ARE BETTER: FEE-ONLY OR COMMISSIONED PLANNERS?

Many mutual fund brokers are financial planners. They are experienced professionals who specialize in helping people set financial goals for retirement, children's college, and the like, and putting the financial pieces in place to achieve those goals. They know the markets for investment and insurance products, and they can help you find the right products to meet your needs.[2]

There is no such thing as a free financial plan. (Except for the one you get from your brother-in-law, and that one is worth exactly what you pay for it.) Financial planners are compensated for their services in either of two ways:

- By charging a fee for the financial plan (a *fee-only planner*)
- By receiving a commission on the sale of the products used to implement the plan

---

2 When shopping for a financial planner, we recommend selecting only those who have the *CFP* designation. See *Certified Financial Planner* in the glossary for more information.

And that brings us to another angels-on-the-head-of-a-pin question: Are fee-only planners better than commissioned planners?

It doesn't matter. Period. Yes, there are snake-oil salesmen who push bizarre investments on the unsuspecting public, wrapped in schemes that can only with great charity be called financial plans. But there are frauds in any business. And there are certainly charlatans on the fee-only side, self-styled gurus who dispense downright lousy advice in seminars and books (present company excepted, of course).

THE BOTTOM LINE

If you are feeling at all confused, it's because we have two sets of angels dancing on the head of the same pin. Here is how to sort it all out:

- If you don't need a financial plan or investment guidance, then ask yourself, "What service is the broker or financial planner providing to earn the commission?" Their funds aren't any better (or any worse) than no-load funds, so what is it that they are doing that justifies their commission?
- If you do need a financial plan or if you want someone to counsel you as you make your investment decision, then ask yourself, "How do I want to *pay* for the financial plan: through a commission, or through a fee?" One may be less expensive than the other, or there may be some other advantage to paying one way or another.

Once you know the commission amount, you are in a position to shop for a financial planner or counselor the same way you would shop for animal crackers. Experience and a willingness to provide service distinguish financial planners from each other. There are no angles, no secret investments in all this. If a planner, or any investment salesperson, makes you a special offer, turn 180 degrees and run as fast as you can. And keep your hand on your wallet.

OTHER SALES CHARGES

There is one other sales charge with which you should be familiar. It's called a 12b-1 fee, and it usually runs about 0.25 percent. You never see 12b-1 fees; they are deducted from the earnings of a mutual fund, along with management fees and expenses, before the earnings are ever credited to your account. Not all mutual funds charge 12b-1 fees, but an increasing number have adopted the practice.

LOADS AND SAVINGS PLANS

Investors in 401k and other company savings plans *generally* don't pay loads on their investments. Loaded funds often waive their sales charges (but not their management fees) for 401k plans and other company savings plans. So, one benefit of participating in your company savings plan is that it may enable you to invest in a loaded fund without the load.

That isn't always the case, however. Small businesses, those with fewer than 100 employees or so, don't always qualify for a sales charge waiver. If you work for a small business with a savings plan and you don't know whether you are paying a load on your contributions to the plan, check your savings plan materials or ask your plan administrator. If you are paying a load, ask if there are other fund companies your employer could use that wouldn't charge a sales load on contributions to the plan.

MUTUAL FUND ADVANTAGES

Mutual funds offer two key benefits to individual investors:

- They help individuals diversify their investments. If I invest $100 directly in stocks or bonds, I might be able to buy a few shares of a single stock. Bonds generally have $1,000 minimums, so I would be out of luck there. If I invest the same $100 in a mutual fund, my investment would be spread among all the investments in the fund. [That won't give me the same degree of diversification I would get by allocating my investment among different types of funds (stable values, bonds, and stocks). But fund investing is one of the best ways to diversify *within* an asset class.]
- Mutual funds provide the benefits of professional investment management. Investment managers aren't gurus, but they do tend to be more consistent than individuals. Professional managers not only stick to a

particular asset class but they also generally follow a
particular *style* of investing.

MUTUAL FUND DISADVANTAGES

Before we start sounding like a cheerleading squad for the mutual
fund industry, let's state clearly that mutual funds are far from the
ideal investment vehicle. Here are some of their significant disadvantages:

- They can be pretty expensive. The average stock mutual
  fund charges a management fee of about 1.25 percent. That
  may not seem like much, but over the course of a career it
  can amount to over $13,000. (If an individual invests $2,000
  per year for 30 years at an average rate of 10 percent and
  pays 1.25 percent per year in management fees, the total
  management fees come out to $13,283.) As mutual funds
  grow in popularity, fees are on the rise.
- They are surrounded by much more hype and hoopla than
  they warrant. If the companies that make animal crackers
  made as much noise about their packages as the mutual
  fund companies make about their funds, we would all
  laugh at them.

The ideal investment vehicle wouldn't have any of these disadvantages. Unfortunately, the ideal investment vehicle doesn't exist. At
least for now, mutual funds really are one of the best deals going, as
long as the investor can sift through all the nonsense.

ANNUITIES

Variable annuities enjoy unprecedented popularity right now. Everyone is selling them, and no one seems terribly sure of what they
are. Half the people who buy them shouldn't, and half the people
who don't buy them should. Here's the story.

An *annuity* is simply a promise by an insurance company to
pay you an income for as long as you live. For example, let's say
that at age 65, I buy an annuity contract from The Enormous Life
Insurance Company of America. I give my friendly Enormous Life
agent a check for $100,000, and Enormous Life gives me a piece
of paper.

The piece of paper is my *annuity certificate*. It says Enormous Life will pay me an income of $825 per month as long as I live. If I live to be 120 (or longer), my $825 check will continue to arrive like clockwork every month. If I live that long, I will have made out like a bandit—Enormous Life will have paid me $544,500. Not a bad return on my hundred grand.

But notice that my piece of paper says "as long as I live." If I die the month after I buy the annuity, the checks stop. Enormous Life got $100,000 from me, and all I got from them was $825.

VARIABLE ANNUITIES

The type of annuity we have just been talking about is called a *fixed annuity*. These annuities have been around for a hundred years or more, and they have been used for generations to pay fixed, monthly pensions to retirees.

But in the past 40 years, another type of annuity has become popular—the *variable annuity*. A variable annuity has been characterized as a mutual fund wrapped inside a tax shelter. Mutual funds are, by themselves, *after-tax investments*. You don't get any sort of a tax deduction for the money you invest in a mutual fund, and you have to pay income tax on the investment earnings paid to your account. In many cases, you have to pay income taxes even on earnings that aren't distributed to your account![3]

The situation is very different if you invest in a mutual fund through your company savings plan or an *individual retirement account* (IRA). In both cases, you receive a tax deduction for the amount of money you invest in the mutual fund each year, and you don't pay income taxes on your investment earnings from the fund. As a result, your savings grow much faster in a savings plan or IRA mutual fund than they would in the same mutual fund on an after-tax basis.

The problems with savings plans and IRAs are that not everyone can contribute to them, and there are limits on how much one can contribute even if eligible. Those factors are responsible for the rise of variable annuities.

---

3 It's called a *capital-gain distribution*, and it can affect the type of mutual fund you select. See *capital-gain distribution* in the glossary for more information.

HOW A VARIABLE ANNUITY WORKS

From an investment standpoint, a variable annuity is nearly identical to a mutual fund. In fact, many variable annuities offer name-brand mutual funds as their investment vehicles. But variable annuities provide a death benefit. The investor is guaranteed to receive back at least what he or she invested in the annuity. That guarantee makes a variable annuity an insurance policy. And that qualifies them for a bit of tax magic.

The owner of an insurance policy isn't taxed on its growth each year. Instead, the policy owner is taxed when he or she withdraws funds from the policy. It's called *inside buildup*, and it's a key feature of most insurance policies.

A variable annuity acts as a shell for an investment fund that operates like a mutual fund. Since the variable annuity qualifies for inside buildup, the owner isn't taxed on the annual earnings of the investments inside the shell. In other words:

- You don't get a tax deduction for the amounts you invest in a variable annuity.
- But once dollars are invested in a variable annuity, the *investment earnings* on those dollars are sheltered from income tax until you withdraw them from your account.
- And you can transfer money between the different investment funds offered by your variable annuity (so long as you don't take money out of the annuity itself) without paying taxes on your investment gains.

That tax-shelter feature is what has made variable annuities very popular with individual investors.

ADVANTAGES AND DISADVANTAGES OF VARIABLE ANNUITIES

Variable annuities provide all the benefits we described above for mutual funds, plus the tax shelter of inside buildup. The biggest disadvantage of variable annuities is their fee structure. Variable annuities typically charge the same management fees and sales loads that mutual funds charge. But they charge an additional layer of fees on top of these, the *profit and risk charges*.

These charges are ostensibly for the death benefits provided by the annuity. But most investors don't buy variable annuities for a lifetime income—they buy them for the tax advantage offered by inside buildup. So, in reality, the profit and risk charges are the price the investor pays for the tax benefit. These charges can run to another 1.25 percent or so, on top of the management fees the investor would pay in a mutual fund. That makes them an expensive investment proposition.

WHEN DO VARIABLE ANNUITIES MAKE SENSE?

Variable annuities generate as many teapot tempests as load versus no-load funds and fee-only versus commissioned planners. Some financial professionals swear that, because of their high fees, variable annuities are rip-offs. Intelligent investors, they say, should *never* buy them.

That's far too extreme a position to take. Yes, variable annuities are expensive. They are *very* expensive, compared to similar investments. And there are times when they are questionable investments. For example, some company savings plans (which are already tax-sheltered) offer variable annuities as investment vehicles. Why in the world would I pay double fees for the tax shelter a variable annuity provides and then stick it inside *another* tax shelter? It simply makes no sense.

For years, one type of savings plan, known as a *403b plan*, could be invested only in variable annuities. These plans were offered by nonprofit institutions, such as hospitals and colleges. For employees in these savings plans, variable annuities were the only investments permitted by law, and that justified their use.

But in recent years, many nonprofit organizations have gained the right to offer "custodial accounts" or 401k plans to their employees, which can use lower-fee mutual funds, rather than variable annuities, as investment vehicles. That makes the continued use of variable annuities by many nonprofit organizations somewhat questionable.

Despite their high fees, there are circumstances in which variable annuities can make sense:

- If you and your spouse are currently contributing the maximum annual amounts to your company savings plans
- If you are currently contributing as much as you can to an IRA account
- If you plan to save still more money

In that case, a variable annuity will provide you with a tax benefit you can't get with an after-tax IRA—inside buildup.

Just because you get the benefit of inside buildup, that doesn't mean it will be worth anything to you. Remember the 180 degree rule. (Any time anyone offers you an investment deal that sounds too good to be true, turn 180 degrees and run as fast as you can, as far as you can.) Inside buildup will benefit you only to the extent that it actually lowers your taxes. The 1997 Taxpayer Relief Act lowered *everyone's* tax rate, which took a good bit of the wind out of variable annuities' sails. Before you let someone talk you into buying a variable annuity on the grounds it will lower your taxes, make him or her *prove* to you that it will do so. If it can't be reduced to plain common sense, then it doesn't *make* sense, and your best course of action is to say "No, thank you."

COMMON FUNDS

Common funds are a third type of box animal crackers come in. Banks, through their trust departments, offer common funds to individual investors and corporate pension or savings plans. Typically, a bank will offer a number of common funds, in all five of the basic asset classes. Investment management fees for these funds are typically lower than either variable annuities or mutual funds. Fees can run as little as one-third of the fees mutual funds charge for the same type of investment.

Common funds have declined in popularity in recent years, as mutual funds have risen in popularity. Banks don't advertise their common funds on television or in the popular press, and they don't generally offer amenities like toll-free-call centers or free software in connection with their common funds. That, combined with banks' general reputation for stodginess, has resulted in common funds' being consigned to the stuffed-shirt crowd.

ADVANTAGES AND DISADVANTAGES OF COMMON FUNDS

In a way, that's a real shame. If the five flavors of animal crackers are 90 percent the same, no matter whose box they come in, then common funds would be the house brand of animal crackers—as good as the name brands, but at a fraction of the price. There are a lot of investors out there who subscribe to this approach, and it makes a lot of sense.

The major disadvantages of common funds are the following:

- They don't provide the amenities that mutual funds provide.
- They can be a hassle to deal with.
- Their cost advantages may be more smoke than fire.

We said earlier that common funds don't provide the toll-free-call center, free software, and other amenities one typically receives with a mutual fund. However, common funds can provide a level of personal service, in the form of a bank trust officer, that mutual funds can't begin to approach.

Trust officers can provide considerable handholding and one-to-one attention. They generally have the same qualifications as a capable financial planner in investing, taxes, and estate planning. And the relationship is personal and ongoing. Trust officers meet with their customers in person, and a client works with the same trust officer, not whichever customer service representative happens to answer the phone.

That's the good news. The bad news is that one has to enter into a trust agreement and pay trustees' fees on top of investment management fees. The trustee may be able to provide a mini-trust agreement that covers just investment management, or the individual may have to get a lawyer to prepare a full-blown trust agreement.

As to the fees, nothing comes for free. All that personal attention and handholding cost money, and the trustees' fees cover that expense. By the time those fees are added to investment management fees for the common funds themselves, the whole arrangement may end up costing more than a mutual fund.

WHEN DO COMMON FUNDS MAKE SENSE?

The questions you should ask yourself if you are considering common funds are similar to the questions you would ask about a financial planner:

- Do I need the level of service an investment trustee can provide?
- Will the trustee I am considering provide the level of service I expect?

Trustees can be excellent resources for surviving spouses of deceased retirees. Let's say one person in your family has handled the family finances and investments. What will happen when that person dies? The surviving spouse (husband or wife) would probably be totally lost in the world of investing and could be easy prey for the charlatans and snake-oil salesmen we talked about earlier in the chapter.

For that reason, many families use trust agreements and common funds to manage investment assets in retirement. The spouse who has handled the investments can continue to take an active role in the direction of the investments during his or her lifetime. Later, the trustee can take over direction of the investments and can make sure that necessary tax returns are filed and that any other required steps are taken.

A mutual agreement on the level of service that will be provided is key to a successful trust relationship. Not every bank provides the level of handholding you or your spouse may expect. You should make sure there is a clear understanding of your expectations and the bank's capabilities at the outset of the relationship.

Many investment brokers offer the same types of services that are offered by a trustee. They will provide handholding, they will make investment recommendations, and they will watch over loose ends. But an investment broker is not making a living unless you are buying investment products or paying a separate fee for his or her investment management services. (Many brokerage firms offer *wrap accounts* that carry separate fees for investment management and personal attention.) If you plan to work closely with an investment broker as a quasi-trustee, make sure you understand the broker's expectations for product sales and the broker understands your expectations for service.

SHOPPING FOR ANIMAL CRACKERS

That just about covers the major types of animal cracker boxes you are likely to encounter. We can summarize our advice on choosing among the different vehicles as follows:

- For most people, a mutual fund will probably be the best vehicle for individual investing.
- Mutual funds in company savings plans are the best investment vehicles for long-term savings, such as retirement or college education expenses. They provide a

tax deduction for the amounts you invest, and the earnings on your investments in the plan accumulate free of taxes.

- If you and your spouse are already contributing the maximum amount allowable to a company savings plan or if you don't have a savings plan, find out if you qualify for an individual retirement account. If you do, the amounts you contribute to the account will receive the same tax benefits as contributions to a company savings plan.

- If you have "maxxed out" on your company savings plan and an IRA (or if you don't qualify for one or both), consider using a variable annuity for additional tax-sheltered savings. But make sure you will actually benefit from inside buildup before you buy.

- Once you have exhausted all opportunities for tax-sheltered savings, your next best investment vehicle is probably an after-tax mutual fund.

- If you need or prefer personal attention, you may want to consider using the services of a trustee or a brokerage firm wrap account. These arrangements are generally more expensive than mutual funds, but the additional services that come with them can justify the additional fees.

The one basis on which you *shouldn't* choose a vehicle is that "they have better investments than the others." Animal crackers are animal crackers—they come in five basic flavors. The animal crackers you find in one box really aren't going to be very different from the same flavor of animal crackers you find in another company's box.

19
CHAPTER

We'll Have Funds, Funds, Funds Till Daddy Takes the T-Bird Away

Choosing the right mutual funds for your portfolio.

So, where are we, and where are we going? By this time you should have fixed your mix, which was the most important part of investing. As we have said repeatedly, it determines 90 percent of your investment performance.

You should also have decided what vehicle you plan to use for your investments. For most people, the vehicle of choice will probably be mutual funds. They may be funds in a company savings plan, they may be funds in an IRA account, or they may be after-tax funds. Now the time has come to choose the funds in which to invest.

THE STARTING POINT

The starting point in picking funds is your *asset allocation*, the mix you selected earlier. Let's say, for example, you decided to use Portfolio 30, *The Jogger*. Your mix will look like Figure 19–1.

All we have so far is a pie chart. To get anywhere, we have to select funds to fill each of the slots in the portfolio. We need:

FIGURE 19-1

Asset Allocation for Portfolio 30

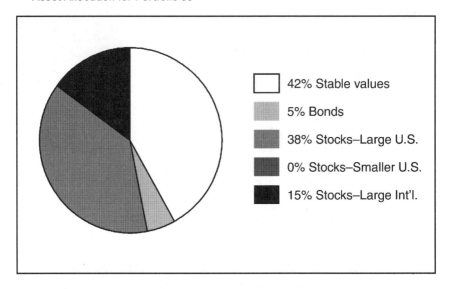

42% Stable values

5% Bonds

38% Stocks–Large U.S.

0% Stocks–Smaller U.S.

15% Stocks–Large Int'l.

- A stable value fund, to which we will allocate 42 percent of our investments
- A bond fund, to which we will allocate 5 percent
- A large U.S. stock fund, to which we will allocate 38 percent
- A large international stock fund, to which we will allocate 15 percent

INVESTING WITH STYLE

Now that we have defined the slots we need to fill, we will go about the task of finding funds to fill those slots. The usual procedure for picking mutual funds is to find those that have performed particularly well compared to similar funds. Oddly enough, that's not the way most professionals go about it. Instead, they look at something called *investment style*. Experience has shown that approach is far more effective at making sure our return will be as predictable as we can make it.

Why not simply use return? Well, if I am a fund manager, the easiest way to improve my performance relative to similar funds is to take more risk than they do. We saw in Chapter 2 that, by cranking up the risk in my fund's portfolio, I can crank up the return. And we saw in the *Star* portfolios what happens to riskier portfolios when the market turns really ugly. So, if all I am looking at is performance, I'm liable to end up on a black diamond when I thought I was simply over the hump!

We can easily adjust the fund's return to account for risk taken by the manager. But that alone won't solve the problem. Suppose I select a fund that was in large stocks last year, small stocks the year before that, and is in bonds this year. How do I know whether I am jogging or skydiving? And even if I know what I am doing this year, how can I tell what I am going to be doing next year, or next week?

That sort of opportunistic investing used to be very popular, and it remains so in some quarters. (So-called hedge funds often pursue a strategy of investing wherever opportunity seems the greatest. Some hedge funds have been quite successful. But, because of their risk, they are recommended for skydivers only.) But it makes a hash of the *Star* strategy of controlling risk, and it destroys whatever level of predictability we have. It takes us back to the realm of gambling, and of luck. To deal with these issues, academics and investment professionals have come up with a variety of tools to measure a fund's style and the consistency of its style.

THE ELEMENTS OF STYLE

There are a number of different definitions of *investment style*. We will use the definitions suggested by Morningstar, Inc., a leading analyst of mutual funds. Morningstar data are readily available to the public through publications such as the *Morningstar 500* (discussed later in this chapter) and through online services.

Morningstar doesn't include stable value funds in its mutual fund "universe." And the whole idea of style isn't terribly relevant to stable values, anyway. The fact that stable values are very liquid, low-return investments renders style analysis superfluous.

- *Bonds.* Funds are grouped by the length of the bonds in which they invest (short, intermediate, and long), and the credit quality of the bonds (high, medium, and low). These factors are arranged on a two-dimensional grid, as shown in Figure 19–2. For example, the fund shown in Figure 19–2 invests in high-quality, long-term bonds.

FIGURE 19–2

Fixed-Income (Bonds) Style Box

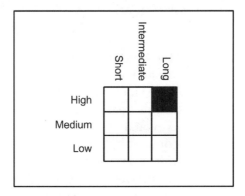

- *Stocks.* Stocks are grouped by the size of the company (large, medium, and small) and the manager's approach (growth, blend, and value). These factors are also arranged on a two-dimensional grid, as shown in Figure 19–3. For example, the fund shown in Figure 19–3 invests in medium-sized, growth and value companies.

Yes, we argued in Chapter 3 that the Great Growth versus Value Debate amounts to angels dancing on the head of a pin, yet here it is again. Growth versus value certainly has less of an impact

FIGURE 19–3

Equity (Stocks) Style box

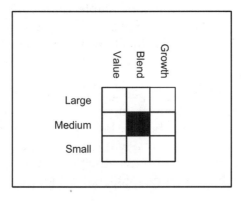

on long-term returns than, say, stocks versus bonds. Still, we can get a better picture of a manager's consistency by seeing whether a fund sticks to one or another or jumps around.

REVENGE OF THE NUMBER CRUNCHERS

Style boxes can be very useful in identifying a fund's style. We'll see later in the chapter that we can use style boxes for each year over the past decade or so to determine whether a manager has been true to its style. But as useful as style boxes are, they are at best an approximation, a rough estimate of a fund's consistency.

Long before style boxes came into vogue, number crunchers had come up with a statistic that does a remarkably good job of measuring style consistency. It's called *r squared,* and it measures the degree to which a fund's return is attributable to a particular index or a combination of indexes. (*Real* number crunchers call it the *coefficient of determination.*) An *r* squared of 0.00 would mean no part of a fund's return can be explained by the market. An *r* squared of 1.00 means 100 percent of a fund's return is determined by the market.

Let's use two funds as examples:

- The first fund is the *Vanguard Index 500* fund, which is designed to mirror the performance of the Standard & Poor's 500 Index. This fund has an *r* squared of 1.00, which makes sense since the fund is supposed to do just what the index does.

- The second fund is the *Centurion Tactical Asset Allocation Fund.* (We aren't trying to pick on this fund or say that it's a bad fund. What we will say is that it's just about as unpredictable as a fund can get.) Its strategy is to move around between different asset classes in order to take advantage of market opportunities. The index that comes closest to "fitting" the fund is a long-term U.S. Treasury Index, and even at that, the fund has an *r* squared of only 0.16. The performance of this fund is not at all predictable relative to any one market or type of investment.

If one is trying to fill a large U.S. stock slot in a portfolio, which choice would give the investor more control over risk? Obviously the first fund. We're not saying it's a *better* fund, only that it will make it easier to control risk. And we don't mean that index funds are the best choices simply because they have high r squared values. But, generally speaking, the higher a fund's r squared, the more consistent and predictable that fund is likely to be.

HOW IMPORTANT IS THE MANAGER?

So far, we haven't said the first word about the manager of the fund. Conventional wisdom says that an investor should carefully consider a fund manager's background and experience. And that's good advice. But the role of the manager is often overemphasized in the popular press, and even in some of the professional literature. It's not that the manager isn't important, far from it. A fund's manager is the person responsible for charting a steady course through stormy waters. However, the emphasis on management turnover at mutual funds has fostered a cult of guruism. Is the new manager a genius, or a dolt? Years ago mutual funds began promoting their most successful investment managers as their firm's "stars." But stars don't generate returns; the market generates returns, a point that has been the basic theme of this book from the beginning. Over 90 percent of your risk and return is generated by how you allocate your investments among the basic asset classes.

Does that mean the manager is irrelevant? Not at all. Frequent management changes at a fund can mean frequent changes in direction. That's not good if consistency is important. That's one of the reasons why a number of large mutual fund companies have abandoned their star system in favor of a team approach to managing funds. If one of the managers on the team leaves or is reassigned, the remaining members can continue managing the fund without disruption or a change in direction.

What impact should a change in managers have on your consideration of a fund?

- First, look to see if the fund has had a consistent style in the past. Use the style boxes and the r squared in the fund's *Morningstar* profile to decide how consistently the fund has followed a style.[1]

---

1 *Morningstar* profiles are explained later in the chapter.

- Second, look to see if an individual or a team has managed the fund. Team-managed portfolios are less susceptible to style disruption when a manager leaves.
- Finally, look to see what the fund company has said recently about the direction of the fund. Often a fund company will make it clear that a change in direction is coming before it puts it into place.

If a fund has shown consistency in the past, and if there are no indications that a change of direction is in the wind, there is no reason why a change in the fund's manager should disqualify a fund from consideration.

MUTUAL FUND FEES AND EXPENSES

A few years ago, a mutual fund broker with whom I was having lunch said, "Do you know what's the greatest thing about this business? None of the customers have any idea what they are paying in fees!"

Sadly, that's pretty much the case. At 401k investment seminars, participants are sometimes shocked to learn they are paying investment management fees. Many assume their employer pays the fees. In the vast majority of cases, these expenses are borne by the employees, along with the administrative expenses of the plan.

Some employees have brought their savings plan account statements forward after a seminar and demanded to know where on the statement these fees and expenses are shown. Try as you may, you will never find them on your statement because they are not there.

Management fees and expenses, along with some sales charges, are deducted from the earnings of the fund before those earnings are ever credited to your account. (The sales charges are called *12b-1 fees*, and they are being adopted by an increasing number of mutual fund companies.) If your large U.S. stock fund earns 10 percent and the management fee is 1 percent, then 9 percent is credited to your account. If your fund *loses* 10 percent, then 11 percent is deducted from your account. Management fees aren't charged as a percentage of the fund's income. They are charged as a percentage of the total amount invested. Win or lose, the manager still takes its fee.

Mutual fund fees are notoriously difficult to decipher. To make the job easier, mutual funds are required to include an *expense ratio* in their funds' prospectuses. The expense ratio tallies up all the fees and expenses charged to the fund as a percentage. You can find a fund's expense ratio by looking in its prospectus, under *"Fees,"* or you can find the expense ratio in a *Morningstar* or similar profile. We will show you how to do that later.

CHOOSING FUNDS IN A COMPANY SAVINGS PLAN

For most investors in company savings plans, the job of selecting funds is pretty easy. As we said in the last chapter, many savings plans offer one fund in each of the five basic asset classes. If your plan is like that, then you need to simply identify which fund belongs to which asset class, then fill out your investment election form or call the service center and tell them how you want to allocate your savings.

Some plans offer more than one fund in a particular asset class. As we said in the last chapter, savings plans sometimes offer two large U.S. stock funds. If that's the case, then how do you choose between them? Here are some suggestions and guidelines:

- Read the fund descriptions to see how the two funds differ. For example, savings plans often offer a growth and income fund along with a fund that invests 100 percent in large U.S. stocks. A *growth and income fund* invests *most* of its assets in large U.S. stocks, but it holds up to 20 percent of its investments in stable values or bonds. The stable value and bond holdings are intended make the fund a bit less aggressive than other stock funds. But a growth and income fund duplicates part of what you have already done in fixing your mix, so you are probably better off picking a fund that invests only in large U.S. stocks. In that case, you are probably better off with the 100 percent stock fund.
- Sometimes plans offer an actively managed fund and an index fund. (An *actively managed fund* is one in which the fund manager attempts to outperform an investment market by selecting investments that achieve above-average performance. Most active managers of large U.S. stock funds have failed to beat the market in recent history, which has led to the current popularity of index funds. An

index fund is one in which the manager buys all stocks in a particular market index. The strategy virtually guarantees the fund will perform as well as the market, neither outperforming it nor underperforming it to any significant degree. These funds are popular because they have outperformed most active managers in recent years and because the investment management fees for these funds are generally a fraction of what active managers charge for their services.) If that's the case, then the index fund will usually have the lower fees. If you believe the manager of the active fund can consistently beat the market by enough to justify its higher fees, then the actively managed fund may make sense. Otherwise, you are probably better off with the index fund. (Index funds consistently beat most active managers of large U.S. stocks, but the same cannot be said of other asset classes. For example, active managers of small U.S. stocks have a much better track record against their indexes, as do managers of international stock funds.)

If all else fails and you simply can't decide between two funds, simply split your stock allocation between them. Remember that 90 percent of your performance comes from the asset class, not the specific fund.

LIFESTYLE FUNDS

An increasing number of savings plans now offer so-called lifestyle funds. These funds are similar to the *Star* portfolios—they are mixes of different asset classes. The mixes generally range from conservative to aggressive, much as the *Star* portfolios do, and they are sometimes accompanied by explanations of the type of person for whom they are considered appropriate. Figure 19–4 shows an example of a lifestyle fund array.

If your savings plan offers lifestyle funds, they may be a good choice for you. Lifestyle funds can make your investment election easier, and they can reduce the chores involved in maintaining your portfolio. But here are some things to watch out for in lifestyle funds:

- Check the funds' fees very carefully. Lifestyle funds are often more expensive than funds that invest in single asset

FIGURE 19-4

Lifestyle Fund Example

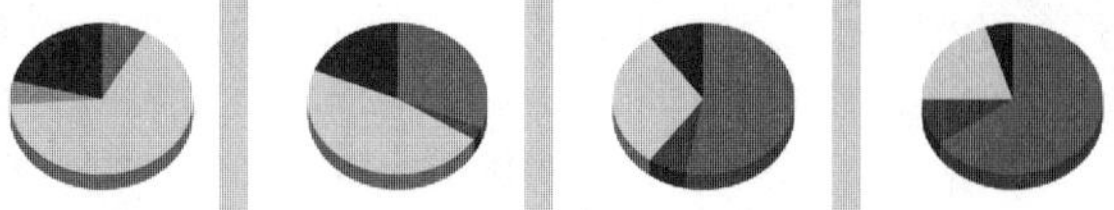

	Young and Single	Married with Children	College Bound	Ready to Retire
Stable values	8	31	53	65
Bonds	0	3	7	10
Stocks - large U.S.	66	47	30	20
Stocks - smaller U.S.	5	0	0	0
Stocks - large Int'l.	21	19	10	5

classes. You pay fees to the stock and bond managers in the fund, and then you pay another fee to a manager who maintains the mix. (As we mentioned earlier, you never actually see these fees since they are deducted from the funds' earnings before they are credited to your account.)

• If the funds have names that suggest the sort of investor for whom they might be suitable, take the names with a grain of salt. For example, you may be young and single but if you have a low Ouch Factor, you might find a portfolio made up of 92 percent stocks far too aggressive for your tastes.

• Some lifestyle funds switch their mixes around in an attempt to time the market.[2] That hasn't been a very successful strategy for these funds, and you are probably better off avoiding funds that do so.

Some funds have *year labels* instead of the lifestyle labels shown in Figure 19–4. For example, the funds might be named (from left to right) *The 2030 Fund, The 2020 Fund, The 2010 Fund,* and *The 2000 Fund.* The idea behind the names is that each fund is considered most appropriate for individuals retiring in that year. If you are 30 years

---

2 Funds that do so are called *tactical asset allocation funds.* See that entry in the glossary for more information.

old (and planning to retire around 2030), the theory goes, the 2030 Fund would be best for you. Again, take these names with a grain of salt. The 2030 Fund might be too aggressive for your tastes, and you might not leave your money in the plan until retirement. For example, what would happen if you needed to borrow from the fund to pay for a child's college education? As you have seen from the earlier chapters of the book, there is a lot more to fixing your mix than making a mechanical choice based on your age.

If your plan offers lifestyle funds, if they stick with their mix, and if their fees are reasonable, there is no reason not to use them. Compare the percentages of the *Star* portfolio you selected (or your own percentages) to the percentages in each lifestyle fund. If one of the lifestyle funds comes close to your own mix, then it's probably a good fit. But if your mix falls between two lifestyle funds, you are probably better off allocating your investments to your savings plan's asset class funds rather than its lifestyle funds.

DOES YOUR SAVINGS PLAN DO WINDOWS?

No, we aren't talking about computers. Some savings plans have begun to offer mutual fund "windows" in the past couple of years. The idea is illustrated in Figure 19–5. A savings plan with a window arrangement typically offers a set of *core funds,* which often corresponds to the five basic asset classes. In addition, the plan offers a sixth fund, which is a window into a mutual fund family designated by the plan. Participants can elect to allocate part of their savings to the window. If they do so, they contact the mutual fund company directly and tell them how they want their window allocation spread among the fund company's funds.

If your plan offers a mutual fund window, and if you prefer investing in name-brand mutual funds, then you will probably find a window option very attractive. But remember what we said about animal crackers in the last chapter—other than coming in five flavors (the five basic asset classes), there isn't as much difference among funds as mutual fund marketers would have us believe. So, before you make a beeline to jump through the window, compare the fees on your plan's core funds with those of the funds offered through the window. In many cases, the core funds are much less expensive, and they offer performance equal to or better than the window funds.

FIGURE 19–5

A Mutual Fund Window Arrangement

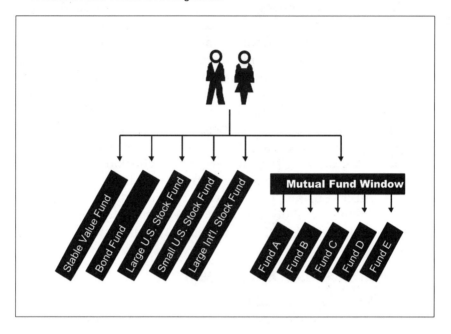

FINDING THE NEEDLE IN THE HAYSTACK

What if you don't have a company savings plan? In that case, the job of picking funds is a little more involved. No one has selected a half-dozen or so funds to choose from. You have to come up with the funds yourself.

The job is actually a lot easier than it sounds. In the rest of this chapter, we are going to walk you through a step-by-step process you can use to select the right funds for your portfolio. It starts at your local library. They have a number of resources you can use to pick a fund. We will cover two of them here:

- *The Individual Investor's Guide to Low-Load Mutual Funds*, published by the American Association of Individual Investors

- Various publications from Morningstar, Inc., such as *The Morningstar 500*

Both publications are also available at bookstores, and both publishers offer computerized versions of their information.

USING THE LOW-LOAD GUIDE

The Individual Investor's Guide to Low-Load Mutual Funds used to be called "The Guide to *No-Load* Mutual Funds."[3] With the advent of 12b-1 fees and other sales charges that get buried in management fees, the American Association of Individual Investors has changed the title to more accurately reflect the sales charges imposed by many funds that were formerly no-load.

The low-load guide contains tables that group different funds by category and performance. For example, one of its tables ranks small-stock funds by their annual returns. The tables can be helpful in narrowing down the list of prospective funds in a particular category, but don't take them as gospel. Since all they show is return, they don't provide a complete picture of a fund's performance. As we saw earlier, it is all to easy to crank up return by cranking up risk.

The second part of the low-load guide contains profiles of over 850 no-load and low-load funds. The guide is also available as a computer program for MS-DOS and Windows-based systems.

Figure 19–6 shows a sample page from the guide. We show the page for the *Vanguard Index 500* fund, a popular index fund that tracks the S&P 500. Here is how to use the guide to narrow down your search:

A. *Name and address.* The name, address, phone number, and Internet address of the fund's parent company is shown at the top of the page.

B. *Inception date.* The fund's inception date is shown next. As a general rule, the longer a fund has been around, the better. You should look only at funds that have at least a 3-year track record.

C. *Return.* The next section shows the return history of the fund. The 3-, 5-, and 10-year returns are less informative than the "bull" and "bear" returns. These items show the

---

3   American Association of Individual Investors, 625 North Michigan Avenue, Chicago, IL 60611; (800) 428-2244.

FIGURE 19-6

A Sample Page from the *AAII Low-Load Fund Guide*

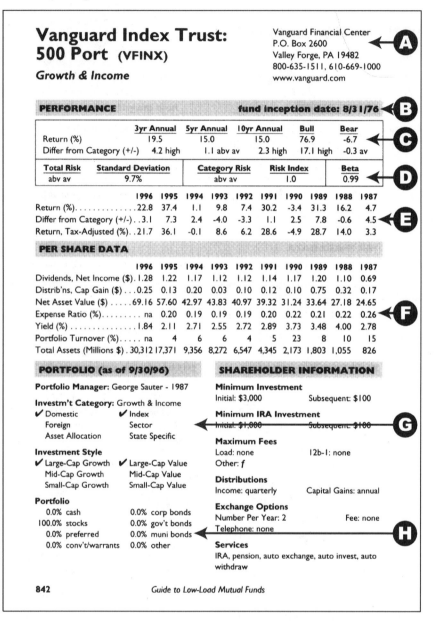

	3yr Annual	5yr Annual	10yr Annual	Bull	Bear
Return (%)	19.5	15.0	15.0	76.9	-6.7
Differ from Category (+/-)	4.2 high	1.1 abv av	2.3 high	17.1 high	-0.3 av

Total Risk	Standard Deviation	Category Risk	Risk Index	Beta
abv av	9.7%	abv av	1.0	0.99

	1996	1995	1994	1993	1992	1991	1990	1989	1988	1987
Return (%)	22.8	37.4	1.1	9.8	7.4	30.2	-3.4	31.3	16.2	4.7
Differ from Category (+/-)	3.1	7.3	2.4	-4.0	-3.3	1.1	2.5	7.8	-0.6	4.5
Return, Tax-Adjusted (%)	21.7	36.1	-0.1	8.6	6.2	28.6	-4.9	28.7	14.0	3.3

PER SHARE DATA

	1996	1995	1994	1993	1992	1991	1990	1989	1988	1987
Dividends, Net Income ($)	1.28	1.22	1.17	1.12	1.12	1.14	1.17	1.20	1.10	0.69
Distrib'ns, Cap Gain ($)	0.25	0.13	0.20	0.03	0.10	0.12	0.10	0.75	0.32	0.17
Net Asset Value ($)	69.16	57.60	42.97	43.83	40.97	39.32	31.24	33.64	27.18	24.65
Expense Ratio (%)	na	0.20	0.19	0.19	0.19	0.20	0.22	0.21	0.22	0.26
Yield (%)	1.84	2.11	2.71	2.55	2.72	2.89	3.73	3.48	4.00	2.78
Portfolio Turnover (%)	na	4	6	6	4	5	23	8	10	15
Total Assets (Millions $)	30,312	17,371	9,356	8,272	6,547	4,345	2,173	1,803	1,055	826

fund's return under favorable and unfavorable market conditions. They are analogous to the asset class ranges we looked at earlier in the book, and they can give a pretty good idea of the earnings range you might expect from a fund.

D. *Risk.* The next line gives different measures of the fund's risk. *Total Risk* shows how the fund compares to all other funds in the book, and *Category Risk* shows how the fund compares to other funds in the same category.[4] The *Risk Index* is simply the ratio of the fund's risk to the average risk of the category. It's a numerical version of the *Category Risk* item. We discussed *Beta* in Chapter 2, and we will return to it in the next chapter. The low-load guide's beta has limited usefulness. The Standard & Poor's 500 Index is used to calculate every stock's beta. The S&P 500 is a useful index for measuring large U.S. stock funds (like the Vanguard Index 500), but it's far less useful for smaller and international stocks. The guide doesn't calculate a beta for bonds.

E. *Year-by-year returns.* The next section of the profile shows a year-by-year return history for the fund and a comparison of its returns to similar funds. The thing to look for here is consistency. If a fund outperforms the category one year and underperforms it the next, the manager probably isn't following a consistent strategy.

F. *Year-by-year expenses.* The next section shows various pieces of information on the same year-by-year basis as the returns. The guide explains all the items, but the most important by far is the *expense ratio.* It is with this figure that the mutual fund industry discloses what you are being charged for the management of your investments. (See the discussion later in the chapter for more information.)

---

4   Categories can be somewhat confusing in the AAII guide, because they use a classification system based on mutual fund objectives, rather than asset classes. Appendix C, "Types of Mutual Funds," shows the standard investment objective categories used by mutual funds and the corresponding asset classes.

G. *Investment category and style.* At the bottom of the page, the fund is classified in an investment category. These categories are used by the mutual fund industry. Just below that, the *Investment Style* section shows the type of investments made by the fund. These style categories generally correspond to the asset classes we used to build the *Star* portfolios.

H. *Holdings.* At the bottom of the page, in the *Portfolio* section, the profile shows the composition of the fund's investments. For example, the fund in Figure 19–6 is classified as a growth and income fund, but about 95 percent of its assets are invested in stocks. That makes the fund a bit more aggressive than the typical growth and income fund, but it might be suitable for an investor looking for a fund that keeps nearly all its assets invested in stocks.

The low-load guide can be a good resource to use in narrowing down your search. Its chief drawbacks are:

- Its fund groupings are based on the mutual fund industry's investment objective classification system, which is less helpful than style or asset class in choosing funds.
- The way that it calculates betas limits their usefulness in evaluating the performance of a fund.

Those shortcomings are addressed in our next resource, the *Morningstar Reports.*

USING MORNINGSTAR PROFILES

Morningstar reports come in several different packages:

- Morningstar publishes a monthly loose-leaf newsletter titled *Morningstar Mutual Funds.* It covers several thousand mutual funds in the profile format shown in Figure 19–7. The newsletter service may be purchased from Morningstar, Inc.,[5] and it is available in the reference section of many local libraries.

---

5   Morningstar, Inc., 225 West Wacker Drive, Chicago, IL 60606; (800) 735-0700.

FIGURE 19-7

A Sample *Morningstar* Profile

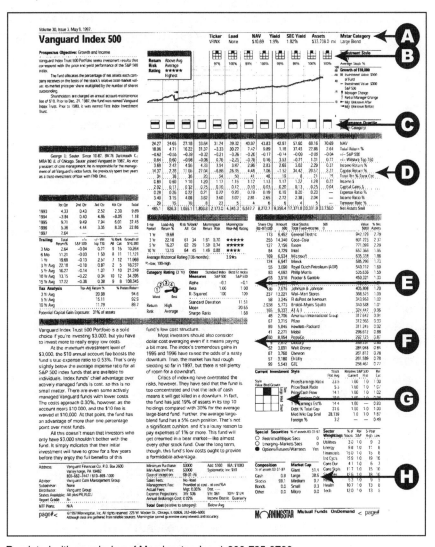

Reprinted with permission of Morningstar, Inc. 1-800-735-0700.

- Morningstar publishes an annual compilation of the 500 top-performing mutual funds titled *The Morningstar 500*. It is available at most bookstores around February of each year, and it sells for about $35.[6] The book is a subset of *Morningstar Mutual Funds;* the profile format is the same as that shown in Figure 19–7.
- Morningstar publishes a Windows software program titled *Morningstar Principia.* The program covers Morningstar's full database of over 8,000 mutual funds and allows the investors to screen funds on over 100 factors. The *Principia Plus* version of the program also includes profiles of the sort shown in Figure 19–7.
- Morningstar maintains several online areas. On America Online, type the keyword "morningstar" to go to the Morningstar area of the service. Morningstar also maintains a World Wide Web site at www.morningstar.net. The Web site contains fund profiles with all the information described in this chapter and the next, but they are in a slightly different format than Figure 19–7.

Morningstar's publications are organized in a manner similar to the low-load guide. The first part of each publication contains rankings, and the second part of the book contains profiles. Since the format is similar across publications, we will refer to them simply as "*Morningstar.*" A sample *Morningstar* profile is shown in Figure 19–7. Again, we have used the popular Vanguard Index 500 fund as our sample profile.

Here is how to use *Morningstar* to narrow down your search:

A. *Morningstar category.* Morningstar uses the style-based categories we looked at earlier, rather than the mutual fund industry's investment objective categories. The sample fund we have shown in Figure 19–7 invests in large stocks, using a value approach. Use this box to identify the type of fund.

---

6 A monthly newsletter, *Morningstar Investor,* updates the book and contains articles of general interest to mutual fund investors. It is available by subscription from Morningstar, Inc.

B. *Style history.* The Morningstar page shows a history of the fund's style. The history is shown in a series of year-by-year style boxes. You can use this box to decide whether a fund has been true to its style. The style history in Figure 19–7 shows that the Vanguard Index 500 has consistently invested in large U.S. stocks, both growth and value. We would expect no less of a fund designed to mirror the Standard & Poor's 500 Index.

C. *Performance quartile.* The boxes below the line chart show how the fund has fared against its peers over the past several years. The horizontal line in this box shows whether the fund's return was in the top, second, third, or last quarter of its group. The Vanguard Index 500 suffered relative to its peers in 1990, but it has turned in consistently strong performance since 1994.

D. *Historical data.* The table below the performance boxes shows several pieces of information on a year-by-year basis. The most important items in the table are the fund's returns and its expense ratio. The trend of the expense ratio will show you whether the fund is becoming more expensive (as seems to be the case with most funds) or is holding the line on fees and expenses. You can compare the fund with others you are considering by looking at the most recent expense ratio of each.

E. *Other measures.* Morningstar calculates a beta and an alpha for each stock fund in the book. Like the low-load guide, Morningstar calculates a *beta* based on the Standard & Poor's 500 Index. As we said earlier, that's a useful benchmark for large U.S. stocks, but it doesn't provide as meaningful data for other types of stock, or for bonds. So Morningstar calculates a second beta, based on whatever major index is the best fit to the fund. You will also find the fund's alpha and its *r* squared in this table; the *Best Fit Index* column provides the most useful information. The *alpha* statistic indicates whether the manager has added value, and you can use the *r* squared statistic as a measure of the fund's consistency. (If the alpha is positive, the fund earned more than would be predicted by the markets and the fund's risk. Many

experts interpret a positive alpha as "value added" by the
manager, additional return that the fund generated
without additional risk. Others argue that positive alphas
are illusory. See Chapter 2.)

F. *Analysis.* Morningstar provides a short commentary on
the performance of the fund, any changes in its
management, and its current direction. This analysis can
provide useful insights into a fund's past and current
performance.

G. *Style box.* This box shows the fund's style as of the time
the report is published. Next to the box, there is a table
that shows various characteristics of the fund's portfolio
relative to the market as a whole.

H. *Composition.* This table shows how the fund's
investments are allocated among stocks, bonds, and cash.
It also shows the size companies in which the fund
invests.

MAKING THE CUT

The best way to go about choosing your funds is to go through
Morningstar, the low-load guide, or some similar resource, and
compile a list of a half-dozen or so funds for each slot you need to
fill in your portfolio. The fund rankings are a good place to start.
Look for funds with good performance over the past 5 years or so.

Once you have identified your half-dozen or so candidates for
each slot, look at each fund's profile. Weed out inconsistent funds or
funds whose styles don't seem to fit the slot well. Also, make sure
the amount you plan to invest when you open the account meets the
fund company's minimums. You should be able to narrow the list
down to two or three contenders for each slot.

Finally, look at the expense ratios for each fund. Funds with
lower expense ratios will make you more money, all other things
being equal, since less goes to the manager and more goes to your
account for reinvestment. If one contender's expense ratio is significantly lower than the others' are, then that fund may be the logical
selection. If the contenders' expense ratios are all pretty close, then
you will have a couple of finalists to choose from.

What if different fund companies offer the finalists for different slots? You have a couple of alternatives. You can certainly select funds from different companies, such as a large U.S. stock fund from Vanguard and an international fund from American Funds. But, as we will see in Chapter 21, dealing with different fund companies can be a hassle when the time comes to transfer money between funds.

Many major brokerage houses offer "one-stop shopping" for funds from different "families." Money can be transferred between funds with a single phone call to the broker. Charles Schwab & Co. offers the best-known program, under the name *Schwab OneSource.* Schwab offers no-load funds under this program, so you don't get stuck paying up-front sales commissions. (However, many funds in the program charge 12b-1 fees, which are sales charges added on to the fund's management fees and expenses.)

If you prefer to buy your funds from a single mutual fund company, then let the largest slot in your portfolio determine your choice. If your largest allocation is to large U.S. stocks, and if you have a strong candidate for that slot, look at other funds offered by the same mutual fund company for the other slots in the portfolio. You may find funds that are nearly as strong as the other candidates you previously identified.

PULLING THE TRIGGER

Once you have decided which funds you want to use, call the mutual fund company's or the brokerage firm's toll-free number. Their customer service representatives will send you the paperwork you need to complete to open your account. Once the paperwork is done, return it to the mutual fund company with a check for your initial investment. Then call the toll-free number a few days later to confirm that the fund company or broker received your money and invested it as you directed.

Once you have done all that, you can breathe easy for a while. Unless, or course, the market drops the day after you make your investment. *Murphy's first law of investing* says it will.

20 CHAPTER

Changing the Oil

Evaluating the performance of your funds and deciding if changes are needed.

Once you have fixed your mix and picked the funds to fill the slots in your portfolio, you don't need to do a whole lot to keep things on track. "Pick and stick" is the slogan for the *Star* approach to investing. But there are certain things you will still need to do. "Pick and stick" doesn't mean "set and forget."

A portfolio is a lot like a car. It needs to have the oil changed periodically to keep it running smoothly. That doesn't mean you take it into the shop every 3 months for an engine overhaul. You don't do that unless there is definitely something wrong with your car. But even when the car is running well, we all know it needs routine maintenance.

This chapter is about performing routine maintenance on your investment portfolio—a 3,000-mile checkup, as it were. Many of us aren't as good as we should be about getting our cars serviced regularly. It's one of those things, like flossing our teeth, we know we should do but often don't.

One of the greatest benefits of the *Star* system is that it does little harm if you miss an oil change or two. Let's face it, if you change the oil next month instead of this month, your car isn't going to fall apart. But if you *never* change the oil, your car probably won't last as long as you expect it to. Your investments won't fall apart either if you let them go for a time. But you will still need to sit down with them for some routine maintenance every once in a while, just to make sure they still have at least one-eighth-inch tread left on the tires.

FLAVOR OF THE MONTH

One of the companies I worked with recently considered whether to add additional investment options to its 401k plan. One of the members of the plan committee was reluctant to do so. "I think it may be more trouble than it's worth," he said. "It seems like every time I sit down with my financial planner, I'm 6 months behind the times, and I have to change everything."

Welcome to the Flavor of the Month Club, where we specialize in chasing the latest and greatest investment fads. (Also known as the "Churn 'em and Burn 'em Club." *Churning* is the practice of encouraging clients to buy and sell frequently, in order to increase brokerage commissions. The practice is frowned upon by most brokers, and in some cases is downright illegal.) If large U.S. stocks underperformed large international stocks in the past 3 months, dump the U.S. and go international! Or if your large U.S. stock fund underperformed the Hi-Flyer Large Cap Equity Fund for 3 months running, dump your dog and jump on the Hi-Flyer bandwagon!

Both of those examples may seem a bit silly, but they happen every day. Investing isn't a horse race. Well, maybe it is a horse race, but it's a very long one. Three months isn't nearly long enough to make a judgment about how your investments are doing. Three *years* is more like it.

"But if I let my investments go 3 years and something goes wrong, I'm likely to end up in a very deep hole," you might say. Probably not. Remember, the asset mix determines over 90 percent of your performance. Unless you did a particularly bad job of picking your fund in the first place, your performance won't be that far off the market.

Besides, we aren't saying you should wait 3 years to monitor your portfolio. You should probably do it at least once a year, every 3 or 6 months if a fund isn't performing the way it is supposed to. Some people feel more secure if they check their performance every month. If it makes you feel better, then, by all means, go for it! But you probably won't come up with very much information that's useful.

WHAT ARE WE MEASURING, ANYWAY?

New investors often assume that if the value of their investments is going up, they are doing well, and if the value is going down, they're not. Nothing could be further from the truth. Consider the following:

- The value of your large U.S. stock fund went down 5 percent last year, but the stock market went down 12 percent. You actually did pretty well.
- The value of your large U.S. stock fund went up 10 percent this year, but the stock market went up 18 percent. You didn't do so well.

It's not a question of whether your funds went up or down. The market is the rising tide that lifts all boats, and all boats do down when the tide goes out. The important question is: *How did your portfolio perform relative to the market?*

"Okay," you say. "If I go down less than the market when it's down, and if I go up more than the market when it's up, then I am doing well." That would be a neat trick, if you could pull it off consistently. (And if you can, Fidelity Funds is always on the lookout for portfolio management talent for its flagship Magellan Fund. But Peter Lynch, who ran the fund during its glory years, never did it and said he didn't think anyone could.)

BACK TO BETA

In Chapter 2, we looked at *beta,* one of the number crunchers' favorite statistics. A fund's beta tells us how risky a fund is compared to the market. A beta of 1.0 means a fund is just as risky as the market. When the market goes up 5 percent, the fund will go up 5 percent. And when the market is down 5 percent, so is the fund.

A beta greater than 1.0 means the fund is riskier than the market. Take the example of a stock fund with a beta of 1.2. That means it is 120 percent as risky as the market. When the market is up 5 percent, the fund should be up 6 percent (5 percent × 1.2). [The number crunchers have asked (insisted, actually) that we offer a disclaimer at this point. For the sake of clarity, we have oversimplified the process just a bit. Later, we will add one other step, which involves the *risk-free rate,* to make a more accurate measurement.] And when the market is down to –5 percent, the fund should be down to –6 percent. The fund goes up higher than the

How a Fund with a Beta Greater Than 1.0 Performs

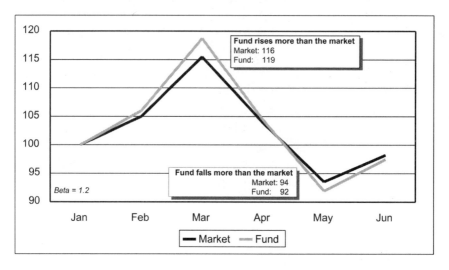

market, and falls lower than the market, as well. Figure 20–1 shows this relationship.

By the same token, a beta less than 1.0 means the fund is less risky than the market. When the market is up, the fund will be up, too; just not quite as high. When the market drops, the fund will drop, too; only not quite so far. For example, a fund with a beta of 0.8 is only 80 percent as risky as the market. When the market is up 5 percent, the fund will rise only 4 percent. And when the market drops 5 percent, the fund will only drop 4 percent. Figure 20–2 shows that relationship.

In short, if a fund outperforms the market on the upside, then it will *under*perform the market on the downside. Put another way, if I want a fund that doesn't fall as far as the market during tough times, I have to make a tradeoff—the same fund won't rise as much as the market in good times.

Betas aren't snapshots—they do not measure risk at a specific time. Instead, they are more like movies. They measure a fund's average risk over a *period* of time. For example, Morningstar calculates its betas from the most recent 36-month performance of the fund and the index used to measure its market.

FIGURE 20–2

How a Fund with a Beta of Less Than 1.0 Performs

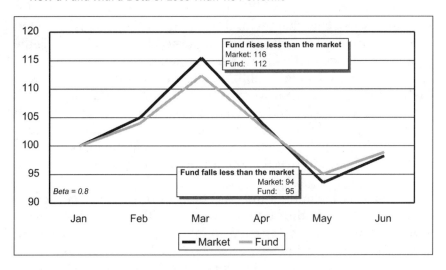

GREAT EXPECTATIONS

So, what *are* we measuring, anyway? We're measuring whether the fund has done *what we expected it to do*. Consider the following examples:

- Last year, George invested in a large U.S. stock fund with a beta of 0.8, because he doesn't want to fall as far as the market when it goes down. He accepts the tradeoff of not having his fund rise as far as the market when it goes up. Last year the Standard & Poor's 500, our index for large U.S. stocks, rose 10 percent. George's fund went up 12 percent. Is that good news or bad news?
- This year, Martha invested in a stock fund with a beta of 1.2, because she wants to do better than the market in good times. Martha has a long time frame, and she doesn't mind losses. This year, the Standard & Poor's 500 was down 10 percent, but Martha's fund is only down 8 percent. Is that good news or bad news?

(*Note:* In Chapter 2 we discussed the term *alpha*, which some investors use to measure the value added by a fund manager. Many experts argue that in a well-diversified fund, there is very little room for a manager to generate a positive alpha, that alphas "tend toward zero" with increased diversification. We accept that argument for the purposes of this chapter, and we make an implicit assumption that any variance from the return suggested by a fund's beta is the result of a change in the fund's risk characteristics.)

As crazy as it sounds, both pieces of news are potentially bad. Certainly not terrible, but worth a second look. Here's why: With a beta of 0.8, George's fund is what is known as a *defensive fund*. It should have underperformed the stock market last year—it should have been up only 8 percent. The fact that it beat the market means that its manager did *something* that dramatically increased the risk of the fund.

That may mean the fund has changed direction since George bought it. The new direction has increased the fund's beta to 1.2, which means it can be expected to fall further than the market in a correction. It's no longer a defensive fund. George bought the fund for downside protection; upside profits were a secondary goal. George's fund would probably be a better fit for Martha's goals, not his.

Martha's fund is probably a better fit for George than for her. She is concerned primarily with outperforming the market on the upside. That's why she selected a fund with a beta greater than 1.0. It's nice that her fund hasn't fallen as far as the market, but it may signal a change in direction as pronounced as George saw in his fund. That change in direction may make the fund a poor match for Martha's investment objectives.

HOME ON THE RANGE

There is another possibility for George's and Martha's funds, as well. George's manager may have guessed correctly that the market was about to take off, so he or she made a *temporary* change in the fund to take advantage of it. Likewise, the manager of Martha's fund may have guessed correctly that the market was about to drop, and he or she successfully headed for the exits with the fund before it happened.

Both of these moves may sound like shrewd money management, but in the view of many academics and investment professionals, both managers have "gone cowboy." That's not such a good thing to do, which comes as a surprise to many people. "After all," you might say, "isn't that precisely what an investment manager is supposed to do—anticipate changes in the market and act on them?"

That takes us back to Chapter 2. Guessing the next move of the stock market is like guessing the next flip of a coin. I should be able to do it 50 percent of the time, but not more. The most famous "cowboy call" in recent history occurred in February 1996, when the manager of Fidelity's flagship Magellan Fund decided technology stocks were about to go into a steep decline and that bonds were about to soar. He pulled 20 percent of the $56 billion fund out of the stock market and invested it in long-term bonds instead.

Had the markets moved as the manager expected, the switch would have been hailed as audacious and brilliant. Unfortunately, the stock market continued its upward march, and bonds went south instead. The Magellan Fund now has a new manager, one who is more committed to maintaining a consistent style.

Does that mean it's impossible to rise more than the market in good times, but fall less than the market in bad times? "Impossible" might be too strong a word, but both experience and the number crunchers tell us it's very unlikely. Your best bet is to assume that any fund that will rise higher than the market will also fall lower than the market, as well.

BENCHMARKS BY THE BUSHEL

The process we have been looking at is called *benchmarking a fund*. The toughest part of the process is picking an appropriate market index to use as a benchmark. We made it easy in our George and Martha examples. We gave both investors large U.S. stock funds, and that let us use the Standard & Poor's 500 Index as our benchmark. But we can't use the S&P 500 for everything. Our benchmarking needs to compare apples to apples.

For example, it would make no sense to use the S&P 500 to benchmark a bond fund. Bonds behave very differently from large U.S. stocks, so the S&P 500 won't give us any useful information about whether the bond fund is meeting our expectations. By the same token, the S&P 500 is not a very useful benchmark for stable values either.

What about other kinds of stock? The S&P 500 is commonly used to benchmark all kinds of stock, including international stocks and smaller U.S. stocks. Even the AAII low-load guide uses the S&P 500 to calculate small and international stock betas. But that's an apples-to-oranges comparison. Large U.S. stocks and large international stocks behave differently enough that they are considered separate asset classes. Benchmarking needs to be based on a market index for the same type of investments.

It is at least arguable that the S&P 500 is an appropriate index for smaller U.S. stocks. We previously discussed Professor Siegel's contention that smaller U.S. stocks really haven't outperformed large domestic stocks (see Chapter 4). If U.S. stocks, large and small, behave that similarly, then perhaps one index should be used for all of them. But if that's the case, then the S&P 500 may still not be the right index to use. A broader market index that includes smaller stocks would be a better fit.[1]

Table 20–1 shows several market indexes commonly used to benchmark funds in different asset classes. The choice is somewhat subjective—investment professionals argue these points the way barflies argue politics. These indexes have the virtue of being readily available in the financial pages of most newspapers and at a number of sites on the Internet.

When you look up the beta of a fund, make sure the beta was calculated by comparing the fund to an appropriate index. The *Morningstar 500* can make your life easier in this area. Each fund

TABLE 20–1

Indexes Commonly Used for Benchmarking

Asset Class	Index
Stable values	U.S. 3-month Treasury bills
Bonds	Lehman Bros. Government/Corporate Bond Index
Stocks, large U.S.	Standard & Poor's 500 Index
Stocks, smaller U.S.	Russell 2,000 Index
Stocks, large int'l.	MSCI EAFE Index

---

1 Two indexes that are often used by proponents of the all-U.S.-stocks-are-alike approach are the *Russell 3000*, which includes the S&P 500, plus the next 2,500 companies; and the *Wilshire 5000*, which is similar but includes 5,000 companies.

profile contains a beta for the fund. The beta is calculated by comparing the fund to a *best-fit index*—the index that comes the closest to matching the fund's risk and return characteristics. Morningstar also publishes the results for each of these indexes in the summary section of the *Morningstar 500*.

The one type of fund for which you won't find a beta is a stable value fund. Morningstar doesn't include stable value funds in its universe, and neither do most other fund rating services. Your best bet is to use a beta of 1.0 for your stable value fund and compare it to 3-month treasury bill returns.

BUILDING A BETTER YARDSTICK

In the end, what we are measuring is *how well the fund lived up to our expectations*. Obviously, our expectations have to be realistic, or our measurements will be meaningless. The description of beta we have given so far has been intended to explain the concept and how it works. But we need to add another step to make it a truly useful tool for measuring the performance of our investments.

Let's start with what beta is supposed to do: It measures the risk of an investment relative to the risk of the market. To figure that out, we have to be able to measure the risk of the market. We can measure the risk of the market by comparing our market index to a *risk-free rate*. That's the rate on the least risky investment available. Most professionals use the rate on 3-month U.S. Treasury bills as the risk-free rate.

If I subtract the risk-free rate from the market rate, the difference will be equal to what I got paid for taking on the risk of investing in the market. For example, in 1996 the Standard & Poor's 500 earned a return of 23.1 percent. In the same year, 3-month U.S. Treasury bills earned 5.3 percent. Since they could have earned the 5.3 percent rate without any risk, stock market investors were paid 17.8 percent for taking the risk involved in large U.S. stocks. Professionals call this excess a *risk premium*.

We can also calculate the risk premium associated with a fund by subtracting the risk-free rate from its return. Once we have done that, we have the basis for a better yardstick. When we say that Martha's fund has a beta of 1.2, what we are actually saying is that the fund's *risk premium* is 120 percent of the market's risk premium.

That's a subtle difference, but in this one instance it amounts to much more than angels dancing on the head of a pin. If we leave the risk-free rate out of beta, the result understates the true volatility of an investment relative to the market. In other words, it leads to unrealistic expectations.

YOU, TOO, CAN BE A NUMBER CRUNCHER

Let's say you want to benchmark the performance of a fund over the past year. Here are the steps you need to take, using the *Morningstar 500* as your information resource (the approach we are presenting is a version of the *Jensen Performance Index,* which compares a realized return to a risk-adjusted expected return):

Step 1. Select an appropriate market index to use as a benchmark for the fund. Morningstar's recommendation for each fund is shown in the best-fit column of their beta calculation.

Step 2. Look up the returns for the market index and the risk-free rate over the past year. (The 3-month Treasury bill return is the appropriate rate to use in benchmarking with Morningstar data since that's the rate they use to construct their betas.) The *Morningstar 500* includes returns for its market indexes and the risk-free rate in its summary section.

Step 3. Subtract the risk-free rate from the market index return for the past year. That will give you the risk premium for holding that type of investment.

Step 4. Multiply that figure by the fund's beta (the best-fit figure from *Morningstar*). That will give you the *fund's* risk premium.

Step 5. Finally, add *back* the risk-free rate we subtracted earlier to the fund's risk premium. The result is a *target return* that approximates the performance we can expect from the fund during the period we are benchmarking.

Let's benchmark the performance of a popular international fund, the *EuroPacific Growth Fund*. Its Morningstar profile is shown in Figure 20–3.

FIGURE 20-3

Morningstar Profile: EuroPacific Growth Fund

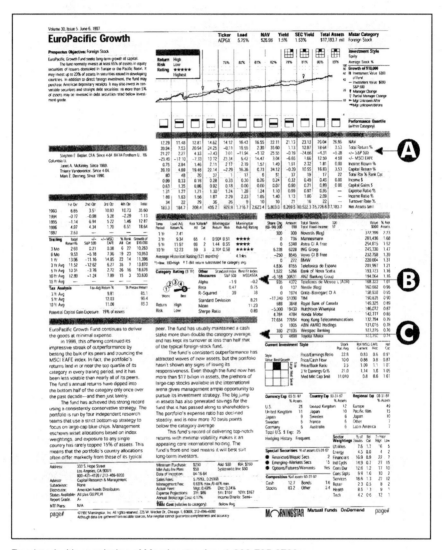

Reprinted with permission of Morningstar, Inc. 1-800-735-0700.

- From the Morningstar profile, we see that the fund earned 18.64 percent in 1996 (see *A* in Figure 20–3).
- We also see that the best-fit index for the fund is the MSEASEA (see *B* in Figure 20–3).[2]
- Finally, we see that the EuroPacific Growth Fund's beta relative to its best-fit index is 0.75 (see *B* in Figure 20–3).
- We turn to the summary section of *Morningstar,* and we find that in 1996, the MSEASEA Index earned 20.96 percent. In the same section, we find that 3-month treasury bills earned 5.02 percent. (We use 3-month treasury bills because that's what *Morningstar* uses to construct their betas. By using the same indexes, we keep our comparisons apples to apples.
- We subtract the 5.02 percent treasury bill rate from the MSEASEA's return of 20.96 percent. The result, 15.94 percent, is what investors earned in 1996 for taking on the risk of investing in large international stocks. (Since we're using the MSEASEA, it actually measures what investors were paid for taking on the risk of investing in international stocks *outside Japan.*) That's our market risk premium.
- We multiply the market risk premium by 0.75, the fund's beta, which gives us 11.96 percent. That's the 1996 risk premium we *expect* to see for taking on the risk of investing in the EuroPacific Growth Fund.
- Finally, we add back the 5.02 percent we subtracted in the second step. The result is our *target return* of 16.98 percent.

Now we simply compare the EuroPacific Growth Fund's actual 1996 return of 18.64 percent to the 16.98 percent we expected of it. We can see that the EuroPacific Growth Fund earned about 1.66 percent *more* in 1996 than we would have expected.

READING THE TEA LEAVES

So, what do we do with our benchmarking results? Let's continue with our EuroPacific Growth Fund example. Based on its beta, we

---

2   The *Morningstar* glossary tells us that the MSEASEA Index is an international index published by Morgan Stanley. It is similar to their widely used EAFE Index except that is excludes Japanese stocks.

had expected the fund to earn about 17.0 percent. We saw that it actually earned about 18.6 percent percent. That tells us the fund was probably a bit riskier in 1996 that it had previously been.

Whether that's good news or bad news depends on what we had expected from the fund. Let's assume we had selected the EuroPacific Growth Fund as a defensive international fund, one that wouldn't be expected to fall in a downturn as far as international stock markets generally. The fund's conservative beta would be expected to "buy" us that protection, at the cost of lower upside potential.

But the fund did better than expected in 1996's "up" market. Does that signal a change in direction for the fund? If it means the fund is moving to a more aggressive posture, we might lose the downside protection we are counting on. It's time for a bit of detective work.

Our first stop should be the fund's Morningstar profile to see if we can figure out whether the 1996 return is an aberration or if the fund really is moving in a more aggressive direction.

The *Analysis* section (see C in Figure 20–3) of the fund's Morningstar profile says that in 1996, the fund "continued it's impressive streak of outperformance by besting the bulk of its peers and trouncing the MSCI EAFE index." That's great, but is it really what I expected from the fund? Given its low beta, it shouldn't turn up at the top of the pack in a bull market.

The analysis continues, "The fund has achieved this strong record using a consistently conservative strategy. . . . [It] has usually maintained a cash stake more than double its category average." That sounds more like the fund I selected. So, how is it performing this well in a bull market? The analysis says the fund "eschews asset allocations based on index weightings, and exposure to any single country has rarely topped 15 percent of assets."

INTERNATIONAL COWBOYS?

That's probably the key. International indexes, such as the EAFE or the EASEA, assume a fund will allocate set percentages of its investments to particular countries in the index. Many managers, including the EuroPacific Growth Fund, don't do that. A quick look at the fund's *r* squared confirms the hunch. It tracks only 78 percent to its best-fit index, which means only 78 percent of the manager's performance can be accounted for by the index. Consequently, the beta isn't quite as reliable as it would be for a manager with a very high r squared.

An r squared of 78 would be pretty low for a large U.S. stock manager. An r squared below 80 would suggest that the manager doesn't follow a consistent style. A *Star* investor should think about replacing such a fund with one that follows a more consistent style.

Turning back to the EuroPacific Growth Fund, does its relatively low r squared mean a cowboy manager is running the fund? Not necessarily. International markets aren't as efficient as the U.S. stock market, and there are many more international stock markets than there are U.S. stock markets. International funds often have lower r squared values than U.S. funds, and an r squared below 80 doesn't necessarily suggest that a fund has "gone cowboy." (The same also holds true for smaller U.S. stocks. Smaller companies are not as widely followed as the largest companies, which leaves a bit more room for a manager to add value.)

OVERREADING THE TEA LEAVES

So where does that leave us? The EuroPacific Growth Fund did perform more as we would have expected from a more aggressive fund, but the Morningstar analysis suggests that its basic characteristics haven't changed. In other words, the signals are mixed. We don't want to overreact to the situation, so our best course of action is to probably take another look at the fund in 6 months to see if the signals are any clearer.

Keep in mind that no fund ever performs *exactly* as the target return would predict. It is only an approximation. There is no cause for alarm if either of the following occurs:

- Your fund is over or under the target return by a relatively small amount, even over a longer period. Investing is like horseshoes and hand grenades—close counts.
- Your fund is over or under the target return by a larger amount, but only for a period or two. Investment managers aren't perfect (but don't tell them that), and even very consistent funds occasionally need to make changes that throw them temporarily out of whack.

In short, don't get worked up about a fund's being off its target unless it is *significantly* off the mark and stays off for several periods.

HOW OFTEN IS TOO OFTEN?

As we said earlier, it doesn't really make sense to benchmark your fund every day. Benchmarking once a month is too often, unless you are seriously lacking for things to do in your life. For most people, even 3 months is probably too often. It's questionable whether you get any useful information out of the exercise, and you will most likely cause yourself to lose at least a few nights' sleep somewhere along the line.

Benchmark your funds once a year. Do it just after the New Year—it feels better than making a list of resolutions, and you don't feel guilty later. If any of your funds looks off-kilter, don't pull the plug just yet. Do some homework first, as we did with the EuroPacific Growth Fund:

- Take another look at the fund's Morningstar profile. Check the mutual fund company's quarterly newsletter. Call their toll-free number and ask for the most recent reports on the fund. There may be a simple explanation for the result.
- Take another look at the fund 3 or 6 months later. Is it moving back toward where you expect, is it moving in the other direction, or is there no clear direction? If the fund isn't moving back toward the kind of performance you expect from it, then it's probably time to start thinking about replacing it.
- But again, don't pull the trigger quite yet unless the fund is so far off its mark as to be alarming. Give it another 3 months before you begin looking for a replacement fund.

Obviously there are exceptions to the rule, extreme cases where the investor should shoot first (managers who have gone seriously cowboy come to mind) and ask questions later. But in most situations, a calm, deliberate approach will serve you far better than an immediate reaction to the most recent 3 months.

BENCHMARKING YOUR PORTFOLIO

We said earlier that we shouldn't use the S&P 500 to benchmark a bond fund. The worst trap we can fall into is trying to benchmark an entire *portfolio* against the S&P 500, or against any market index.

Financial planners get apoplectic when a client compares a 50 percent stock–50 percent bond portfolio against the S&P 500 and then complains that the portfolio fell substantially below the bench-mark. Well, of course it did! The only portfolio the S&P 500 can be used to benchmark is one that's made up 100 percent of large U.S. stocks. Otherwise, the comparison is between apples and a crate of apples, oranges, raspberries, and bananas.

If we want to measure how our portfolio performed, we have to measure it against a *weighted index.* A weighted index is made up of the market indexes used to measure the performance of each fund in the portfolio. Each market index is given a weight equal to its fund's weight in the portfolio. That weight is assigned to the fund's target return and its actual return. We total these weighted returns to come up with a target return for the portfolio and its actual return.

Table 20–2 illustrates how to benchmark a portfolio. For our mix, we have chosen Portfolio 30, *The Jogger.* We have filled the slots in the portfolio with the Vanguard Index 500 Fund, the EuroPacific Growth Fund, and two other funds. (We chose these funds for this example more or less at random. We don't recommend them over other funds for Portfolio 30, or for any other portfolio.)

There are four steps involved in benchmarking a portfolio:[3]

Step 1. Enter each fund's name, its weight (portfolio percentage), and its beta. These items are shown in the first three columns of Table 20–2.

Step 2. Calculate the target return for each fund in the portfolio, as we did for the Guardian Fund earlier. In Table 20–2, the three center columns under *Unweighted Returns* show these items. The *Bench* column shows the return for each fund's benchmark, the *Actual* column shows the fund's actual return, and the *Target* column shows the fund's target return.

Step 3. Multiply each fund's actual return by its weight, and do the same thing for the fund's target return. These results are shown in the two *Weighted Returns* columns on the right in Table 20–2.

Step 4. Total the two weighted return columns. The results are the actual return for the portfolio and its target return.

---

3 If you find that you really enjoy this exercise, then you may qualify for an exciting career as a tax return preparer. If not, then you might want to download *Benchmarking.xls* from the www.veeneman.com Web site. It does the benchmarking calculations for you.

T A B L E   20–2

Benchmarking a Portfolio

Fund	Weight, %	Beta	Bench	Unweighted Returns Target, %	Actual, %	Weighted Returns Target, %	Actual, %
Enormous Life Stable Value Fund	42	1.00	5.02	5.02	5.35	2.11	2.25
Stein Roe Intermediate Bond Fund	5	0.87	3.62	3.80	4.57	0.19	0.23
Vanguard Index 500 Fund	38	1.00	22.95	22.95	22.89	8.72	8.70
EuroPacific Growth Fund	15	0.75	20.96	16.98	18.64	2.55	2.80
Totals	**100**					**13.57**	**13.97**

Note = Note: Risk-free rate=5.02 percent.

We can draw several conclusions from the information in Table 20–2. Let's start with the portfolio as a whole:

- We expected the portfolio to earn about 13.57 percent. It actually earned about 13.97 percent. That's close to what we ex-pected, and it suggests the portfolio is basically in good shape.
- The Enormous Life Stable Value Fund is slightly over its benchmark but not enough to cause any concern.[4]
- The Stein Roe Intermediate Bond Fund was a bit above its target, which suggests the fund may be just a bit riskier than we had thought. But it is such a small part of our portfolio that it doesn't raise any concern.
- The Vanguard Index 500 Fund was right on its target, as we would expect of an index fund.
- As we discussed earlier, the EuroPacific Growth Fund over-performed its target. We will revisit the fund in 6 months to see if the fund's direction has become any clearer.

In short, our portfolio seems to be in pretty good shape. All our funds are performing more or less as we had expected, and there

---

4   This fund name is fictitious. Any resemblance to actual insurance companies, living or dead, is purely coincidental.

are no situations that call for immediate action. We will take another look at the EuroPacific Growth Fund in another 6 months to see if it has moved any closer to its target. Until then, we can put our portfolio away.

CAUTION: ANGELS DANCING AHEAD

It's easy to get carried away with benchmarking. If my large U.S. stock fund uses a value style, then maybe I should use a value stock index to measure it. If my bond fund invests in reverse upside-down mortgages,[5] then maybe I need to find a reverse upside-down mortgage index. Pretty soon we are back to angels doing the fox-trot on the head of a pin.

The two most important things to remember about benchmarking are:

- It is at best an approximation.
- The simpler, the better.

Remember that all we are trying to do is reach a reasonable, common-sense conclusion about whether our funds are performing as we expected them to. If they are, then we can put our funds folder away for another year and get back to the rest of our lives.

---

5   I made this up. There is no such thing as a reverse upside-down mortgage—yet.

21
CHAPTER

Midcourse Corrections

Rebalancing your portfolio as your investments grow and your goals change.

In the last chapter, we said a portfolio is a lot like a car. Well, this is a different chapter, and a portfolio isn't like a car any more. Now, it's like an airplane—an airplane on a cross-country flight from New York City to Los Angeles.

It would be nice to think that all the pilot has to do is get the plane off the ground, aim it toward L.A., and watch the in-flight movie. But that's not the way it works. From the moment the plane leaves the runway, winds are pushing it off course. We aren't talking about the gentle breezes you and I sometimes encounter on our way to lunch. At the altitudes at which jet aircraft customarily fly, wind speeds can exceed 100 miles per hour. So during the entire flight to L.A., the airplane is blown back and forth by winds that can be fierce at times.

Before the flight leaves, the pilot files a flight plan for the trip to L.A. showing the intended route across the country. At regular intervals during the flight, the pilot checks the plane's actual position against its intended position. Each time, the pilot expects to find the plane to be off course. That doesn't mean there is anything wrong with the flight; it's just a normal part of flying. Consequently, the pilot makes constant midcourse corrections to bring the plane back on course. The pilot's motto could be "Adjust, adjust, adjust."

You are the pilot of your portfolio. "Pick and stick" doesn't mean "choose and snooze." If you do, you will land somewhere in Canada, instead of Los Angeles. In the last chapter, we looked at one aspect of portfolio navigation. In this chapter, we will look at two others:

- How do you keep the risk of your portfolio under control once you have set the mix and selected funds?
- What should you do about risk as you get nearer to your goals? How do you do it?

A technique called *rebalancing* will help you control risk on an ongoing basis. It has the same effect as the midcourse corrections the pilot makes between New York and Los Angeles. Another technique, called a *step transfer,* will help you land the plane as you approach your destination. This technique will also help you change your destination if your goals change and make a smooth transition into your new flight plan.

THE BALANCING ACT

When we create our portfolio, we balance the return we want to earn against the risk we are willing to live with. Those forces may start out in balance, but the winds of the investment markets immediately begin blowing the portfolio out of balance. Here is an example.

Let's say that on January 1, 1996, we invested $10,000, and that we chose Portfolio 30, *The Jogger,* as our mix. Portfolio 30 sets a *target weight,* or percentage, for each asset class in the mix. We invest that percentage of our $10,000 in each of the four funds we selected for our portfolio. (We are using the same portfolio we benchmarked in Chapter 20.)

Table 21–1 shows what our portfolio would have looked like on the day we set it up. Now let's look at the same portfolio 1 year later. 1996 was a good year in the market, and all our funds made money. (The fund rates of return for 1996 are shown in Table 20–2.) And that means our funds have grown. But they haven't all grown at the same rate, and that has changed our portfolio weights. Table 21–2 shows the situation on January 1, 1997.

TABLE 21–1

Sample Portfolio Weights on January 1, 1996

Fund	Value, %	Weight, %
Enormous Life Stable Value Fund	4,200	42
Stein Roe Intermediate Bond Fund	500	5
Vanguard Index 500 Fund	3,800	38
EuroPacific Growth Fund	1,500	15
Total	**10,000**	**100**

TABLE 21–2

Sample Portfolio Weights on January 1, 1997

Fund	Value, $	Weight, %
Enormous Life Stable Value Fund	4,425	38
Stein Roe Intermediate Bond Fund	523	5
Vanguard Index 500 Fund	4,670	41
EuroPacific Growth Fund	1,780	16
Total	**11,398**	**100**

The stock funds have grown more than our bond fund and our stable value fund. That growth has increased its weight in the portfolio. They haven't grown enough to throw things seriously out of whack, but they have changed enough to be noticeable.

As the percentages change, so does the risk of our portfolio. We have said all through the book that "the fix is in the mix"—asset allocation determines over 90 percent of investment performance. In 1996, the weight of stocks in our portfolio increased by 4 percent, and the weight of stable values decreased by the same percentage. A 4 percent shift in our asset allocation isn't going to make or break the portfolio. But it has moved us about one-third of the distance from Portfolio 30 to Portfolio 40. At some point, we're going to need to act, or we will find ourselves with a *Center Line* portfolio instead of a *Jogger*.

In short, our portfolio has become out of balance. Some of the funds are overweighted, and some are underweighted. At some point we are going to have to *rebalance* the portfolio, or we will lose control over its risk. The *r* in *Star* could stand for "rebalancing"— that's how important it is to keep a portfolio in balance over time.

THE PORTFOLIO DIET DOCTOR

We said in Chapter 5 that a key to effectively regulating a portfolio, or maintaining control over its risk, is to "bump, don't jump." Take small steps, not big leaps. That's how rebalancing works. To rebalance, sell just enough of the funds that are over their target weights to bring them back to their targets. Reinvest the proceeds of those sales in the funds that are under their targets to bring them back up to theirs.

Here is an example. Table 21–3 shows the amount by which each fund is over or under its target weight. Our stable value fund is underweighted by $362, and our bond fund is underweighted by $47. We will need to invest a total of $409 in these funds to bring them back up to their target weights.

Our U.S. stock fund is overweighted by $339, and our international stock fund is overweighted by $70. We need to sell $409 of these funds to bring them back *down* to their target weights. That's where we will get the money to reinvest in the stable value and bond funds.

T A B L E   21–3

Rebalancing Transfers for January 1, 1997

Fund	Value, $	Target, $	Over or Under, $
Enormous Life Stable Value Fund	4,425	4,707	–362
Stein Roe Intermediate Bond Fund	523	560	–47
Vanguard Index 500 Fund	4,670	4,331	220
EuroPacific Growth Fund	1,780	1,681	99
Total	**11,398**	**11,398**	**0**

MAKING THE TRANSFERS

The process of actually making the *rebalancing transfers* is a whole lot easier if you use funds from one mutual fund family or if you select funds through a brokerage program that allows telephone transfers between funds of different families.[1] To make the transfer, you simply phone the fund company or broker and go down your list. In the example we used above, the instructions would be, "I want to transfer $339 out of my Vanguard Index 500 Fund and $70 out of my EuroPacific Fund, and I want to transfer $362 into my Enormous Life Fund and $47 into my Stein Roe Bond Fund." The fund company or broker will execute the transfers and send you confirmations. And at that point, your portfolio is back in balance.

BUYING LOW AND SELLING HIGH

There's another reason to rebalance, as well. Somewhere along the line, when you were very young, someone probably said to you, "Investing is very easy. All you have to do is buy low and sell high." Look what happens when we rebalance:

- We took money out of our two stock funds, which had the highest returns in our portfolio. That's selling high.
- We put money into our stable value and bond funds, which had the lowest returns in our portfolio. That's buying low.

Regular rebalancing enforces a discipline of taking our gainers and investing in the portions of our portfolio that haven't "had their run" yet.

Rebalancing also answers the age-old question, "How long should I let a winning investment run before I cash it in?" The answer is to forget the question. Instead of fund-jumping, take just enough of your winners on a regular basis to bring them back to their target weights.

Some investors can't bear to take anything out of an investment that is in the middle of a strong run. "It makes no sense," they say, "to pull money out of an investment that is doing well and put it in

---

1   The *Schwab OneSource* program is an example of such a brokerage program. Most company 401k plans also provide the same feature.

a dog." Well, as the saying goes, every dog has its day. Sooner or later, that investment will probably have its run, and if you keep it at its target weight, you will get the performance you expected when you created the portfolio.

Another important reason for rebalancing winners takes us back to fear and greed. Remember that bulls get rich and bears get rich; pigs and chickens get slaughtered. By rebalancing our winners, we reduce the risk of losing all our gains because of a sudden and unexpected drop in a winner's value.

HOW OFTEN IS TOO OFTEN?

Three of the most frequent questions in seminars are the following:

- Should I rebalance my portfolio at regular time intervals, or should I rebalance it when my investments go over or under their target weights by a certain percentage?
- If I rebalance at regular time intervals, how often should I do it?
- If I rebalance when the weights go off target, what's the right percentage to let them go over or under before I rebalance?

There are no right or wrong answers to these questions. Some general guidelines may be helpful:

- Rebalance your portfolio at least once per year, and rebalance then even if the changes in fund weights are small.
- Rebalance any time changes in fund weights have moved your mix more than halfway to the next portfolio in the *Star* series. For example, let's say your mix is Portfolio 30, *The Jogger*. If the weight of your large U.S. stock fund has increased to 42 percent, it's probably time to rebalance.

During a time when markets are particularly strong or particularly weak, the second guideline may mean you rebalance your portfolio every 6, or even every 3, months.

CHANGE IN DIRECTION

What do you do if you suddenly decide to make a major change in your investment strategy? In most cases, we recommend you sit down, take a few deep breaths, and remember the Second Best Piece of Investment Advice Ever Given.[2] But there are a few situations where a major change can make all the sense in the world:

- If your Ouch Factor changes; for example, a *Mattress* investor who decides to move to a more aggressive strategy
- If your time frame changes; for example, a father saving for a child's college education who learns the child has been awarded a full scholarship

Either of these situations may call for a move from one portfolio to another. You might move from *The Mattress* to *The Jogger*, or you might move from a moderate or aggressive portfolio to one more conservative. In either case, "bump, don't jump" should remain your motto.

THE TEXAS TWO-STEP

Step transfers will help you make a major change smoothly and with minimal risk. Step transfers combine rebalancing with the *dollar cost averaging* we talked about in Chapter 5. We said that you can reduce the risk of jumping into the market at a bad moment by making investments gradually, over time. In Chapter 5, we talked about using dollar cost averaging to buy investments. Now let's talk about how to use it to *change* investments.

A step transfer is simply a transfer of an investment from one fund to another in a series of steps. Here is a simple example: Let's say I have my entire savings of $10,000 in a stock fund, and I decide I would like to move the entire amount to a stable value fund. How should I make the change?

I could simply move the money today, in which case I would run the risk of making the move at a bad time. If the stock market takes off tomorrow, I am going to wish I had waited. But if I do wait and the stock market takes a tumble, I am going to kick myself for not making the move sooner.

Or I could transfer one-tenth of the stock fund each month to the stable value fund. If the stock fund stays exactly where it is today, I will transfer $1,000 per month, and it will take me 10 months to make the move. But we know that the one thing the stock market does *not* do is stand still. It is a moving target that doesn't always

---

2   Have you forgotten already? It was, "Don't make any sudden moves, pilgrim!" See Chapter 5.

move at the same speed or in the same direction. At $1,000 a month, it could take me a couple of years to make the transfer.

PENNIES FROM HEAVEN

To understand how a step transfer solves this dilemma, set 10 pennies on the left side of your desk or table. We are going to move these pennies to the right side of the table in 10 steps.

When we begin, there are 10 pennies on the left. If we move 1 penny to the right, we are moving *one-tenth* of the pennies on the left. That leaves 9 pennies; if we move 1 of those, we are moving *one-ninth* of the pennies on the left. That leaves 8 pennies; our next move affects *one-eighth* of those. And so it goes, until we have 2 pennies on the left. We then move *one-half* the pennies to the right, leaving 1 on the left. Our final move transfers *all* the pennies from the left to the right.

HITTING THE MOVING TARGET

A step transfer works the same way. To make our 10-step move, we would transfer one-tenth of the stock fund this month. Next month, we would transfer one-ninth of the stock fund, and we would transfer one-eighth of the stock fund the month after that.

We would keep doing that each month; in the ninth month we would transfer half of the stock fund, and in the tenth month, we would transfer all of the remaining stock fund. Whether the market goes up or down, we will complete our transfer in the 10 steps we had originally planned.

In the real world, I probably will not have the luxury of transferring from a single fund to another fund. It is much more likely that I will need to move from one mix to another. Consequently, I will need to determine the correct transfer amount for each fund in my portfolio, using the percentage applicable to that step.

Needless to say, this can all get mind-numbingly complicated very quickly. In case you decide to use step transfers to make a major move, *Appendix C* contains a worksheet that will help you calculate the amounts for each transfer.[3]

---

3   A computerized version of the worksheet, *Step Transfers.xls*, is available on the www.veeneman.com Web site.

HOW MANY STEPS?

In our example, we made our transfer in 10 steps a month apart. There is nothing magical in either the number of steps or the interval. In theory, the more steps the better, and the longer the period they are spread over, the better. But there is a practical limit to the number of steps an investor may be willing to go through. Beyond a certain point, it all becomes angels dancing on the head of a pin.

If you stagger your steps over a year-long period, you will dramatically reduce your risk of bad timing. Four steps, one every 3 months, should suffice, although more certainly wouldn't hurt. However many steps you decide to take, space them evenly over the period of your transfer. If you forget to make one of the step transfers, you can make it when you remember, or you can let it go. Your next transfer will bring you back to where you should be.

WHEN TO USE STEP TRANSFERS

Not every transfer needs to be made in steps. Let's say my retirement account has $400,000, and I plan to move $10,000 from one asset class to another. The transfer involves such a small portion of my portfolio that it probably isn't worth making the transfer in steps. But if I plan to move the entire $400,000, or even half of it, a step transfer strategy makes a lot of sense.

COMING IN FOR A LANDING

Throughout this chapter, we have used the metaphor of a cross-country plane trip. If you follow the pilot's golden rule of "Adjust, adjust, adjust," you will stay on course until you reach your destination. What do you do then? As one pilot once said, "Adjusting is fine, but sooner or later I have to actually land the plane!"

As you get closer to your goal, you can take either of two approaches:

- You can use step transfers to gradually liquidate your portfolio. The proceeds from your stepped sales should be put into a stable value fund, such as a savings account or a money market fund, until you actually need them.
- You can use the *Star* portfolios to gradually move toward more conservative asset allocations. For example, if you are

an *Over the Hump* investor who is approaching retirement, you could move from Portfolio 60 to Portfolio 50 this year, then to Portfolio 40 next year, and so on.

The first approach works well with savings goals that have definite ending dates, such as saving for a child's college education. The second approach works well for indefinite goals, such as retirement.

HOW LONG AN APPROACH?

Our cross-country pilot doesn't cruise along at 35,000 feet until the plane is over the airport, then dive for the runway. Instead, the plane makes a gradual approach and touches down on the runway smoothly and gently.[4] How long an approach do you need to make as you near your goal?

For most investors, 5 years out is not too soon to start thinking about the landing. Most financial planners suggest that a 5-year time horizon is about the minimum needed to maintain a significant stock exposure. So, at the time you are 5 years from your goal, you should begin to think about transitioning to more conservative investments.

THE LENGTH OF THE RUNWAY

Everything we have said about the length of the approach assumes that on one day, at some definite point in the future, you will need a pile of cash. In some cases, that may be very realistic. If you are saving for your first house or for a retirement home, you will need a down payment. That's a pile of cash.

What about retirement? It depends a lot on what you want to do. If your company savings plan account is earmarked for the purchase of a land-yacht to take you and your spouse cruising the highways and byways of America, you will need a pile of cash. But that's not the case for most of us. Our retirement savings are supposed to provide us with a steady income during our golden years.

Those golden years can last a couple of decades. A 65-year-old man has a life expectancy of about 15 years.[5] A woman's life

---

4   Anyone who does any flying at all knows this is pure fantasy.

5   National Center for Health Statistics, U.S. Department of Health and Human Services (1993). Reported in *1997 Information Please Almanac*, Houghton Mifflin Company, Boston, 1997, pp. 849–850.

expectancy at that age is even longer—about 19 years.[6] So, unless you are in poor health or unless you need that pile of cash we have been talking about, you have a very long time frame at retirement. A *Mattress* investment may not serve you well unless your number 1 goal is to avoid all market risk.

Parents saving for college will also need a pile of cash—and a big one at that. But they won't need it all at once. Most students incur their college expenses over a period of 4 years. So when the child begins college, there is still a 3-year time frame on the money needed for their senior year. So as you begin moving a college savings fund toward more conservative investments, don't move all of them at the same rate. The fact that college tuition is staggered over 4 years gives you an opportunity to leave at least some of your college savings invested for growth just a bit longer.

REGULATING YOUR INVESTMENTS

Rebalancing is a key strategy for maintaining control over the risk of your investment portfolio. Bumping the funds back to their target weights, rather than jumping from fund to fund, lets you regulate the flow of risk the way a faucet regulates the flow of water. Along the same lines, step transfers help you maintain control over your portfolio any time you need to make a major change. Both techniques will enable you to "adjust, adjust, adjust" your portfolio as you navigate toward your financial goals.

---

6   Ibid. Does this strike anyone else as unfair?

22 CHAPTER

Reaching for a Star

Review of key concepts. Now it's up to you.

We began this book 22 chapters ago with a story about Karen and the star she reached for. You now have the tools you need to reach for your own star, whatever it might be. All it takes is time, desire, and commitment. But if you want to, there is no reason why you should not retire with at least a million dollars.

You have at your disposal a different way to invest. It is designed to take the gambling out of investing, to reduce the element of chance and let the probabilities work in your favor. It is a way of investing that doesn't depend on picking the next hot fund or timing the market. It is based on a very simple premise: Investments are unpredictable in the short run but very predictable over the long haul.

Simplicity is the key to making the *Star* system work. Many of the debates over this style or that, or over whether risk "really" goes down over time, amount to little more than arguing over how many angels can dance on the head of a pin. Investing really boils down to three simple rules, which we have called the *three laws of investing:*

1. *Nobody beats the system:* A higher return means higher risk.

2. *Risk goes down over time:* The longer your time frame, the less you can be hurt by day-to-day swings in stocks and bonds.

3. *The fix is in the mix:* Asset allocation determines over 90 percent of performance.

Simplicity carries over to the five basic types of investments, that is, to the asset classes that make up the building blocks of investing. Nearly every fund an individual investor is likely to come across falls into one these asset classes: stable values, bonds, large and small U.S. stocks, and international stocks.

The *Star* system uses these building blocks to create predictable portfolios with controllable risk. The system itself is based on four key strategies, which together make the acronym *Star:*

-   **Spread** your investments—diversify.
-   Use **time** to protect yourself against risk.
-   Understand your **attitude** toward risk. Don't get carried away by either fear or greed.
-   **Regulate** your investments. Make any changes to your portfolio gradually.

You learned how to choose an asset allocation (your investment mix). In the *Star* system, your asset allocation is based on your time frame and your Ouch Factor. Both are critical factors in making an investment decision, and both are very personal. Nobody knows what's better *for* you *than* you.

You learned how to estimate the return you can expect from your mix of investments and how widely the return might vary from what you expect. And then you looked at 11 model mixes, from *The Mattress* to *The Sky Dive,* and you selected the portfolio that best fit your time frame and your Ouch Factor.

Once you selected a mix, you learned what types of funds are available for your investments and how to select funds to fill the slots in your portfolio. You learned how to read fund reports, including those published by the AAII and Morningstar, and how to select funds based on the information in those reports.

Then you learned how to evaluate the performance of your investments and how to act on your evaluation. It matters less whether a fund is up, or whether it beat the market, than whether it performed as you expected it to. You learned how to set reasonable expectations for performance and how to benchmark a portfolio to see if it met those expectations. You learned when to replace a fund and when to give it more time.

And finally, you learned how to maintain the balance of your portfolio and how to make major changes in direction. In both cases, it is most important to "bump, don't jump." Small changes bring the portfolio back into line, and gradual changes, made in small steps, change direction.

You have learned, and done, quite a lot. The tools you have used and the techniques you have mastered are much the same as those used by the professional investors who run some of the nation's largest pension plans and endowment funds.

And now the rest is up to you. No one can guarantee you will have a million dollars, but if you want it, you have every prospect in the world of succeeding. Take a few minutes after you put down this book and ask yourself, "What would it mean to me to have a million dollars by the time I retire? What would it mean to me to have $2 million? What would it mean for my family?"

Then take a few days to really think it over. Having done that, if you decide you are serious about your million, then you are ready to go to work. All you need to do is find $3,500 a year. That's $9.59 a day; $67.31 per week. If you can find it, then you have in your hands the tools you need to retire with one million dollars or more.

I wish you the best of luck! But knowing what you now know, you won't need it.

How the *Star* Portfolios Were Created

The Fortune in Your Future is based on two types of investment modeling:

- Historical modeling
- Forecasting

Historical modeling looks into the past. Basing decisions about the future solely on historical results is a lot like driving a car by looking through the rear-view mirror. Forecasting looks into the future. But we saw early on that attempts to predict the future are notoriously unreliable. Consequently, neither approach is foolproof, and neither should be relied upon to the exclusion of common sense.

FORECASTING

We used an approach called *mean-variance optimization* to develop the *Star* portfolios. The approach is more commonly referred to in the investment business as *efficient frontier modeling*. Under this approach, a computer model is used to create a series of portfolios with specific risk and return characteristics. For *The Fortune in Your Future,* we set up the model to generate 11 portfolios based on five asset classes:

- Stable values
- Bonds
- Large U.S. stocks
- Smaller U.S. stocks
- Large international stocks

The model set stable values and large international stocks as the conservative and aggressive "anchor points" of the risk spectrum. The conservative anchor point was designated 0, and the aggressive anchor point was designated 100. The 11 portfolios were calculated to fall at even 10-point increments along the risk line; point 0, point 10, point 20, and so on.

Efficient frontier modeling uses mathematical formulas to search out combinations of investments that are efficiently diversified. Each efficient portfolio has the highest expected return available at its given level of risk. The model bases its calculations on a series of investment assumptions. These assumptions are based largely on the historical performance of the investments used in the model. However, the historical returns are modified to take into account inflation expectations and other changes in expectations for the long-term performance of the model's investments.

We used *EnCORR* optimization software, published by Ibbotson Associates, Chicago, to construct the *Star* portfolios. We built our efficient frontier from the *Optimizer Inputs* (2nd Quarter 1997) published by Ibbotson Associates for use with *EnCORR* software. Those assumptions are listed in Table A–1.

The Ibbotson *Optimizer Inputs* contain assumptions for a number of asset classes. We used the following indexes:

- *Stable values.* 3-month U.S. Treasury bills
- *Bonds.* Lehman Bros. government and corporate bonds
- *Stocks, large U.S.* Standard & Poor's 500
- *Stocks, smaller U.S.* Russell 2,000
- *Stocks, large international.* MSCI EAFE

TABLE A–1

Assumptions Used to Create the *Star* Portfolios

	Stable Values	Bonds	Stocks		
			Large U.S.	Smaller U.S.	Inter-national
Expected return	5.41	6.7	14.28	14.25	15.67
Standard deviation	3.21	8.09	20.32	26.35	28.34
Correlations					
Stable values	1	0.12	−0.03	−0.03	−0.07
Bonds	0.12	1	0.55	0.22	0.22
Stocks,,large U.S.	−0.03	0.55	1	0.85	0.51
Stocks, smaller U.S.	−0.03	0.22	0.85	1	0.41
Stocks, large int'l.	−0.07	0.22	0.51	0.41	1

These assumptions created the efficient frontier shown in Figure A–1. The vertical gridlines show the 10-point intervals at which the portfolios were calculated. The circles represent the *Star* portfolios, and the rectangles represent the indexes used to create the portfolios.

In some cases, the portfolios do not fall precisely on their 10-point intervals. Certain asset classes have a tendency to "dominate" an efficient frontier model. We used a sensitivity analysis to reduce the domination effect. This reduction had a slight impact on the risk and return of some portfolios.

HISTORICAL MODELING

We used historical modeling to calculate the past performance figures for the *Star* portfolios. Here's how we did it:

- We used five market indexes to represent our five asset classes. We gave the annual returns for each index the same weight as its asset class had in each *Star* portfolio.
- We used these weightings to create a blended rate for each year for each of the 11 portfolios.

Wherever possible, actual data were used. In several cases, data were not available back to 1926. In these cases, derived series were used:

- *Stable values.* The Smith Barney 3-month T-bill series goes back only to January 1978. We used this series and the Ibbotson 30-day T-bill series to create a derived series for 3-month T bills going back to 1926. The average monthly geometric return spread between the two series was calculated for the period January 1978 through June 1997. The spread was then added to the 30-day series for the period January 1986 through December 1977.
- *Bonds.* The Lehman Bros. Government/Corporate Bond Index goes back only to 1978. Ibbotson publishes three separate bond indexes that go back to 1926; one for long-term government bonds, one for long-term corporate bonds, and one for intermediate-term corporate bonds. The three indexes were used to calculate a melded bond return, with the three indexes were weighted evenly with no rebalancing.

272

FIGURE A-1

Efficient Frontier for the *Star* Portfolios

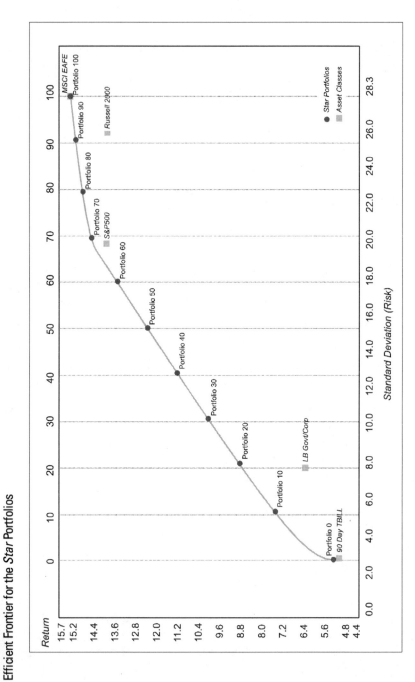

- *Stocks, large U.S.*   We used the S&P 500 for the period January 1926 to June 1997 to represent this asset class.
- *Stocks, small U.S.*   The Ibbotson Associates Small U.S. Stock Index for the period January 1926 to June 1997, from *Stocks, Bonds, Bills and Inflation,* was used to represent this series.
- *Stocks, large international.*   The MSCI EAFE Index goes back only to 1970. The average monthly geometric return was calculated for the EAFE Index and the S&P 500 Index for the period January 1970 through June 1996. The spread between the two means was added to the S&P 500 for the period January 1926 through December 1969.

What a Return Will Earn

This appendix will help you translate rates of return into dollars earned (or lost!) on your investments. Here is how to use it: Table B shows how much each dollar you invest will grow to at different rates of return over various time frames. For example, let's say you plan to invest $1,000, and you want to know how much you would have after 5 years if you earn an average of 11.6 percent on your investment.

Start with the rate of return. Various rates of return are shown in the first column of each table. Find the row for the rate that's closest to the rate of return you want to translate. Time frames from 1 to 20 years are listed across the top of the table. Read across the rate of return row until you come to the column that matches the time frame you want.

In the example above, you would read down the table until you get to 11 percent, which is the closest rate to the one you want. You read across the 11 percent row to the 5-year column, where you see that every dollar you invest would grow to $1.69 after 5 years. Since you plan to invest $1,000, that means your investment would grow to $1,690.

As another example, if you lost 3 percent for 5 years, how much of your $1,000 would you have left? From the table you can see that you would have $0.86 of each dollar you invested, or $860.

TABLE B

Growth of 1 Dollar at Various Rates of Return

Return	1	2	3	4	5	6	7	8	9	10
					Time Frame, Years					
65%	$1.65	$2.72	$4.49	$7.41	$12.23	$20.18	$33.30	$54.94	$90.65	$149.57
63%	$1.63	$2.66	$4.33	$7.06	$11.51	$18.76	$30.57	$49.83	$81.22	$132.40
61%	$1.61	$2.59	$4.17	$6.72	$10.82	$17.42	$28.04	$45.14	$72.68	$117.02
59%	$1.59	$2.53	$4.02	$6.39	$10.16	$16.16	$25.69	$40.85	$64.95	$103.27
57%	$1.57	$2.46	$3.87	$6.08	$9.54	$14.98	$23.51	$36.91	$57.96	$90.99
55%	$1.55	$2.40	$3.72	$5.77	$8.95	$13.87	$21.49	$33.32	$51.64	$80.04
53%	$1.53	$2.34	$3.58	$5.48	$8.38	$12.83	$19.63	$30.03	$45.94	$70.29
51%	$1.51	$2.28	$3.44	$5.20	$7.85	$11.85	$17.90	$27.03	$40.81	$61.63
49%	$1.49	$2.22	$3.31	$4.93	$7.34	$10.94	$16.30	$24.29	$36.20	$53.93
47%	$1.47	$2.16	$3.18	$4.67	$6.86	$10.09	$14.83	$21.80	$32.05	$47.12
45%	$1.45	$2.10	$3.05	$4.42	$6.41	$9.29	$13.48	$19.54	$28.33	$41.08
43%	$1.43	$2.04	$2.92	$4.18	$5.98	$8.55	$12.23	$17.49	$25.00	$35.76
41%	$1.41	$1.99	$2.80	$3.95	$5.57	$7.86	$11.08	$15.62	$22.03	$31.06
39%	$1.39	$1.93	$2.69	$3.73	$5.19	$7.21	$10.03	$13.94	$19.37	$26.92
37%	$1.37	$1.88	$2.57	$3.52	$4.83	$6.61	$9.06	$12.41	$17.00	$23.29
35%	$1.35	$1.82	$2.46	$3.32	$4.48	$6.05	$8.17	$11.03	$14.89	$20.11
33%	$1.33	$1.77	$2.35	$3.13	$4.16	$5.53	$7.36	$9.79	$13.02	$17.32
31%	$1.31	$1.72	$2.25	$2.94	$3.86	$5.05	$6.62	$8.67	$11.36	$14.88
29%	$1.29	$1.66	$2.15	$2.77	$3.57	$4.61	$5.94	$7.67	$9.89	$12.76
27%	$1.27	$1.61	$2.05	$2.60	$3.30	$4.20	$5.33	$6.77	$8.59	$10.92
25%	$1.25	$1.56	$1.95	$2.44	$3.05	$3.81	$4.77	$5.96	$7.45	$9.31
23%	$1.23	$1.51	$1.86	$2.29	$2.82	$3.46	$4.26	$5.24	$6.44	$7.93

(Continued)

TABLE B

Growth of 1 Dollar at Various Rates of Return

Return					Time Frame, Years					
	1	2	3	4	5	6	7	8	9	10
21%	$1.21	$1.46	$1.77	$2.14	$2.59	$3.14	$3.80	$4.59	$5.56	$6.73
19%	$1.19	$1.42	$1.69	$2.01	$2.39	$2.84	$3.38	$4.02	$4.79	$5.69
17%	$1.17	$1.37	$1.60	$1.87	$2.19	$2.57	$3.00	$3.51	$4.11	$4.81
15%	$1.15	$1.32	$1.52	$1.75	$2.01	$2.31	$2.66	$3.06	$3.52	$4.05
13%	$1.13	$1.28	$1.44	$1.63	$1.84	$2.08	$2.35	$2.66	$3.00	$3.39
11%	$1.11	$1.23	$1.37	$1.52	$1.69	$1.87	$2.08	$2.30	$2.56	$2.84
9%	$1.09	$1.19	$1.30	$1.41	$1.54	$1.68	$1.83	$1.99	$2.17	$2.37
7%	$1.07	$1.14	$1.23	$1.31	$1.40	$1.50	$1.61	$1.72	$1.84	$1.97
5%	$1.05	$1.10	$1.16	$1.22	$1.28	$1.34	$1.41	$1.48	$1.55	$1.63
3%	$1.03	$1.06	$1.09	$1.13	$1.16	$1.19	$1.23	$1.27	$1.30	$1.34
1%	$1.01	$1.02	$1.03	$1.04	$1.05	$1.06	$1.07	$1.08	$1.09	$1.10
−1%	$0.99	$0.98	$0.97	$0.96	$0.95	$0.94	$0.93	$0.92	$0.91	$0.90
−3%	$0.97	$0.94	$0.91	$0.89	$0.86	$0.83	$0.81	$0.78	$0.76	$0.74
−5%	$0.95	$0.90	$0.86	$0.81	$0.77	$0.74	$0.70	$0.66	$0.63	$0.60
−7%	$0.93	$0.86	$0.80	$0.75	$0.70	$0.65	$0.60	$0.56	$0.52	$0.48
−9%	$0.91	$0.83	$0.75	$0.69	$0.62	$0.57	$0.52	$0.47	$0.43	$0.39
−11%	$0.89	$0.79	$0.70	$0.63	$0.56	$0.50	$0.44	$0.39	$0.35	$0.31
−13%	$0.87	$0.76	$0.66	$0.57	$0.50	$0.43	$0.38	$0.33	$0.29	$0.25
−15%	$0.85	$0.72	$0.61	$0.52	$0.44	$0.38	$0.32	$0.27	$0.23	$0.20
−17%	$0.83	$0.69	$0.57	$0.47	$0.39	$0.33	$0.27	$0.23	$0.19	$0.16
−19%	$0.81	$0.66	$0.53	$0.43	$0.35	$0.28	$0.23	$0.19	$0.15	$0.12
−21%	$0.79	$0.62	$0.49	$0.39	$0.31	$0.24	$0.19	$0.15	$0.12	$0.09
−23%	$0.77	$0.59	$0.46	$0.35	$0.27	$0.21	$0.16	$0.12	$0.10	$0.07

(Continued)

TABLE B

Growth of 1 Dollar at Various Rates of Return

Time Frame, Years

Return	11	12	13	14	15	16	17	18	19	20
65%	$246.79	$407.20	$671.88	$1,108.60	$1,829.19	$3,018.17	$4,979.97	$8,216.96	$13,557.98	$22,370.66
63%	$215.81	$351.76	$573.38	$934.60	$1,523.40	$2,483.14	$4,047.52	$6,597.46	$10,753.86	$17,528.80
61%	$188.40	$303.33	$488.36	$786.25	$1,265.87	$2,038.05	$3,281.25	$5,282.82	$8,505.34	$13,693.60
59%	$164.20	$261.08	$415.11	$660.02	$1,049.44	$1,668.61	$2,653.08	$4,218.40	$6,707.26	$10,664.55
57%	$142.86	$224.28	$352.12	$552.83	$867.95	$1,362.68	$2,139.41	$3,358.87	$5,273.43	$8,279.29
55%	$124.06	$192.30	$298.07	$462.00	$716.10	$1,109.96	$1,720.44	$2,666.68	$4,133.35	$6,406.69
53%	$107.55	$164.55	$251.76	$385.19	$589.35	$901.70	$1,379.60	$2,110.79	$3,229.51	$4,941.16
51%	$93.06	$140.52	$212.18	$320.39	$483.79	$730.52	$1,103.08	$1,665.65	$2,515.14	$3,797.86
49%	$80.36	$119.74	$178.41	$265.83	$396.09	$590.17	$879.36	$1,310.25	$1,952.27	$2,908.88
47%	$69.26	$101.81	$149.67	$220.01	$323.41	$475.42	$698.87	$1,027.33	$1,510.18	$2,219.97
45%	$59.57	$86.38	$125.25	$181.62	$263.34	$381.85	$553.68	$802.83	$1,164.10	$1,687.95
43%	$51.13	$73.12	$104.56	$149.52	$213.82	$305.76	$437.23	$625.24	$894.10	$1,278.56
41%	$43.79	$61.75	$87.07	$122.76	$173.10	$244.07	$344.13	$485.23	$684.17	$964.68
39%	$37.43	$52.02	$72.31	$100.51	$139.71	$194.19	$269.93	$375.20	$521.53	$724.93
37%	$31.91	$43.72	$59.89	$82.05	$112.41	$154.00	$210.98	$289.05	$396.00	$542.51
35%	$27.14	$36.64	$49.47	$66.78	$90.16	$121.71	$164.31	$221.82	$299.46	$404.27
33%	$23.03	$30.64	$40.74	$54.19	$72.07	$95.86	$127.49	$169.56	$225.52	$299.94
31%	$19.50	$25.54	$33.46	$43.83	$57.42	$75.22	$98.54	$129.09	$169.10	$221.53
29%	$16.46	$21.24	$27.39	$35.34	$45.59	$58.81	$75.86	$97.86	$126.24	$162.85
27%	$13.86	$17.61	$22.36	$28.40	$36.06	$45.80	$58.17	$73.87	$93.81	$119.14
25%	$11.64	$14.55	$18.19	$22.74	$28.42	$35.53	$44.41	$55.51	$69.39	$86.74
23%	$9.75	$11.99	$14.75	$18.14	$22.31	$27.45	$33.76	$41.52	$51.07	$62.82

(Continued)

TABLE B

Growth of 1 Dollar at Various Rates of Return

Time Frame, Years

Return	11	12	13	14	15	16	17	18	19	20
21%	$8.14	$9.85	$11.92	$14.42	$17.45	$21.11	$25.55	$30.91	$37.40	$45.26
19%	$6.78	$8.06	$9.60	$11.42	$13.59	$16.17	$19.24	$22.90	$27.25	$32.43
17%	$5.62	$6.58	$7.70	$9.01	$10.54	$12.33	$14.43	$16.88	$19.75	$23.11
15%	$4.65	$5.35	$6.15	$7.08	$8.14	$9.36	$10.76	$12.38	$14.23	$16.37
13%	$3.84	$4.33	$4.90	$5.53	$6.25	$7.07	$7.99	$9.02	$10.20	$11.52
11%	$3.15	$3.50	$3.88	$4.31	$4.78	$5.31	$5.90	$6.54	$7.26	$8.06
9%	$2.58	$2.81	$3.07	$3.34	$3.64	$3.97	$4.33	$4.72	$5.14	$5.60
7%	$2.10	$2.25	$2.41	$2.58	$2.76	$2.95	$3.16	$3.38	$3.62	$3.87
5%	$1.71	$1.80	$1.89	$1.98	$2.08	$2.18	$2.29	$2.41	$2.53	$2.65
3%	$1.38	$1.43	$1.47	$1.51	$1.56	$1.60	$1.65	$1.70	$1.75	$1.81
1%	$1.12	$1.13	$1.14	$1.15	$1.16	$1.17	$1.18	$1.20	$1.21	$1.22
-1%	$0.90	$0.89	$0.88	$0.87	$0.86	$0.85	$0.84	$0.83	$0.83	$0.82
-3%	$0.72	$0.69	$0.67	$0.65	$0.63	$0.61	$0.60	$0.58	$0.56	$0.54
-5%	$0.57	$0.54	$0.51	$0.49	$0.46	$0.44	$0.42	$0.40	$0.38	$0.36
-7%	$0.45	$0.42	$0.39	$0.36	$0.34	$0.31	$0.29	$0.27	$0.25	$0.23
-9%	$0.35	$0.32	$0.29	$0.27	$0.24	$0.22	$0.20	$0.18	$0.17	$0.15
-11%	$0.28	$0.25	$0.22	$0.20	$0.17	$0.15	$0.14	$0.12	$0.11	$0.10
-13%	$0.22	$0.19	$0.16	$0.14	$0.12	$0.11	$0.09	$0.08	$0.07	$0.06
-15%	$0.17	$0.14	$0.12	$0.10	$0.09	$0.07	$0.06	$0.05	$0.05	$0.04
-17%	$0.13	$0.11	$0.09	$0.07	$0.06	$0.05	$0.04	$0.03	$0.03	$0.02
-19%	$0.10	$0.08	$0.06	$0.05	$0.04	$0.03	$0.03	$0.02	$0.02	$0.01
-21%	$0.07	$0.06	$0.05	$0.04	$0.03	$0.02	$0.02	$0.01	$0.01	$0.01
-23%	$0.06	$0.04	$0.03	$0.03	$0.02	$0.02	$0.01	$0.01	$0.01	$0.01

(Concluded)

Step Transfer Worksheet

The worksheet provided in this Appendix will help you calculate the amount to transfer among your funds to make a step transfer (step transfers are discussed in Chapter 21):

Step 1. Enter your target percent for each asset class in *column B*.

Step 2. Enter your funds in *column C*, next to their asset class.

Step 3. Enter the target percentage for each fund in *column D*.[1]

Step 4. Multiply the current balance of your entire portfolio by each target percent in *column D* to get the target balance for each fund. Enter that amount in *column E*.

Step 5. Enter the current balance for each fund in *column F*.

Step 6. Subtract *column F* from *column E*. The result, the *off-target amount,* is how much the balance of each fund is over or under its target balance. If the off-target amount is positive, the fund is below its target. If the amount is negative, the fund is over its target.

Step 7. Enter the *step percent* in *column H*. For example, let's say you are taking a total of 12 steps to move to your new asset allocation. If your current transfer is the fifth step, then your step percentage is 5/12, or 41.66 percent.

Step 8. Multiply the off-target amount in *column G* by the step percent in *column H*. Enter the result in *column I*. That's the amount you need to transfer to or from each fund to keep your portfolio on track to your new asset allocation. If the amount in *column I* is positive, you will need to transfer that amount to the

---

1 The target percent for each fund is equal to the target percent for the asset class times the target for the fund within the asset class. For example, if the target percent for bonds is 20 percent, and a bond fund's target is 50 percent of my bond investment, then the fund's target percent is 10 percent (20 percent × 50 percent) of my portfolio. I enter 10 percent in *column D*.

fund; if it is negative, you will need to transfer that amount from the fund. You can verify your calculations by adding the amounts in *column I.* They should total zero.

A computerized version of the worksheet, *Step Transfer.xls,* is available for download from the www.veeneman.com Web site.

APPENDIX C

Step Transfer Worksheet

A	B	C	D	E	F	G	H	I
	Target	Fund	Target	Target	Current	Off-Target	Step	Step Transfer
Stable values								
Bonds								
Stocks, large								
Stocks, small								
Stocks, large								
Total								

283

GLOSSARY

12b-1 fee A sales charge that is added to the annual expenses charged by a fund.

180 degree rule, the Any time anyone offers you an investment deal that sounds too good to be true, turn 180 degrees and run as fast as you can, as far as you can.

401k plan A special type of company savings plan, named after the section of the tax law that authorizes the plan. Employees designate a portion of their salary (1 to 15 percent) to save in a personal account under the plan. Each employee chooses his or her own investments from a menu offered by the plan. Employees receive a tax deduction for all amounts they save (up to specified maximums), and employers often match their employees' contributions. Fifty cents on the dollar is the most common match.

403b plan An employee savings plan offered by hospitals, universities, and other nonprofit institutions. A 403b plan works similarly to a 401k plan, with one big difference: 403b savings are generally invested in *variable annuities*. These investments are issued by insurance companies, and they look like mutual funds or other pooled funds. But technically, they are considered annuities. As a result, the insurance company adds a risk charge onto their expenses, which generally makes these funds more expensive than other funds.

active management A strategy of using investment selection, market timing, or both to increase the earnings of an investment portfolio. Market timing has been largely discredited. Most active managers try to add value by picking investments that will outperform others.

actively managed fund See *active management*.

after-tax investments Investments you make outside your company savings plan (*401k, 403b,* and so on) and outside an IRA plan. You get no tax deduction on after-tax savings, and the earnings from your investments are taxed each year.

aggressive fund A fund that is expected to outperform the market when it is rising and underperform it when it is falling. Aggressive funds have betas greater than 1.0.

Alpha A statistic used in the Capital Asset Pricing Model (CAPM) to measure company risk. Some investors also use it to measure the value added to an investment portfolio by a manager. It represents the return of an investment over what the investment's beta would have predicted.

American Stock Exchange (ASE) An exchange where large U.S. stocks are traded. It is generally considered to be secondary in importance to the New York Stock Exchange, the so-called Big Board.

annuity A contract issued by an insurance company in which it agrees to pay someone (called the *annuitant*) a regular income for life. For example, a retirement annuity from Enormous Life might cost $100,000. In return, Enormous Life will pay you $825 a month for as long as you live, even if you live to 120 or more.

arithmetic mean A simple average. The arithmetic mean of 1, 2, and 3 is 2—it's the average of the three numbers.

asset allocation The basic mix of stocks, bonds, and stable values in an investment portfolio. You should decide on this mix before you even begin looking at particular investment funds. A number of research studies have concluded that this mix determines as much as 90 percent of the risk and return in your investment portfolio. In other words, the percentage of my savings that I commit to stocks is 9 times more important than *which* stock fund I use for that percentage. See also *strategic asset allocation* and *tactical asset allocation*.

asset allocation fund A fund that attempts to increase earnings by shifting its asset allocation to take advantage of changing market conditions. This sort of "tactical" asset allocation is very different from the "strategic" asset allocation on which the *Star* system is based. The evidence to date suggests tactical asset allocation does not outperform longer-term approaches.

asset class A basic investment category, or type. These categories are used to determine the basic investment mix, or *asset allocation*, in an investment portfolio. Not everyone agrees on how many asset classes there are. It's sort of like asking "Into how many slices can we divide a pie?" In this book we work with three major asset classes: *stocks, bonds,* and *stable values.* We break stocks into three subclasses: *large U.S. company stocks, smaller U.S. company stocks,* and *large international company stocks.*

back-end load A sales commission that is paid when a fund is sold; also

called an *exit fee* or a *surrender charge.* Most back-end loads decline over time according to a fixed schedule, reducing to zero after 5 years or so.

balanced fund A balanced fund contains both stocks and bonds, usually in a 50-50 mix, or a 60 percent stock–40 percent bond mix. The fund manager of a balanced fund keeps the mix at whatever mix has been set as they target for the fund. If stocks rise, the fund manager sells enough stocks to bring the fund back to its target percentages. In other words, unlike *tactical asset allocation funds,* the manager doesn't try to increase returns by switching back and forth between stocks and bonds. For years, balanced funds have been used by investors who prefer not to set their own asset allocation. See also *tactical asset allocation.*

basis point A percent of a percent, or 0.01 percent. For example, 25 basis points equals 0.25 percent. Investment returns and fees are often expressed in basis points.

bear market A prolonged downturn in stock or bond markets. Bear markets are usually associated with recessions, as opposed to *corrections,* which are not. The stock market has been known to lose one-third or more of its value in a bear market before recovering.

beta A measure of the risk of an investment relative to the market in which it trades. Investments with a beta higher than 1.0 are riskier (more volatile) than their market; investments with betas lower than 1.0 are less risky than their markets. To calculate the beta for an investment, subtract the risk-free rate of return (U.S. Treasury bills or a similar investment) from the fund's earnings over a 3- to 5-year period, and do the same with the market return. The results are the *risk premiums* for the investment and the market, respectively. The ratio of the investment's risk premium to the market's risk premium is its beta.

board of directors A group charged with responsibility for managing the affairs of a corporation. Directors, who are elected by a company's shareholders, hire, fire, and review the performance of a company's senior management.

book value The value at which an asset is carried on the books of a corporation.

bull market A market environment in which prices are rising.

business cycle The cycle of growth and recession that drives the American economy and its investment markets.

Capital Asset Pricing Model (CAPM) A model of investment behavior originally developed by Professor William F. Sharpe. CAPM has dominated academic and professional approaches to investing for the past 20 years. The *Star* system is based largely on CAPM.

CAPM See *Capital Asset Pricing Model.*

capital gain Investors generally pay income taxes on the profits from sales of their investments. These profits are called *capital gains.* Investors in company savings plans (401k plans, 403b plans, and the like), IRAs, and certain other savings plans aren't required to pay taxes on capital gains. That's one of the benefits of these plans.

capital-gain distribution Mutual fund investors are required to pay income taxes on their pro-rata share of the profits realized by a mutual fund during the year. This taxable amount is called a *capital-gain distribution.*

Certified Financial Planner (CFP) *Certified Financial Planner*, a designation

awarded by the Certified Financial Planner Board of Standards. To qualify for the CFP designation, an individual must complete courses in insurance, investments, income taxation, employee benefits, estate planning, and the financial planning process. They must also pass a comprehensive national examination and meet continuing-education requirements set by the board. You can receive referrals to CFPs in your area, or check the status of a planner with the designation, by calling the board's consumer information line at (303) 830-7543.

CFP See *Certified Financial Planner.*

churning When a broker recommends that his or her clients buy and sell frequently, when the only result of the trading is to increase brokerage commissions, the broker is churning the accounts.

commercial paper Short-term (30 days to 1 year) IOUs issued by major corporations. Money market funds invest heavily in commercial paper.

common fund Any investment fund managed for the benefit of many investors. Mutual funds are technically common funds. The term is usually applied to funds offered by banks and trust companies.

common stock Units of ownership in a company. Large companies raise money to expand their operations by selling their ownership to the public. When an individual buys *shares* (units) of a company's stock, they actually become a part-owner of the company. As an owner, they become entitled to a share of the company's profits, called a *dividend.* Individuals can also invest in investment funds that buy stocks, in which case they become indirect owners of the stock.

confidence level The reliability of a return or dollar range. The higher the confidence level, the more we can rely on it. For example, if we calculate a range to a 66 percent confidence level, we can say only that the return will probably fall inside the range 4 out of 6 years, or 66 percent of the time. In one of the remaining years, it will probably fall above the range, and in the other remaining year, it will probably fall below it. On the other hand, if we calculate a range to a 90 percent confidence level, we can say the return will fall inside the range 90 years out of 100. The tradeoff for a higher confidence level is a wider range. The return and dollar ranges in this book are calculated to a 90 percent confidence level.

correction   A short-term drop in prices in the stock or bond markets. A market drop is generally considered to be a correction if prices decline 10 percent or more. If a correction lasts more than 90 days or so, it is considered a bear market.

coupon rate   The interest rate stated on the face of a bond.

cowboy manager   See *go cowboy*.

Crash That Nobody Heard, The   A nickname for the infamous bear market of 1973 to 1975. U.S. and international stock markets went into a steep decline at the same time, and the slide affected both large and smaller stocks. The bear market didn't begin with a crash, as the Depression bear market had. Instead, the market lost ground steadily over a period of almost 2 years in the wake of ongoing bad news, including the Watergate scandal and the first oil crisis of the 1970s.

credit quality   The creditworthiness of a bond or a stable value investment.

credit risk   The risk that the issuer of a bond or stable value will be unable to pay off the obligation when due.

dartboard portfolio   An investment portfolio chosen at random. Dartboard portfolios often outperform actively managed portfolios. Proponents of "passive management" cite these results as evidence in their favor.

defensive fund   A fund that will fall less than its market in a downturn. Defensive funds typically underperform their markets on the upside; that's the tradeoff for the downside protection. Defensive funds have betas less than 1.0.

deferred annuities   See *variable annuities*.

defined benefit pension plan   An old-style pension plan. The employer promised to pay the employee a specific amount each month for life during retirement. In other words, the amount of the benefit is defined in the plan. See also *defined contribution plan*.

defined contribution plan   A defined contribution plan can be a pension plan or a savings plan. It works the same way in both cases. The employer promises to deposit a specified amount (or percentage) to a plan account maintained for the employee. In some cases, the employee may contribute his or her own money to the account by payroll deduction. The employee is typically given a choice of several different investments for his or her account. When the employee dies, retires, or terminates employment, the balance of the account is turned over to him or her. In other words, it's the contribution to the account that's defined in the plan, not the benefit amount the employee will ultimately get. That depends largely on how well the employee's investments perform. See also *defined benefit pension plan*.

dividend   A shareholder's pro-rata share of corporate profits. Dividends are declared by a company's board of directors, usually four times per year.

dollar cost averaging   Investing a fixed

amount of money at regular intervals. For example, a 401k plan deducts a regular amount from your paycheck for investment in the funds you select. Dollar cost averaging can be used to reduce risk (see *step transfer*). It can also help you buy at a cost that is actually lower than the average price of the investment over the period of your purchases.

dollar range How much an investment will be worth at some point in the future if an investment earns a certain return. For example, over a 5-year time frame, the dollar range of an investment in Portfolio 30 is $1,118 to $2,290, depending on whether the portfolio earns the low or high end of its return range. See also *return range*.

Dow Jones Industrial Average An index of 30 large industrial and service corporations, chosen by Dow Jones & Co. as representative of blue-chip stock performance. "The Dow" is widely reported in the press, and it is the most widely used barometer of market activity in general. But it is rarely used to measure the performance of stock funds or asset classes because of the relatively small number of stocks in the index.

downtick A decrease in the price of an investment. To "sell on the downtick" means to sell while the price is falling.

EAFE Index See *MSCI EAFE Index*.

earnings multiple See *price-earnings ratio*.

efficiency See *portfolio efficiency* and *market efficiency*.

efficient frontier Pioneers with really good managers (just kidding).

efficient market hypothesis See *market efficiency*.

emerging-market funds Funds that invest in companies located in less-developed countries in Asia, Africa, and South America. These markets are less well established than those of the major industrialized nations, and they are extremely volatile.

excess return The return generated by an investment over and above what was predicted by the investment's beta.

expected return An estimate of what an investment is likely to earn over some period in the future. In most cases, the expected return is calculated as a simple average of the investment's returns over some historical period. By itself, an expected return isn't all that meaningful. After all, the investment may or may not earn that return—it's a coin toss. What's really important is understanding what might happen if the investment doesn't earn that return. For example, say we have two investments with expected returns of 9 percent. Both look the same, right? But now let's say that the first investment's return can range from 8 to 10 percent, while the second investment can run anywhere from –14 to 32 percent. Do they still look the same? The second investment swings much more wildly than the first. It's more *volatile*, which most of us view as riskier.

expense ratio The fees and expenses charged by a fund, expressed as a percentage of the fund's price.

face amount The amount for which a bond (and some stable values) will be redeemed.

fee-only financial planner A financial planner who does not sell financial products or accept commissions. Be careful: Some financial planners who advertise themselves as "fee based" charge fees *and* accept commissions.

fixed annuity An annuity that promises to pay a specific periodic income for the life of the holder of the annuity.

front-end load A sales commission that is paid from an amount being invested. If I invest $1,000 in a fund with a 5 percent front-end load, only $950 goes into the fund.

fund jumping An investment strategy of frequent switching between funds to earn a higher return. Some fund-jumpers simply follow the current fad, while others use investing rules or formulas to determine when to jump. The strategic approach of the *Star* system is at the opposite end of the spectrum from fund-jumping.

future value How much will a dollar invested today grow over time? For example, let's say I invest $100 at an expected return of 9 percent. If I earn that return, how much will my investment be worth in a year? The answer is $109, which is the future value of $100 in 1 year at 9 percent. See also *present value.*

geometric mean The rate of return that will grow a starting investment to a particular amount over a specific time frame. The geometric mean is different from the simple average (see *arithmetic mean*) with which we are most familiar. Here is an example. Let's say I invest $1,000 for 3 years. I earn 8.9, 10.2, and 7.6 percent in each of the 3 years, so at the end of the period my investment is worth $1,291.28. A simple average of my 3-year return is 8.90 percent. But if I compound my $1,000 investment at that rate for 3 years, I end up with $1,291.47. The simple average *overstates* my average return by just a bit. The geometric mean is 8.89 percent; that's the rate of return that will grow my $1,000 to $1,291.28 over 3 years. It may seem like we are splitting hairs, but when money gets compounded for 20 years, those hairs grow to the size of sewer pipes.

go cowboy To abandon an investment management style in pursuit of short-term opportunity, such as when an aggressive manager pulls out of the market in the face of bad news.

going rate The prevailing rate of interest.

growth and income fund A "growth and income" fund invests *most* of its assets in large U.S. stocks, but it holds up to 20 percent of its investments in stable values or bonds. The stable value and bond holdings are intended to make the fund a bit less aggressive than other stock funds.

growth fund A stock fund that invests in companies its managers expect to grow faster than the average company.

growth investing An investment approach, or style. A growth investor buys the common stock of companies that are expected to grow faster than the average company in the near term. These companies are typically the darlings of Wall Street, and their shares are generally more expensive than the average company when measured as a multiple of their current earnings. That's okay with the value investor because he or she expects the *future* growth of the company to offset the current high price of the shares. See also *value investing* and *price-earnings ratio.*

hedge funds Funds that invest in a wide variety of investments with relatively little consideration for investment style. Many experts consider these funds to be tantamount to gambling.

incremental return How much additional return we earn as we move to more aggressive portfolios. For example, Portfolio 0's expected return over 1 year is 5.6 percent, and Portfolio 10's expected return over the same period is 7.8 percent. The *incremental return* provided Portfolio 10 is the difference between the two, or 2.2 percent.

independence The extent to which you can use one event to predict another. The odds that a coin toss will come up heads is 50 percent. But coin tosses are independent events, so just because the coin came up heads this time doesn't mean it will come up tails the next time. Stock market returns are highly independent, which means that what happened today isn't generally very useful in predicting what will happen tomorrow. See *serial correlation*.

index See *market index*.

index funds Investment funds that try to mirror the performance of specific market indexes, such as the Standard & Poor's 500.

individual retirement account (IRA) An investment account established by an individual that qualifies for certain federal and state income tax breaks.

inside buildup An accumulation of earnings free of income tax inside an investment vehicle. Company savings plans, IRAs, and variable annuities all provide this feature.

interest rate The interest earned by an investment, expressed as a percentage of its price.

international stocks Stocks of companies headquartered outside the United States.

investment company A company registered with the federal government as being in the business of investing other people's money. In plain English, a mutual fund.

IRA See *individual retirement account*.

junk bonds Low-quality bonds with higher-than-average interest rates.

large U.S. stocks An asset class that represents the stocks of major U.S. corporations. The performance of this asset class is generally measured by the *Standard and Poor's 500 Index*.

lifestyle fund A fund that invests in several different asset classes, using a mix that its managers consider suitable for investors of a particular age or lifestyle.

load A sales commission.

locking in a loss (or gain) Selling an investment while its value is below (or above) the price at which the investor purchased it.

lockup Buying an investment that pays a set interest rate for a period of time. If I buy a 7 percent, 30-year bond, I have bought a 30-year interest rate lockup. Even if interest rates rise above 7 percent, I will receive no more than that from my bond.

loss year A year in which a portfolio suffers a loss, or a decline in value. The number of loss years in a decade is one way of measuring how well or poorly a portfolio performed.

management fees Compensation paid to the manager of an investment fund.

market efficiency The degree to which an astute investor can earn a higher return without greater risk. A market with a significant number of undervalued investments is said to be *inefficient*. In a market where all investments are fairly valued, the investor cannot increase return without buying riskier investments. Such a market is said to be *efficient*.

market index A benchmark used to measure the performance of a market. Indexes are usually created by compiling the returns of a large number of investments in the particular market.

For example, the Standard & Poor's 500, which is used to measure the performance of the large U.S. stocks market, compiles the performance of the stocks of the 500 largest companies in the market.

market value The value at which an investment actually trades.

market risk What market professionals call *volatility*, the ups and downs of the stock and bond markets. When pros use the term *market risk*, they are generally referring to something else entirely. In this book, we use the term as a synonym for *volatility*.

mature When a bond or a stable value is paid off. The maturity date is generally stated on the face of the investment. There is an old joke (mainly told by women) that asks the difference between a guy and a government bond. Answer: A government bond eventually matures.

maturity date The date a bond is repaid to the lender. If I buy a $1,000 Raintree County bond with a maturity date of December 31, 1999, then on that date the county will pay me the $1,000 they borrowed when they originally sold the bond. Of course, until that date I will also receive interest on the bond.

MSCI EAFE Index A widely used index published by Morgan Stanley. It measures the performance of markets in Europe, Australia, and the Far East.

mutual fund An investment fund managed by a professional manager and offered to the general public.

mutual fund window An arrangement in some company savings plans that allows participants to direct their savings to a family of mutual funds.

NASDAQ Exchange NASDAQ is an abbreviation for the National Association of Securities Dealers, Automated Quotations. The NASDAQ Exchange is an exchange on which shares of mid-sized and large U.S. companies are traded. This exchange has overshadowed the American Stock Exchange in recent years and is widely considered to the second most important exchange in the United States.

New York Stock Exchange (NYSE) The largest and most prestigious stock exchange in the United States. The shares of the largest companies in the country are traded on this exchange.

no-load fund A fund that does not charge sales commissions on the amount deposited or withdrawn. Many no-load funds add so-called 12b-1 charges to their management fees. These charges amount to a pay-as-you-go load.

number cruncher A statistician. My apologies and a tip of the hat to my friends who are statisticians and actuaries (particularly those who helped with the preparation of this book).

odd lot A stock purchase or sale of less than 100 shares. Small investors often trade in odd lots. The widely followed *odd-lot indicator* assumes these investors always buy and sell at the wrong times. Buy when odd-lot investors are selling, it says, and sell when they are buying.

par value The face value of a share of stock. It bears little relation to the market value of the stock.

passive management A strategy of investing in index funds to secure a market return. Passive investors do not believe that *active management* outperforms the market in the long run. So these investors try to lock in a market return in funds with the lowest management fees they can find.

pension plan An employee benefit plan that promises to pay the employee a fixed monthly income for life, beginning on a retirement date specified in the plan. Also called a *defined benefit plan.*

periodic investment plan (PIP) A plan offered by most mutual fund companies under which an individual commits to invest a specific amount per month in a company's funds. Mutual funds generally waive their minimums for investors with periodic investment plans, allowing individuals to start investing with smaller sums. For the investor, the PIP provides the benefits of dollar cost averaging. See *dollar cost averaging.*

pooled fund See *common fund.*

portfolio efficiency A mix that squeezes the most expected return out of each unit of risk. While return does generally go up with risk, some mixes are more *efficiently diversified* than others, which means they are expected to generate a particular level of return with less risk than other mixes. For example, certain mixes of stocks and bonds can generally generate the same expected return at less risk than bonds alone.

present value What a dollar tomorrow is worth today. For example, let's say I want to have $100 1 year from today, and I can buy a 1-year CD that pays 4 percent interest. How much would I have to put in the CD to have $100 in a year? A financial calculator will tell me it's $96.15. That's the present value of $100 in 1 year at 4 percent.

pretax investments Investments in company savings plans and other arrangements (such as IRAs) that qualify for state and federal income tax breaks.

price-earnings ratio A way of measuring how expensive a company's stock is at any time. Divide the price per share of a company's common stock by its earnings per share of the same stock, and you get a *times-earnings measure* of the cost of the stock. A company that earned $2 per share last year and whose stock is trading at $32 per share is trading at 16 times earnings. That's more expensive than the stock of a company that earned $1 per share last year and whose stock is trading at $11 per share. It's only trading at 11 times earnings.

range The high and low returns you can expect from an investment. A range has two important attributes: *time frame* and *definitiveness* (that is, how *definite* it is). For example, we might say that an investment has a range of 6 to 9 percent over any 1-year period and that it will stay in this range 2 years out of 3. That's only two-thirds of the time, and that's not very definite. The same investment could also have a wider range of 2 to 13 percent over the same 1-year period. But we could say that it will stay within *that* range 95 years out of 100. That's a much more *certain* range. In nearly every case, the more certain the range, the wider it will be. On the other hand, as the time frame gets longer, the range narrows. An investment with a range of 1 to 16 percent over a 1-year period might have a range of 6 to 11 percent over a 20-year period.

real growth See *real return.*

real return An investor's return, adjusted for inflation. Subtracting the inflation rate from the investment return gives an approximation of the real return. For example, if you earn 8 percent on your investments and the inflation rate is 3 percent, then your real return is approximately 5 percent. The real return is important because it lets you see the rate at which your investments are growing after increases in prices.

rebalancing A way of controlling, or regulating, risk in a portfolio. Let's say you set the *target weights* in your portfolio at 60 percent stocks and 40 percent bonds. You invest $6,000 in stocks and $4,000 in bonds. Over the next year, there is a terrific run-up in the stock market, and your stocks' value increases by 50 percent. Bonds go nowhere. Now you have $9,000 in stocks and $4,000 in bonds. That leaves you with about 70 percent in stocks, 30 percent in bonds. Your stocks are over-weighted relative to their target, and your bonds are underweighted. To bring your portfolio back into balance with its target, sell $1,200 of your stocks and reinvest the proceeds in your bond fund. Those moves will bring your portfolio weights back to 60-40, which brings the risk and return of your portfolio back on target.

rebalancing transfer A transfer to or from a fund to bring it back to its target weight. See *rebalancing* and *target weight.*

regulate "Regulating a portfolio" means keeping in on track and under control, in much the same way as a faucet regulates the flow of water. Two key strategies used to regulate a portfolio are *rebalancing* and *step transfers.*

r squared A measure of the strength of an investment manager's investment style. If a fund has a high *r* squared, its performance can be explained to a greater degree by market forces, and the fund will move predictably with the market. A fund with a low *r* squared is less predictable, and its beta will be less reliable in predicting its performance. Also called a *coefficient of determination.*

return What an investment earns over some period of time. These earnings come from two sources: *dividends* or *interest,* and *growth.* Let's say you buy an investment for $100. A year from now, you find that the value of your investment has increased to $105, and it has paid you $3 in dividends. You have made a total of $8, an 8 percent return on your investment. See also *yield.*

return range See *range.*

risk charge An add-on charge imposed by an insurance company on a variable annuity. Ostensibly, this charge compensates the insurance company for its commitment to provide a lifetime income in the future.

risk-free rate The investment return one can expect from the least risky investment available. It is used in calculating betas and other statistics. The rate on 3-month U.S. Treasury bills is often used for the risk-free rate.

risk premium The difference between an investment's return and the risk-free rate. The *risk premium* is the amount investors are paid for taking on the risk of a particular investment.

rollover IRA An individual retirement account created to accept a distribution from a company savings plan or some other employee benefit plan.

Russell 2000 Index An index of the second and third 1,000 largest industrial and service corporations traded on the major U.S. stock exchanges. The Frank Russell Co. maintains an index called the Russell 3,000, which tracks the performance of the 3,000 largest companies. The Russell 2,000 Index tracks all these companies but the top 1,000. This index is often used to measure the performance of the smaller U.S. company stock asset class.

serial correlation A statistical measure that predicts how well you can predict an investment's returns based on its past performance.

shares   Units in which stock is sold.

small-stock effect   Conventional wisdom has long held that small stocks outperform large stocks over the long term. That relationship, called the *small-stock effect*, has been questioned by some academics in recent years.

smaller U.S. company stocks   An asset class that represents the stocks of mid-sized U.S. corporations. These companies are generally smaller than those in the *Standard & Poor's 500 Index*. A variety of indexes are used to measure the performance of this asset class; the most widely used is probably the *Russell 2000 Index*.

stable value funds   Bank accounts and investments that look like bank accounts. They include certificates of deposit, money market funds, and GIC funds found in 401k plans. They are called *stable value* because the value of your savings does not rise and fall with investment markets.

standard deviation   A measure of risk. *Standard deviation* measures how much a series of returns varies from its average.

Standard & Poor's 500 Index   An index of the 500 largest industrial and service corporations traded on the major U.S. stock exchanges. This index is generally used to measure the performance of the large U.S. company stocks asset class.

step transfer   A way to manage risk as you make a major change in your portfolio. Let's say you decide to move 60 percent of your savings from stable values to stocks. Should you move your money now or wait 6 months? If the market crashes in the next 6 months, you're better off waiting. But if it booms, you're better off moving now. You can hedge your bets by transfer-

ring half now and half in 6 months. If the market crashes in the meantime, you buy in with the last half at a lower price. On the other hand, if it booms, you buy in with the first half at a lower price. The result is that you reduce the risk of making your move at a bad time. See also *dollar cost averaging*.

Stock   Units of ownership in a corporation.

strategic asset allocation   The process of setting a long-term mix (percentages of each asset class) for one's investment portfolio. These mixes remain steady as the market changes, and they usually aren't changed for 5 years or so. The *Star* portfolios are examples of strategic mixes. See also *tactical asset allocation*. Strategic asset allocation is built on the premise that the mix of basic asset classes in a portfolio determines over 90 percent of the portfolio's performance.

tactical asset allocation   The process of setting a short-term mix for one's investment portfolio. Proponents of tactical asset allocation accept the proposition that asset allocation determines 90 percent of performance, but they hold that an investor can increase return by shifting the portfolio's mix of asset classes as market conditions change. Critics of the approach claim it amounts to market timing and will underperform portfolios that maintain a long-term, strategic mix. The jury is still out on the viability of the approach, although some preliminary studies have concluded that modest tactical shifts in asset allocation (15 percent or less) can, indeed, add a small amount to a portfolio's return over time.

target return   A benchmark used to determine whether a fund is performing as expected. The beta benchmark is calculated by multiplying the performance of an appropriate market index by the fund's beta relative to that index.

target weight The percentage of a portfolio that should be made up of a particular fund. For example, Portfolio 30, *The Jogger*, assigns a target weight of 38 percent to large U.S. stocks. If I use Portfolio 30 as my mix, I would direct 38 percent of my investment dollars to the large U.S. stock fund I select for my portfolio. As time goes by, some funds in any portfolio grow beyond their target weights, and others fall below theirs. *Rebalancing* is the process of selling just enough of overweighted funds to bring them back to their target weights, and reinvesting the proceeds in underweighted funds, to bring them back up to theirs. See also *rebalancing*.

term The length of time left on a fixed-income investment. All bonds, and most stable values, have a specific term. At the end of the term, the investor turns in the investment and gets the face amount of the investment. For example, if I bought a 10-year, $1,000 bond on December 31, 1989, and I hold it to the end of the term, then on December 31, 1999, if I turn the bond in, I will get my $1,000 back. Of course, I will receive interest on the bond (at the rate shown on the bond) during the term.

three-legged stool An often-used (and some say overused) explanation of how a retirement gets paid for. An old-style pension plan is typically the first leg of the stool. These plans typically fund only about one-third of the amount needed to pay for retirement. So, just as a stool won't stand on one leg, one can't retire on a pension alone. Social security is the second leg of the stool. But it also provides only about one-third of what's needed. The stool won't stand on two legs; what is needed is a third leg—personal savings. The third leg of the stool is typically provided by a company

401k plan. To make the stool stand up, you need to contribute to your 401k plan.

treasury bills Short-term (30 to 90 days) IOUs issued by the federal government. Money market funds invest heavily in treasury bills, and they are often used as the benchmark *risk-free* rate of return.

trust department The division within a bank that performs investment management. Banks can manage investments only when they act as a *trustee* for an investor.

trustee An individual or institution who takes on the responsibility of managing someone else's money for him or her. Not all investment managers are trustees; for example, mutual fund managers are not trustees. In most cases, banks that act as investment managers act in the capacity of a trustee.

uptick An increase in the price of an investment. To "sell on the uptick" means to sell while the price is rising.

value investing An investment approach, or style. The value investor looks for "diamonds in the rough" or "fallen angels." If a company is out of favor, if Wall Street doesn't think much of its prospects, then the value investor is probably checking it out. He or she wants to find a company whose prospects are actually better than what other investors think they are. A classic example is IBM. In the early 1990s, the conventional wisdom said IBM was a dinosaur that had been left in the wake of the personal computer revolution. Its stock traded at less than half its high during the 1980s. Value investors thought otherwise and snatched up IBM's shares at fire-sale prices. Over the next several years, IBM engineered a dramatic turnaround and saw the price of its shares double. Value stocks tend to trade at price-earnings ratios that are lower than the market as a whole; they are cheaper than the average stock. See also *growth investing* and *price-earnings ratio*.

variable annuity A mutual fund wrapped up in a tax shelter. A variable annuity looks, acts, smells, and tastes like a mutual fund, but you don't have to pay income tax on your investment earnings until you withdraw money from your account. These investment vehicles generally charge significantly higher fees than mutual funds, which is the price you pay for the tax shelter. They can make sense if you are already making the maximum allowable contribution to your company savings plan and an IRA (if you are eligible). But their high fees make them questionable investment propositions otherwise.

volatility A measure of the risk of an investment. Think of an investment's return like the pendulum on a clock. Some years, the pendulum swings one way, and the investment makes money. Other years, it swings the other way, and the investment loses money. The center of the pendulum's swing is the average of those years, which is the in-

vestment's *expected return*. If the pendulum doesn't swing very far from its center point, the investment is said to be *stable*. An example is an investment with an expected return of 6 percent, and a range of 5 to 7 percent. A volatile investment is like a much wider pendulum swing. An example of a volatile investment would be one with an expected return of 14 percent and a range of –10 percent to 38 percent. The wider the range, the more volatile the investment.

weighted index A weighted index is a tool used to measure the performance of a portfolio, as opposed to that of a single fund. A weighted index is made up of the market indexes used to measure the performance of each fund in the portfolio. Each of the market indexes is given the same weight as the fund has in the portfolio. For example, if large U.S. stocks make up 38 percent of the portfolio, then the return of the Standard & Poor's 500 would be multiplied by 0.38 and added to the weighted index.

window See *mutual fund window*.

wrap account An investment account managed by a brokerage firm, and for which the firm charges an investment management fee.

yield The annual income paid by an investment; the dividends or interest received on an investment.

INDEX

Index note to the reader: The *n* with an italic number following a page reference refers to a specific footnote on that page. Also, all graphic representations are indicated by the numbers in bold print.

AAII (American Association of Individual Investors), 224, 225, **226,** 227, 228

Active management, 27, 28, 33–34, 220–221
(*See also* Management, investment)

Actuaries, and probabilities, 19–20

Added value, 27, 32, 231–232, 239–240

After-tax investments, 205

Aggressive investment portfolios, **141, 149, 157, 165, 175, 185**
(*See also* Conservative investment portfolios; Moderate investment portfolios)

Alpha, 32, 231–232, 239–240

American Association of Individual Investors (AAII), 224, 225, 227, 228

America Online (AOL), 230

Analysis, Morningstar reports, 232

Annuities, 204–208

Arithmetic mean, 21

Asset allocation:
as crucial to risk and return, 34
investment management and, 33
and mutual fund choice, 213–214, 232–233

Asset allocation *(Cont.)*:
and portfolio creation, 74, 90
tactical, 222*n*2
and time frame, 77, **78**
(*See also* Diversification; Portfolios, Star system)

Asset classes:
and benchmarking, 242
historic earnings of, 93–94
and portfolio creation, 73–74, 89–90, 92
and risk control, 24, 74–75
types of, 52

Average annualized compound rate of return, 21, 40–41, 84

Averages, 21, 84
(*See also* Dollar cost averaging)

Averages, law of, 24, 25

Back-end load, 200

Balanced fund, 198*n*1

Banks, 21–22, 54, 55, 208–210

Bear market (*see* Long-term performance)

Best fit index, 231, 243, 247

Beta:
and benchmarking, 242–243, 244
in indexed funds, 32
low-load guide and, 227
Morningstar reports and, 231–232
performance *vs.* market index, 237–239, **238, 239**
and return targets, 35
vs. risk-free rate, 243
(*See also* Risk)

Board of directors, and
   stockholding, 63
Bond funds, 57
Bonds:
   about, 57–59
   as asset class, 52
   buying and selling, 59–61
   junk, 58
   Morningstar data, 215
   Star 0-60 portfolios, 102, 110,
      118, 126, 134, 142, 150
   types of, **61,** 61–62
Book value of stable values, 60
Breakfast barometer, 16–17
Bull Market, Great (*see* Long-term
   performance)
Business cycle, 58–59, 63
Business Week, 77

Capital-gain distribution, 205*n*3
CAPM (Capital Asset Pricing
   Model), 30–33
Category risk, 227
Certificates of Deposit (CDs),
   21–22, **22,** 23, 54–55
Certified Financial Planner (CFP),
   201*n*2
Chimpanzee portfolio, 26–27
Churning, 236
Coefficient of determination, 217
Coin toss experiment, **18,** 18–19,
   19*n*2
Commercial paper, 56
Commission, financial planner,
   201–202
   (*See also* Expenses)
Common funds, 208–210
*Common-Sense Investing for
   Common-Sense People* seminar, 4
Common stock, 62
   (*See also* Stocks)
Company risk, 30–31, 32
Company savings plans, 221

Company size and stock funds,
   30–31, 64, **64**
Compounding, 41
Computer software, 225, 230
Confidence levels, 21*n*3
Conservative investment
   portfolios, **101, 102, 109, 110, 117,**
   118
   (*See also* Aggressive investment
      portfolios; Moderate
      investment portfolios)
Consistency, 49–50
Core funds, 223
Corporate bonds, 61, **61**
Costs (*see* Expenses)
Crash That Nobody Heard (*See*
   Long-term performance)

Dateline, 26–27
Defensive fund, 240
Depression, Great (*see* Long-term
   performance)
Disco Decade (*see* Long-term
   performance)
Diversification, 23–24, 66, 67,
   74–75, 203
   (*See also* Asset allocation)
Dividends, 62
Dollar cost averaging, 83–85, **84,**
   85, 86, **87**
Dollar range:
   Star 0-50 portfolios, **103, 111,**
      119, 127, 135, 143
   Star 50-100 portfolios, **143, 151,**
      159, 168, 177, 186
   and time frame, 40–41, **41**
   on Web site, 40*n*3
   (*See also* Range of an
      investment; Return range)

EAFE Index, 66, 242
Efficient frontier model, 83, 92–93
Efficient market hypothesis, 33

Elliott Wave Theory, 17
Emerging market stocks, 65
Employer matching contributions, 85–86
Excess return, 32
Expected return, 20–21, 22, **22,** 23, **78**
Expense ratio, 219–220, 227, 232
Expenses:
    for annuities, 206–207
    commissions, 201–202
    fees, 219–220, 222
    for index funds, 28
    loads, 200, 201, 203, 225
    low-load guide, 227
    for mutual funds, 219–220
    sales charges, 201–203, 219
    12b-1 fee, 202–203, 219, 225

401k plan, 59, 85–86, 197–198, 203, 207–208
403b plan, 207
FDIC (Federal Deposit Insurance Corporation), 53, 55
Fear and greed, 79, 82, 95–96, 258
Fees, 28, 201–202, 219–220, 221
Fidelity Investments, 49, 241
Financial Analysts Journal, 34n6
Fixed annuity, 204–205
Forecasts, probabilistic, 24
Fortune 500 stocks, 27
Frank Russell Co., 68
Front-end load, 200

Gallop survey, 59
Garroway, Dave, 26
GIC (Guaranteed investment contract), 56–57
Go-Go Years (*see* Long-term performance)
Going rate of interest, 58
"Gone cowboy," 240–241, 248
Government bonds, 61, **61**

Greed and fear, 79, 82, 95–96, 258
Growth and income fund, 220
Growth companies (*see* Growth investing)
Growth investing, 45n4, 45–48, **48**
Growth stock fund, **64**
Guaranteed investment contract (GIC), 56–57

Hedge funds, 215
Hemline indicator, 17, 45
Historic earnings summary chart, 94–95
Historic performance (*see* Long-term performance)
Hodge, Vernon, 79
Holdings, 228

IBM, 46
Inception date, mutual fund, 225
Independent events (*see* Serial correlation)
Indexed funds, 28–30, 32, 220–222
Indexes, market (*see* Market indexes)
The Individual Investor's Guide to Low-Load Mutual Funds, 224–225, 225, **226,** 227–228
Individual retirement account (IRA), 205
Inflation, CDs *vs.* stocks, 23
Inflation protection:
    Star 0-50 portfolios, 108, 116, 124, 131–132, 140, 148
    Star 50-100 portfolios, 148, 156, 163–164, 172, 182, 192
Inside buildup, annuity, 206
Inside information, 26
Insurance company investments (*see* Annuities)
Interest rate, 54, 55, 58–61, 62
Intermediate-term bonds, 61, **61**

International stocks:
about, 65–68, **67**
benchmarking, 247–248
Star 20-50 portfolios, 118, 126, 134, 142
Star 50-100 portfolios, 142, 150, 158, 166, 176, 186
stock fund grouping, **64,** 65
Internet address (*see* World Wide Web site)
Investing:
after-tax, 205
choice of vehicle for, 210–211, 232–233
as common sense, 11
discomfort with, 5–8
fear and greed, 79, 82, 95–96, 258
laws of, 33–34, 44, 48, 265–266
optimism and pessimism about, 63
regulation of, 83, 85
and Star system, 10–11
(*See also* Management, investment)
Investment, style of:
consistency in management, 49
elements of, 215
and investment indicators, 45
low-load guide, 228
Morningstar reports, 230–231
mutual fund, choice, 214–215
and mutual fund management, 203–204, 218–219
and stock fund types, 64
Investment company, 200
(*See also* Mutual funds)
Investment mix, summary chart, 92
IRA (individual retirement account), 205

The Journal of Financial Planning, 40n2

Junk bonds, 58
Large, U.S. stocks, 41, **42, 43, 44, 64,** 65, 66–67, **67**
Large U.S. stocks (*see* U.S. stocks)
Law of averages, 24, 25
Law of large numbers, 19–20
Laws of investing, 33–34, 44, 48, 265–266
Lifestyle fund, 221–223
Load, 200, 201, 203, 225
(*see also* Expenses)
Loaner *vs.* loaner, 52, 53, 57
Lockup, interest, 55, 59, 62
Long-term bonds, 61, **61**
Long-term performance:
and asset allocation, 48
historic, 231
of index funds, 28
and portfolio creation, 89
small *vs.* large U.S. stocks, **69, 69–71, 70**
Star 0-50 portfolios, 104–107, 112–115, 120–124, 126–131, 136–140, 143–148
Star 50-100 portfolios, 143–148, 152–155, 160–163, 168–172, 178–182, 188–192
(*See also* Performance history, decade by decade)
Loss, locking in, 61
Losses and time frames, **39**
Low-load guide, 224–225, **226,** 227–228
Lynch, Peter, 49, 50

Magellan Fund, 49, 241
Malkiel, Burton, 17–18
Management, investment:
active, 28, 220–221
added value of, 231–232, 239–240
fee *vs.* commission, 201–202
importance of, 218–219

Management, investment *(Cont.):*
  and mutual funds, 203–204
  performance of, 27, 31–32
  Star system for, 8–9, 33–34
  (See also investment, style of)
Management fees *(see* Expenses;
  Fees)
Market:
  beating of, 27, 34
  corrections in, 86–87, **87**
  efficient market hypothesis,
    33
  performance of, 27
  prediction of, 16–20
  (See also Expected return)
Market indexes:
  and benchmarking, 241–243,
    242, 244, 248
  best fit, 231, 243
  MSCI EAFE index, 66, **242**
  Russell 2000 index, 68
  (See also Standard & Poor's 500
    index)
Market risk, 30–31, 34, 53, 61
Market timing, 33–34, 222
Market value, 60
Markowitz, Harry, 9
Matching contributions, employer,
  85–86
Maturity date, bonds, 62
Mean, 21, 24, 25
Me Decade *(see* Long-term
  performance)
Microsoft, 45
Mixed bond funds, 61, **61**
Mixed stock funds, **64**
Mix of investments *(see* Asset
  allocation; Diversification)
Moderate investment portfolios,
  125, 126, 133, 134, **141,** 142
  (See also Aggressive investment
    portfolios; Conservative
    investment portfolios)

Money market funds, 56
Morningstar 500, 215, 224, 230–232,
  242–243
Morningstar, Inc., 215, 224, 228
Morningstar Investor, 230*n*6
Morningstar Principia software, 230
Morningstar reports, 64, 228, **229,**
  230
MSCI EAFE Index, 66
Muggs, J. Fred, 26–27
Mutual funds:
  advantages, 203
  and asset classes, 52
  choice of, 224–225, 232–233
  disadvantages, 204
  lifestyle fund, 221–223
  loads, 200, 201, 203, 225
  overview, 198–200
  prospectus, 220
  sales charges, 201–203, 219
  sales of, 200
  and total risk, 227
  windows, 223, **224**

NBC, 26
News, market impact of, 25
New York Stock Exchange
  (NYSE), 65
Nifty Fifties *(see* Long-term
  performance)
Noble Prize in Economics, 30
No-load funds, 200, 201, 225
Number crunchers, 16, 217–218

Odd lot indicator, 80
180 degree rule, the, 208
Ouch factor, 79, 82, 95–96
Owner *vs.* loaner, 52, 62

Penalties, Certificates of Deposit
  (CDs), 55
Performance:
  beta, 237–239, **238, 239,** 248

Performance: *(Cont.)*
  investment management, 27,
    31–32, 33–34
  (See also Return)
Performance history, decade by
  decade:
  Star 0-50 portfolio, 104, 112, 120,
    128, **136, 144**
  Star 50-100 portfolio, 144, **152,**
    160, 168, 178, 188
  (See also Long-term
    performance)
Periodic investment plan (PIP), 86
The Pit, 25, 33
Pooled fund, 208–210
Portfolio issues:
  chimpanzee stock picks, 26–27
  creation, 73–74, 89–90, 94–97
  and efficient model hypothesis,
    92–93
  mutual fund choice, 224–225,
    232–233
  overview, 90–91
  performance relative to the
    market, 237–241, 248
  rebalancing, 13, 83, 254,
    257–258, 263
Portfolios, Star system:
  0 (The Mattress), **101,** 101–108
  10 (Belt and Suspenders), **109,**
    109–116
  20 (The Shallow End), **117,**
    117–124
  30 (The Jogger), **125,** 125–132
  40 (The Center Line), **133,**
    133–140
  50 (Partly Cloudy), **141,** 141–148
  60 (Over the Hump), **149,**
    149–156
  70 (The Sports Car), **157,** 157–164
  80 (The Deep End), **165,** 165–174
  90 (The Black Diamond), **175,**
    175–183

Portfolios, Star system *(Cont.):*
  100 (The Sky Dive), **185,** 185–
    192
Portfolio summary charts:
  explanation of, **91,** 91–94
  Star 0-50 portfolios, **101, 109,**
    117, 125, 133, 141
  Star 50-100 portfolios, **141, 149,**
    157, 165, 175, 185
Precious metals, 52
Probabilistic forecasts, 24
Probabilities, playing of, 19
Profit charge, annuity, 206–207
Profits *(see* Dividends)
Prospectus, mutual fund, 220
Public information, and stock
  price, 33

A Random Walk Down Wall Street
  (Malkiel), 17–18, **18**
Range of an investment, 21n3,
  21–22, **22,** 35, **39**
  (See also Dollar range; Return
    range)
Rate of return, 40, 96
Real estate, 52
Rebalancing, portfolio, 13, 83, 254,
  257–258, 263
Rebalancing transfers, 257
Recent Past *(see* Long-term
  performance)
Retirement, 3, 209–210, 222–223
Return:
  and asset classes, 27
  efficient market hypothesis, 33
  excess return, 32
  low-load guide, 225, 227
  past *vs.* future, 21
  rate and time frame, 40
  Star system and, 8–9, 35
  10 year example, **160**
  (See also Expected return;
    Performance; Risk and return)

Return range:
  and asset allocation, 39, 44, 77,
    78
  average annualized compound
    rate of return, 40–41
  mixes of stable values and
    stocks, **75**
  summary chart, 92, 93
  (*See also* Range of an investment)
Reversion to the mean, 24, 25
Risk:
  and alpha, 32, 231–232, 239–240
  control through asset allocation,
    24
  efficient market hypothesis, 33
  low-load guide, 227
  market risk, 22–23, 30–31, 34,
    53, 61
  Star system and, 8–9, 35
  and time frame, 38–41, 44
  tolerance for, 82
  (*See also* Beta)
Risk and return:
  and asset allocation, 9–12
  to beat the market, 31, 34
  and mutual fund choices,
    214–215, 232–233
  in portfolio creation, 254–256
  Star 0-50 portfolios, 102–103,
    110–112, 119–120, 126–127,
    134–135, 142–143
  Star 50-100 portfolios, 142–143,
    151–152, 158–159, 166–168,
    177–178, 187–188
Risk charge, annuity, 206–207
Risk-free rate, 237, 243, 244
Risk premium, 243, 244
Risk scale, 92–93
R squared, 217–218, 231, 248
Russell 2000 Index, 68

Savers, and Star system, 10–11
Savings accounts, 54, 55

Seigel, Jeremy, 70, 242
Serial correlation, 16–17, 66–67, **67**
Share, common stock, 62
Sharpe, William F., 9, 30, 49
Short-term bonds, 61, **61**
Simplicity, 50, 265
Skepticism, 11, 38
Small stock effect, 68
Small U.S. stocks, **64,** 65, 68–71, **69,**
  70
Software, 225, 230
S&P 500 Index, 16–17, 27*n*4, 28, 65
Stable values:
  about, 53
  asset allocation, 52, **78**
  book value, 60
  Morningstar data, 215, 243
  Star 0-70 portfolios, 102, 110,
    118, 126, 134, 142, 150
  types of investments, 54–57
Standard & Poor's 500 Index,
  16–17, 27*n*4, 28, 65
Star system:
  asset allocation, 9–12, 74
  investor, 10–11
  laws of investment, 33–34, 41,
    48, 265–266
  portfolio creation, 73–74, 89–97
  risk and return, 8–9, 35
Star system portfolios (*see*
  Portfolios, Star system)
Statisticians, 16, 19–20, 217–218
Step transfers, portfolio, 13, 83,
  254, 259, 260*n*3, 261
Stock Market Crash, 1987, 79–82, **80**
  (*See also* Long-term
    performance)
Stocks:
  about, 62–64
  asset allocation and time frame,
    78
  asset class, 52
  vs. CDs, **22**

Stocks *(Cont.):*
  and expected return, 20–21
  and inflation, 23
  Morningstar data, 216
  Star 10-50 portfolios, 110, 118, 126, 134, 142
  Star 50-90 portfolios, 142, 150, 158, 166, 176
  trading, 25
  types, 27, **64,** 64–71
  value of, 63
  (See also International stocks; U.S. stocks, large; U.S. stocks, small)
Stocks for the Long Run (Seigel), 70
Style boxes, **216,** 217–218
Summary charts *(see* Portfolio summary charts)
Superbowl indicator, 45
Systematic risk, 30

Tactical asset allocation, 222n2
Target return, 244, 248
Target weight, 256
Taxes, 85, 205, 206
T-bills, 56
Time frame:
  to create portfolio, 94–95
  and risk, 38–41, 44, 75–77, **76, 77, 78**
Today Show, 26
Total risk, mutual fund, 227
Trading, stock, 25

Truman, Harry, 23
Trustee, common funds, 209
Trust officer, common funds, 209
12b-1 fee, 202–203, 219, 225

Ultraconservative investment portfolio, **101,** 102
  (See also Conservative investment portfolios)
Unsystematic risk, 30
U.S. stocks:
  large, 41, **42, 43, 44, 64,** 65, 66–67, **67**
  small, **64,** 65, 68–71, **69, 70**
U.S. Treasury bills, 56

Value investing, 45–48, **48**
Value stock fund, **64**
Vanguard Index 500 fund, 225
Variable annuities, 205–208

The Wall Street Journal, 26
War Years *(see* Long-term performance)
Weighted index, 250
Window, 223, **224**
Withdrawals, mutual funds, 200
World Wide Web site:
  Morningstar, 230
  Veeneman, 19, 19n2, 40n3, 45n4, 250n3

Year label, lifestyle fund, 222

ABOUT THE AUTHOR

David Veeneman is an award-winning investment educator, attorney, and principal of investment firm Veeneman Associates. He has helped major employers, including the Federal Reserve, Chrysler, and Xerox, develop investment programs for their employees. Veeneman's investment seminars, including the highly popular *Common Sense Investing for Common-Sense People*, are designed to help everyday Americans save and invest their paychecks for a comfortable lifestyle.